"Applicable to both primary and middle grade classrooms, T[ ]
Karen Biggs-Tucker and Maria Walther, shows us how to in[ ]
ing learning standards, maximize learning time, leverage streng[ ]
opportunities for learning in another, all while keeping the specifi[ ]
at the center of your decision-making."
—Jennifer Serravallo, author of *The Reading Strategies Book* and
The Writing Strategies Book

"*The Literacy Workshop* is the book that helps teachers create classrooms where students
drive their own learning. By looking at common and complementary aspects of reading and writing, Maria and Karen help us envision a less choppy and more connected literacy experience for all students."
—Gravity Goldberg, author of *Teacher's Toolkit for Independent Reading* and
Mindsets and Moves

"*The Literacy Workshop* by Maria Walther and Karen Biggs-Tucker is a professional
gift to us all, offering a thoughtful merger of reading and writing workshop through
a flexible lens of what it might look like when intention centered on students leads the way."
—Dr. Mary Howard , Literacy Consultant, author of *Good to Great Teaching* and
RTI from All Sides

"In *The Literacy Workshop: Where Reading and Writing Converge*, Karen and Maria sit
beside us as classroom teachers and demonstrate the strategic possibilities available
when we weave the common threads of literacy together. "
—Victoria Dotson, 5th grade teacher, Montgomery County Public Schools

"Time is the currency of education. Maria Walther and Karen Biggs-Tucker have written
a smart, practical book that will show teachers how they can find the *time* to engage
students in deep reading and myriad opportunities to write. *The Literacy Workshop:
Where Reading and Writing Converge* includes demonstration lessons for both primary
and intermediate grades with perfect mentor texts and a concise, well-written annotation
and rationale for selecting it.

The effective organization, key chart, and colorful figures make this book readable
and accessible for teachers with a busy, tight, demanding schedule—that's every teacher! "
—Lynne R. Dorfman, co-author of *Welcome to Writing Workshop:
Engaging Today's Students with a Model That Works*

"*The Literacy Workshop* maps out a pathway for re-imagining the reading and writing workshop with authentic and engaging learning opportunities. Built on a foundation of strong pedagogy and diverse mentor text selections, Karen and Maria demystify the relationship between reading and writing with a depth of practitioner insight and rich student work samples. This book provides teachers with everything they need to make savvy decisions to create the cognitively-stimulating and culturally-embracing classrooms our students deserve."

—Dana Onayemi, Founder, Executive Director, and Equity Coach—*Project Imagine, LLC*

"The integrated workshop offers teachers a road map that respects the instructional autonomy of teachers and the learning autonomy of students, making the model responsive and meets all stakeholders where they are."

—Theresa Solomon, Principal, Wild Rose Elementary School, St. Charles, IL

"Imagine that someone took all your favorite professional thinkers—the ones on whom your practice is built—and then intentionally made connections between them in a way that amplifies their impact, both simplifying and adding complexity to the most compelling of reading, writing, and thinking work. *The Literacy Workshop* feels like it's closing an instructional loop that has been begging to be closed."

—Amy Ellerman, Instructional Coach, Maple Grove Elementary, Golden, CO, Contributing Writer for the *Two Writing Teachers* blog

"With *The Literacy Workshop: Where Reading and Writing Converge,* Karen Biggs-Tucker and Maria Walther have bottled up literacy magic. In remixing the reading and writing workshop as literacy workshop, Biggs-Tucker and Walther model how to maximize the precious little time we have with students to reflect our priorities—kids engaging in the real work of readers and writers, questioners and ponderers, global citizens and compassionate humans. This book guides, confirms, lifts, and gently nudges us to take our literacy practices to a place of rich instruction with classroom-ready lessons paired with some of the best titles from today's children's literature landscape. "

—Jessica Walsh, Instructional Specialist, Indian Prairie District 204, Aurora, IL

THE LITERACY WORKSHOP

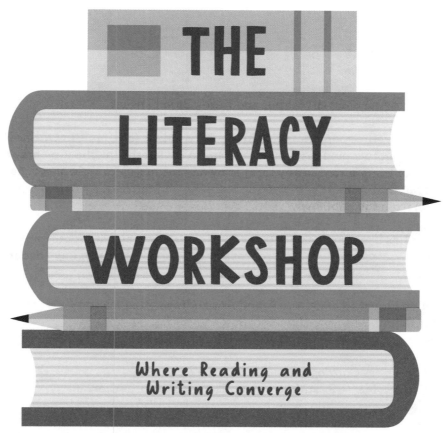

THE
LITERACY
WORKSHOP

Where Reading and
Writing Converge

MARIA WALTHER AND KAREN BIGGS-TUCKER

Stenhouse
PUBLISHERS

Portsmouth, New Hampshire

STENHOUSE PUBLISHERS
WWW.STENHOUSE.COM

Icons used in Figures 2.16, 3.10, 7.3, and Appendixes 3, 5, 12, and 14 are from VectorPortal.com.
Acknowledgments for additional borrowed material begin on page 283.

Library of Congress Cataloging-in-Publication Data
Names: Walther, Maria P., author. | Biggs-Tucker, Karen, author.
Title: The literacy workshop : where reading and writing converge / Maria Walther and Karen Biggs-Tucker.
Description: Portsmouth, New Hampshire : Stenhouse Publishers, [2020] | Includes bibliographical references and index.
Identifiers: LCCN 2019049380 (print) | LCCN 2019049381 (ebook) | ISBN 9781625311962 (paperback) | ISBN 9781625311979 (ebook)
Subjects: LCSH: Language arts (Elementary) | Literacy. | Project method in teaching.
Classification: LCC LB1576 .W25955 2020 (print) | LCC LB1576 (ebook) | DDC 372.6—dc23
LC record available at https://lccn.loc.gov/2019049380
LC ebook record available at https://lccn.loc.gov/2019049381

Cover design, interior design, and typesetting by Cindy Butler

Printed in the United States of America

This book is printed on paper certified by third-party standards for sustainably managed forestry.

26 25 24 23 22 21   4371   8 7 6 5 4 3

TO KATIE

May your life be a perfect blend of professional successes,
personal triumphs, and peaceful moments with friends and family.

MPW

TO MY MOTHER, MARGARET RABORN KRCHOV

Thank you for always blurring the lines between dreams and reality,
giving me the courage to try things I might never have done were it not
for your unwavering support.

KBT

CONTENTS

CHAPTER 3
LAUNCHING THE LITERACY WORKSHOP — DEVELOPING A PURPOSEFUL AND JOYFUL LEARNING COMMUNITY

CHAPTER 4
FOSTERING INDEPENDENCE AND ENGAGEMENT DURING LITERACY WORKSHOP

PART II
ZOOMING IN — LITERACY WORKSHOP DEMONSTRATION LESSONS

CHAPTER 5
DEMONSTRATION LESSONS — LAUNCHING LITERACY WORKSHOP

ACKNOWLEDGMENTS

It seems like just yesterday that our vision for this book began to take shape. But in reality, it was January 2016 in the lobby of the Great Northern Motel in Helena, Montana. We have fond memories of sitting on a comfy leather coach bouncing ideas back and forth. We wouldn't have been together in that lobby if it hadn't been for Steven Layne. Steve, thank you for inviting us both to serve on the Master of Education in Literacy Program's Advisory Board of Judson University. There, we met and discovered we had led parallel lives (a story for another time). We will be forever grateful to you for bringing us together and giving us the opportunity to write a Stenhouse proposal. We value your friendship and appreciate all that you did to make Judson University a place for us both to learn and to grow professionally.

When we reflect on the thinking, ideas, and lessons in this book, we are humbled as we consider the foundation of learning on which our work is built. We would not be the literacy teachers that we are today without the guidance of professional mentors such as Nancie Atwell, Ralph Fletcher, Donald Graves, Debbie Miller, and Katie Wood Ray, who, early in our careers, helped shape our beliefs about reading and writing workshop. As we continued to refine and reenvision workshop practices for our learners, we brought more voices into our conversations. We feel fortunate to have read books and attended presentations created by Ruth Culham, Gravity Goldberg, Peter Johnston, Ellin Keene, Donalyn Miller, Jen Serravallo, and many others about how to foster engagement and independence for our readers and writers. Your wisdom and expertise in the area of literacy instruction have created the canvas on which we painted our version of literacy workshop. We are grateful to be members of a community of educators who support us and guide the work that we have done, and will continue to do, to provide joyful learning experiences for all students!

From the moment we submitted our proposal, to the completion of this manuscript, we've felt welcomed and supported by everyone in the Stenhouse family. Jeff Anderson, you were our first champion. While we were presenting at a conference in Illinois, you encouraged us to pursue this idea and may have nudged a few others to join us on the journey. Thanks to Dan Tobin and Bill Varner for your vision and for continuing to create powerful professional learning opportunities for teachers. To our fellow Stenhouse authors, you are the ultimate encouragers—whether during our quick chats at conferences or via Twitter, your interest in this project has spurred us on. A special thanks to Lynne Dorfman, who has been cheering us on from the inception of this project to its completion. Shannon St. Peter, we can't thank you enough for your attention to detail and determination to help us get the permissions we needed to showcase all the children's literature that teachers will find in this book. We appreciate the support from all of the talented professionals behind the scenes in production, marketing, and editorial, especially Lynne Costa, who coached us through the production process. We are so honored to add our book to the Stenhouse collection.

A special shout-out to our editor, Terry Thompson, who, with every phone call, meeting, text, email, and query in our manuscript, showed us that you believed in us and in the vision of literacy workshop. We appreciate all the time that you invested in this project. You struck the perfect balance throughout this process—encouraging, questioning, guiding, and even a bit of nudging, when we needed it the most. We know how lucky we are to call you our editor and, more importantly, our friend.

We are grateful to the following publishers who have kept us up to date on the latest books for literacy learners and provided us with many of the titles featured in this resource: Candlewick, Chronicle, Disney-Hyperion, Macmillan Publishing Group, Penguin, Random House, and Scholastic. The books you help bring into the world are at the heart of our literacy lessons because they are loved by our students (and their teachers). Our teaching and this book would not shine the way they do without all of the authors and illustrators who create texts that engage learners in conversations that help them grow as readers, writers, and citizens of the world. In addition to the publishers who put books into our hands, we are so appreciative to everyone who works at our favorite independent bookstore, Anderson's Bookshop in Naperville, Illinois. We know that when we walk through the doors of your bookshop, we will always be able to find a title for a lesson or two and inspiration just by sitting among the shelves of amazing children's literature. Thank you for being the place that holds the second mortgage on both of our homes!

FROM MARIA

When you've been in education as long as I have, the lines begin to blur between colleagues, mentors, friends, and family. I feel so fortunate to have spent my career in Indian Prairie District 204 in Aurora, Illinois, where professional learning and innovation are valued and celebrated. While writing this book, I shifted roles from being a full-time first-grade teacher to splitting my time between learning with first graders in our demonstration classroom and supporting teachers as an instructional specialist for our district. This opportunity has provided me with a much broader view of the educational landscape that influenced many of the ideas in this book. I appreciate our superintendent, Karen Sullivan, and assistant superintendent, Laura Johnston, for your support of this unique position and for championing everything that embodies #FutureReady204. Kathy Pease, I'm honored to have ended my career in District 204 with you leading the way. I can't believe all we accomplished in two years to increase the reading volume for children and literacy expertise of teachers. You assembled a top-notch team, including Joan Peterson and Candy Michelli, who supported me as I attempted to balance helping hundreds of teachers better know and guide readers while, at the same time, teaching and writing this book.

In my new position, I was paired with two teammates who were by my side throughout the writing of this manuscript. Nadia Ji, I couldn't have asked for a more perfect colleague with whom to share my first graders. You were willing to "go rogue" and experiment with literacy workshop. Sitting next to you on the "sharing bench" and reading aloud many of the books included in this resource is a memory I will carry with me forever. I wish you the very best as you continue your career as an educator. Then, at the district office, I was fortunate to learn alongside Jessica Walsh, the other half of the #TwoTravelingTeachers. Thanks, Jess, for expanding my view of children's literature, nudging me to select more inclusive and diverse titles, and introducing me to so many talented #ownvoices authors and illustrators. For that, and for your friendship, I will be forever grateful.

As teachers, it is not often that you have the same colleague for a quarter of a century, but I did. Katherine Phillips-Toms, we started the Tuesday Night Team when Brooks opened because we wanted more time to reflect on, revise, and rethink how we learn alongside first graders. Those conversations have fueled a career's worth of professional growth and a willingness to try new things. You've stayed the course with me, supporting me through trying times and celebrating the joyous ones. I'm looking forward to another twenty-five years of friendship and fun.

Every member of our Tuesday Night Team, past and present, has contributed ideas to this book. I feel so lucky to be a member of this community of teachers who pushed me to question, to refine my practice, and to grow as an educator. Speaking of growing as an educator, I always say that the kids will teach you everything you need to know, and they do. The best ideas in this book come from my first graders. Although they probably didn't realize it at the time, observing them in action helped me plot a course to guide other teachers as they journey into literacy workshop.

Karen Biggs-Tucker, over the last decade, we grew to be colleagues, friends, and, now, coauthors! I'm constantly amazed at your ability to balance being a wife, mom, daughter, teacher, professor, writer, and thoughtful friend to so many. Watching you in action, whether in your fifth-grade or university classroom, is inspiring. I'm thankful you were willing to take a chance on writing this book together!

By the time this book is published, I will be nearing the end of my career as a full-time classroom teacher. Over the last thirty-four years, my husband, Lenny, has shown unwavering support of my desire to study, to teach, to write, and to present (and to try to have some fun in between). Whether it's scanning, stapling, videotaping, or pushing me out the door to the gym, he is always willing to lend a helping hand. I'm so excited for this next chapter of my career and for our (hopefully) less busy life together!

FROM KAREN

When you undertake creating a book about reading and writing, you understand the true meaning of being a literacy learner as you read, write, talk, collaborate, and reflect frequently. As I ponder on my experience creating this book, I am reminded that no writer makes that journey alone; they are supported by others. Often, it is that village that helps them make it to the finish line cheering (and sometimes nudging) them along their way. As I find myself at the finish line, my heart is grateful to so many who helped me get to this milestone.

Not many educators can say that they have spent their teaching careers in one district, but I have also spent those years at the same school, Wild Rose Elementary in District 303 in St. Charles, Illinois. It is there that I feel like I have grown up and flourished as a teacher. With the support of my colleagues and the autonomy to do what is in the best interest of learners, there is no other place that I would have wanted to spend the last thirty-four years. A special thank-you to Dr. Bob Allison, who created a culture of lifelong learning within our building, shared the vision of literacy workshop, and supported me throughout the process, always reminding me to find the joy in the work that I was doing with students every day.

But it is ultimately the learners who sat in my classroom each day who brought into focus what was most important about literacy. I learned so much about what it means to be a reader and a writer as I sat with you throughout the school year. I loved watching you fall in love with books and then seeing that love become a passion for creating your own texts. It was in that synergy that I really understood the true meaning of the reciprocity of reading and writing. Listening to you reflect on your learning helped me better understand what is truly important, and it not only guided my instruction but also provided me the inspiration for this book.

Once a week, I drive to Judson University in Elgin, Illinois, to work in the Master of Education in Literacy (MLIT) and Doctor of Education in Literacy (DLIT) Programs. I am blessed to be a part of a community of learners who help me grow in my own understanding about reading and writing instruction. It is through interactions with these amazing educators that I know that I am growing to be a literacy scholar—understanding the "why" of what I do with students, no matter their ages!

In the mid-1980s, Maria Walther and I sat in a room in DeKalb, Illinois, listening to Donald Graves talk about the tenets of writing workshop. We didn't know each other then. Little did we know that, thirty years later, we would be on a journey ourselves to write about a blended workshop. Maria, you have helped me grow in more ways than I could ever imagine, and my only regret is that our paths didn't cross sooner. Thank you for taking this journey with me. In the immortal words of Elephant and Piggie, "We are in a book!"

Learning some of my most important reading and writing lessons comes from being a mom. Thank you, Jason Biggs, for teaching me that literacy looks different for everyone, but when it comes, it is truly amazing. Being your mother has always been one of my favorite jobs, and it has been a joy watching you grow into the man that you are today. I also appreciate you bringing your wife, Sarah, into our family. She has added much joy to our lives, from engaging in book conversations to helping with writing projects when needed but, most of all, just being herself.

Every teacher needs a colleague at school to provide support with instruction and a spouse at home to be their cheerleader. I am blessed that I have someone who fills both roles at the same time! Brian Tucker, my teammate and husband (now, that is a story for another time), fills both roles in a way that I could never imagine anyone being able to do. Thank you for being willing to "think outside the box" and try literacy workshop in your classroom because you saw the power of integrating reading and writing instruction. Teaching alongside you over the last several years has deepened my understanding of what it means to be a reader and a writer, as you demonstrate authentic ways for learners to make meaning throughout their instructional day. You truly are my best friend because you know how to make me laugh, walk me back from the ledge, and help me believe in myself. My heart and life are full because you are in them.

ONLINE RESOURCES ACCESS INFORMATION

The Literacy Workshop Online Resources include access to ten demonstration lessons and reproducible resources for downloading and printing, including a comprehensive big ideas chart. To access the Online Resources, please follow the directions below.

ACCESS INFORMATION:

- Go to **https://page.stenhouse.com/litworkshopolr**
- Fill out the form, click Submit.
- When prompted, enter this passcode: **LitWorkshop20**
- You will immediately receive an email that gives you the link to access the resources. This is the link you will use from here on, so please bookmark it for easy access.
- You may need to enter the passcode each time you access this page.

YOU WILL NOW HAVE ACCESS TO:
DEMONSTRATION LESSONS
BIG IDEA CHARTS

CHAPTER 5
Demonstration Lessons—Launching Literacy Workshop
Common Threads: Big Ideas for Launching Literacy Workshop
    Big Idea: Ideas
    Big Idea: Response

CHAPTER 6
Demonstration Lessons—Fostering Independence and Engagement
Common Threads: Big Ideas for Fostering Independence and Engagement
    Big Idea: Reflect

CHAPTER 8
Demonstration Lessons—Teaching the Elements of Fiction
Common Threads: Big Ideas for Teaching the Elements of Fiction
    Big Idea: Language
    Big Idea: Point of View

APPENDIXES

PREVIEW: SHIFTING PERSPECTIVES

For an educator, perspective shifting is a powerful tool for reflection and a catalyst for peda-gogical change. For us, it was a subtle change in perspective that led to the focal point of this book. About a decade ago, we began reexamining our instructional practices in light of more rigorous literacy standards. As we incorporated this new view into our literacy instruction, we noticed that it made sense to us and to our students to *occasionally* merge our reading and writing workshops. Curious to learn more, we experimented with an inte-grated literacy workshop. We noticed that when the opportunities arose to combine our reading and writing workshops, we had more time to spend on big ideas and students were able to uncover exciting connections. In addition, these blended learning opportunities empowered our learners to explore the natural relationship between reading and writing. As a bit of bonus, we also quickly realized that a literacy workshop approach helped us to better manage our precious instructional minutes.

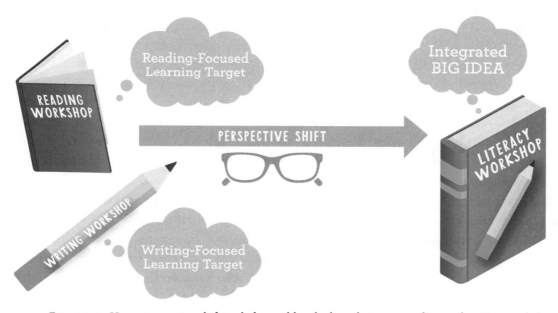

Figure 0.0   How perspective shifting led us to blur the lines between reading and writing workshop.

We shouldn't have been surprised by this, because as these connections were being made organically in our own classrooms, researchers were already at work establishing the power of the reciprocal relationship between reading and writing, confirming that the two are intimately aligned. Think about it—both processes depend on many of the same skills, strategies, and knowledge, though they are demonstrated in different ways by the learner (Shanahan 2008). This echoes Steve Graham and Michael Hebert's *Writing to*

Read study (2010), which found that writing practices can actually enhance our students' ability to read. Graham and Hebert reiterated that the more students read, the stronger their writing becomes, and the more they write, the better their reading develops. Creating intentional links between practices such as written response to boost comprehension and process writing to enhance written pieces helps strengthen the reciprocal processes of both reading and writing (Graham and Hebert 2010).

Another plus in shifting to an integrated literacy workshop is that it can increase the time your students spend engaged in authentic reading and writing rather than "stuff," as Richard Allington (2002) refers to it. Allington's definition of *stuff* is "all the other things teachers have children do instead of reading and writing" (742). Here's the good news: when you weave your reading and writing minilessons together and focus on integrated big ideas, you free up instructional time for children to apply their learning. In her book *Teach Writing Well*, Ruth Culham calls for lessons grounded in "a short instructional burst on a specific topic" (2018, 120). In the chapters that follow, we'll show you how to fuse together reading and writing concepts to create these short instructional bursts we call *demonstration lessons*. As Nell Duke and her colleagues (2018) discovered, demonstration lessons like the ones you'll find in this book have an added benefit: they create a climate where students are motivated to focus, apply themselves, and persist in completing tasks. And these were exactly the results we were getting—stronger readers and writers who were motivated and invested in their learning.

Likely, you've already experienced some of these reciprocal benefits in your own classrooms. So, this begs the question—if we know that reading and writing go hand in hand, doesn't it make sense to integrate our separate reading and writing workshops to cement this connection for students and weave together the common threads of literacy learning? Literacy workshop offers an opportunity to do just that—merge the two workshops into a seamless learning event focused on one literacy-related big idea.

At this point, you are probably thinking to yourself, *Integrate my workshops? What would this look like?* Imagine for a moment that you and your students are exploring nonfiction texts. During reading workshop you plan to introduce text structures such as *question/answer* and *compare/contrast* while, at a separate time, during writing workshop, you'll guide your students as they create nonfiction pieces. *What if*, instead—for a few days—you combined the two workshops and invited learners to study nonfiction text structures from both a reader's and a writer's perspective? After your demonstration lesson, you might find a group of students poring over Jerry Pallotta's *Who Would Win?* series (2009–2019), in preparation for a collaborative effort to write their own version using a question/answer format, while Quentin studies how Jenni Desmond expertly used comparison in her book *The Blue Whale* (2015) as he revises his nonfiction piece. Across the room, some children read while others write, all with a laser focus on learning more about how nonfiction texts are structured. To imagine a scenario like this happening in your classroom, it may help to think of the what-if possibilities. During our literacy workshop journey, we discovered the stunning picture book *What If . . .* (Berger 2018a), where a young artist asks, "What if . . ." as she ponders innovative ways to express her creativity. Literacy workshop invites you and your students to innovate, create, and consider the following possibilities when your reading and writing workshops converge:

- *What if . . .* we found a way to integrate both reading and writing instruction into a single, focused workshop?
- *What if . . .* our learners understood the powerful connections that exist between reading and writing, boosting their confidence in both realms?
- *What if . . .* students had choices within literacy workshop to engage with reading, writing, response, or research in meaningful ways to enhance their learning?
- *What if . . .* we created opportunities for our students to engage in instruction that mirrored the habits, behaviors, and actions of literate citizens?

This book will guide you in making the leap to literacy workshop a reality in your classroom. To support you as you blur the lines between your reading and writing workshops, we've filled the pages that follow with practical ideas, replicable demonstration lessons, and carefully selected book titles straight from our primary- and intermediate-grade classrooms. As we travel with you on this journey, we will examine literacy workshop from different perspectives. In Part I, we'll offer the wide-angle view. Chapter 1 will frame the workshop, highlighting the reciprocal relationships that support literacy workshop. If you're wondering how to plan for literacy workshop, Chapter 2 will shed light behind the scenes. When you're ready to launch literacy workshop, turn to Chapter 3. Then, in Chapter 4, you will find strategies for fostering students' engagement and independence. In Part II, we will zoom in by offering you forty-four demonstration lessons to try out in your primary- or intermediate-grade literacy workshop. You will find an additional ten demonstration lessons in the Online Resources. To set the stage, you'll find demonstration lessons for launching your workshop (Chapter 5) and nurturing student independence (Chapter 6) before moving on to demonstrations that focus on literacy strategies (Chapter 7) and elements of fiction and nonfiction (Chapters 8 and 9, respectively). From the big picture to the helpful details, we'll be right by your side as you blur the lines between your workshops—creating, innovating, and taking risks by continually asking yourself, *What if . . .*

PART I
Exploring the Landscape of Literacy Workshop

Reading is like breathing in and writing is like breathing out.

—Pam Allyn and Ernest Morrell,
Every Child a Super Reader: 7 Strengths to Open a World of Possible

CHAPTER 1

Framing the Literacy Workshop

In literacy workshop classrooms, children inhale authors' words and ideas and exhale their own interpretations and extensions of those thoughts in their conversations and responses. The back-and-forth flow of language helps student discover new ways of thinking about their work as both readers and writers. This breathing in and breathing out is the essence of literacy workshop and an ongoing goal for our students. For this two-way flow of understanding to happen successfully, it will help to begin with a clear picture of what literacy workshop is and how it might look in your classroom. With this in mind, we'll kick things off with a quick glimpse of literacy workshop in action in our classrooms. Then, we'll follow up with a look at some of the foundational elements that support integrating your reading and writing workshop time so you can breathe new life into your literacy instruction.

THE VIEW FROM HERE:
LITERACY WORKSHOP IN A PRIMARY-GRADE CLASSROOM

Let's step into Maria's first-grade class during one of her early literacy workshops. As the music on her iPod sings "Good Morning Baltimore" from the musical *Hairspray*, the children gather in their places for learning. Maria begins by sharing the purpose, or learning target, of the literacy workshop: "Together, during literacy workshop, we are going to try to figure out how drawing and writing make us better at reading. "Think back to the last few days of reading workshop. We've been learning about the difference between fiction and nonfiction texts. Have you ever noticed that when you're reading a nonfiction text, there is a lot to remember? Today, I'm going to show you how drawing and writing while reading a nonfiction text can help you as a reader."

With a clipboard, a pencil, and sticky notes in hand, Maria thinks aloud and sketches and labels (Figure 1.1) as she reads the nonfiction book *Dolphins* (Baines 2016). After reading aloud a few pages, Maria says, "The first three pages are about living in groups, so I'm going to draw a quick sketch of a group of dolphins and label it 'group.' Let me stretch out the word *group*—GR-OO-P. The next page is about how dolphins talk, so I'll add a speech bubble to my sketch."

Maria continues in this fashion until it is time to release the responsibility to her learners: "Now it's your turn to try it! I'm going to keep reading while you draw or write." Ready with their own clipboards, sticky notes, and pencils in hand, first graders sketch and label while Maria reads aloud the next page or two. After a brain break, the children return to their *places for learning* to reflect on the experience. On an anchor chart, Maria records their answers to the question "How did drawing and writing help you better remember key ideas and details in the nonfiction book *Dolphins*?"

Figure 1.1   Maria's Dolphin Sketches

Equipped with the knowledge they gained from the demonstration, first graders are ready for action. Since she's already introduced the routines of independent reading and writing during the separate workshops, Maria explains to them, "Today, I want you to think about the best way to practice what we've just learned. You could choose to do the same exact thing we did in a nonfiction book from your book box, or you could draw and label your own little book to teach someone else about a topic."

After this invitation, some children choose to read and record while others create their own informational text. As they are working independently, Maria confers and guides them in their pursuits. Based on her previous observations and assessments, Maria gathers a small group of learners who need a bit of extra guidance. Together, they draw and label their way through a nonfiction book at their instructional level, providing time for her to prompt, to coach, and to scaffold at points of need. After fifteen minutes or so, she gathers the class back together to share and celebrate.

THE VIEW FROM HERE:
LITERACY WORKSHOP IN AN INTERMEDIATE-GRADE CLASSROOM

Meanwhile, in Karen's fifth-grade classroom, students settle in for learning time during literacy workshop. It may seem like just another morning as her fifth graders unpack and organize their materials, but today, students are buzzing with excitement as they begin their work pondering how figurative language is used in reading and writing.

Some dive into their books to continue reading independently, others grab a pencil and their literacy notebooks to write or sketch, and a few power up computers to record ideas or search for information. It may appear a bit chaotic to some, but during this portion of literacy workshop, students are making deliberate choices about the type of work that they will engage in during their learning time that day.

The orderly chaos can occur because Karen has spent time helping her middle-grade students learn not only what their choices are but also how to manage their time when working on a project. Because time management is an important life skill, Karen teaches (and, yes, reteaches) it throughout the year. To help support her students as they make choices, Karen checks in with them using the same management strategy she uses in both reading and writing workshop called *Status of the Class*. This quick, daily strategy, where learners share what they will be working on, helps Karen's students set realistic goals and alerts her to who might need a bit more guidance once they begin working independently.

After Status of the Class, Karen has quick *mini-conferences* with students who've requested help or those she's identified as needing teacher guidance. She checks in on a group of students wrestling with planning a collaborative book study and makes suggestions for how they might

Figure 1.2   During literacy workshop students make deliberate choices about how to apply their learning.

record and share their thinking. "Remember how we've learned that readers often record their thoughts on sticky notes either while they are reading or at the end of chapters," she coaches the group. "You might consider doing this so you have some notes to start your conversations when you get together. After your discussion, you might want to put the sticky notes in your literacy notebook in case you'd want to do some writing based on what you've learned."

Next, Karen settles in for a more in-depth conference with Cielo, who is working on integrating some figurative language into a book that she's drafting to share with readers in the younger grade levels at her school. She has already gathered some key phrases from her independent reading and is incorporating some of those phrases into her story, but now she is stuck. Karen asks her to share examples from her writing so far and then helps her find a few mentor texts that include more examples of figurative language. Before she steps away, Karen invites Cielo to check back with her to share her revised draft and then scans the room for her next conference.

As you can see, regardless of the grade level, the literacy workshop is a purposeful time when students collaborate, research, converse, and share with others, blurring the lines between reading and writing while finding new purposes for their own learning. Time after time, we've seen the potential of this integrated literacy workshop to build our students' capacity as thoughtful, independent, and captivated literacy learners. And, with these images in your mind, we'll turn our attention to how the concept of literacy workshop came into focus.

Figure 1.3   Fifth graders read, write, collaborate, and converse during literacy workshop.

READING AND WRITING: COMPLEMENTARY COLORS

We're sure that if you pause and ponder for a moment, you can think of some common threads running through the minilessons you teach in your separate reading and writing workshops. Let's say, for instance, you're getting ready to teach a minilesson about characters in reading workshop. You might choose to read aloud a picture book like *Alan's Big, Scary Teeth* (Jarvis 2016) about Alan the alligator, who is best known for scaring the other animals with his "razor-sharp" teeth (Figure 1.4). During your demonstration, you think aloud and say, "As a reader, I learn about Alan as a character by thinking about his actions like brushing his big, scary teeth; practicing his frightening faces in the mirror; and saying scary things. These actions help me to understand that Alan loves being scary." On the flip side, during writing workshop you could use the same book as a mentor text to better understand how writers create memorable characters. Voila! The common thread, character study, emerges. So, instead of doing these two minilessons separately, you can merge them together during an integrated literacy workshop. In Figure 1.5, you'll notice a sampling of some of the other common threads we've identified through the process of developing the literacy workshop demonstration lessons you'll find in Chapters 5–9 and in the Online Resources. We believe that when we weave together those reciprocal concepts to create integrated literacy workshop demonstrations, it helps strengthen our practice as well as deepen our learners' understanding of literacy concepts.

Figure 1.4   Common threads emerge as you explore picture books from both a reader's and a writer's point of view.

READING WORKSHOP	LITERACY WORKSHOP COMMON THREADS	WRITING WORKSHOP
	Response	
What are the different ways I might respond to my own reading?	What are the habits and behaviors of responsive people?	What are the different ways I might respond to my own writing?
How do my reading responses help improve my understanding?	Why is responding in different ways important to my reading and writing life?	How do my writing responses help improve my craft?
Why do the responses of others help me grow as a reader?	How might I use response and input from others when I read and write?	Why do the responses of others help me grow as a writer?
	Ideas (Schema)	
How does activating and building my background knowledge help me better understand texts?	How do I build on what I already know to help me learn new things?	How does accessing my schema help spark ideas for writing?
How does connecting my schema to what is happening in the story help me better understand?	How do I share my ideas and new learning with others?	How does connecting to my readers' experiences help draw them into my writing?
	Structure	
What is happening in the story?	How do the plots in stories help me to better understand my life and the lives of others?	What is the best structure to help move the action of my story forward?
How does figuring out the plot structure help me better understand the story?	How can I apply what I've learned from reading texts with various structures to my own writing?	How can I create plots that will keep a reader on the edge of their seat?

Figure 1.5   **A Sampling of Literacy Workshop Common Threads**
For a complete list of literacy workshop common threads, see Appendix 1 in the Online Resources.

How Writing Colors Reading

Are you a pencil-in-hand reader? Do you jot notes in the margins of your professional books? If so, then writing colors your reading, just as it does the reading of the students in your care. As longtime educators, we've discovered from observation and reflection that our students' reading ability grows when they are immersed in both reading and writing experiences throughout their day. Readers who are writers gain insights into an author's mindset and understand what authors do. This knowledge not only improves student writing but also helps them better comprehend the texts that they read (Shanahan 2008). For instance, when young learners create their own version of a repetitive, pattern book such as *Hello Hello* by Brendan Wenzel (2018), they internalize Wenzel's environmental message as they hone their emergent writing skills.

We have also noticed that when readers write about texts, their emotional connections to those texts increase. Louise Rosenblatt's (1978) transactional theory of reader response reminds us that an aesthetic response to literature, one in which a reader expresses insights, strong emotions, real-life connections, and individual meaning making, cements positive personal encounters with literature. Written response to literature is a tried-and-true means of capturing powerful transactions and promoting positive experiences with books (Hancock 1993).

Developing a relationship with text can be challenging for readers, but writing can often be the vehicle that allows many students to do just that. After Karen shared with her students the story behind the picture book *Beautiful Hands* (Otoshi 2015), she invited them to respond aesthetically by reflecting on what their hands could do (Figure 1.6). As Karen's learners wrote about their reading, they were able to process what the text said, connect to what the author was saying to the reader, and create meaning based on that *transaction*. This personal reaction helped her fifth graders deepen their understanding of the text because, as Sylvia Pantaleo (1995) points out, "The written response, like the reading process, is a way for readers to work through their understanding and interpretations of texts in personally significant ways." (77). Moreover, when readers engage in written response to reading, whether they are answering text-related questions, analyzing the text, or reacting personally to what they have read, they are better able to process the author's meaning (Graham and Hebert 2010). Because writing slows down readers' thinking processes, they are able to dig deeper into the text as they are writing about it. We're guessing you've seen this in your own classrooms as readers jot down their thinking before, during, or after reading.

For our youngest readers, writing about reading provides additional benefits specifically in the areas of phonemic awareness and phonics. When writing or encoding, young learners develop phonemic awareness in a natural and functional manner. In addition, they strengthen their letter-sound knowledge as they spell things the way they sound. Why?

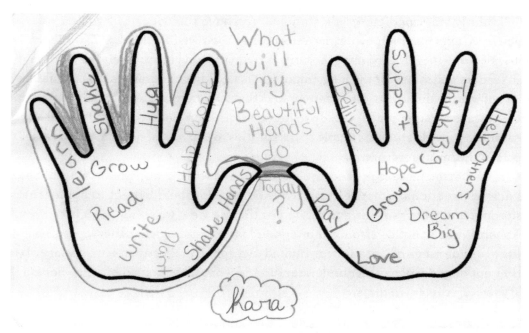

Figure 1.6   A fifth grader's aesthetic response to the book *Beautiful Hands* by Kathryn Otoshi.

Because phonics is so much more transparent and easier to deal with in spelling than it is in reading (Carreker 2011; Foorman and Francis 1994). Finally, writing makes understanding story structure as a reader more concrete. When writers apply their knowledge of story elements to create a piece, they are better able to understand the same elements when they find them in a book (Pearson 2002).

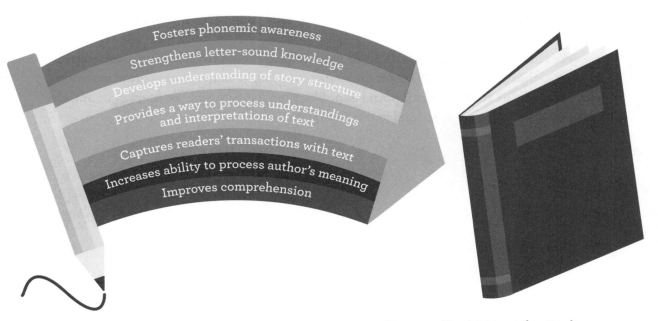

Figure 1.7   How Writing Colors Reading

Similarly, intermediate-grade students who have the opportunity to transfer what they read in texts into their own pieces strengthen their writing. In *How Texts Teach What Readers Learn* (1988), Margaret Meek offers many lessons reinforcing the fact that texts teach readers and stresses "the most important lesson that children learn is the nature and variety of written discourse, the different ways that language lets a writer tell, and the many different ways a reader reads" (21). In a literacy workshop classroom, text-based learning experiences provide students ample opportunities to learn lessons from the diverse landscape of children's literature.

As we started merging our separate reading and writing workshops, we realized that this new instructional practice was providing an additional benefit to our learners by reinforcing many of the skills and strategies that we were teaching them in our reading workshop. We soon noticed from our integrated practices that when literacy learners have access to a wide range of texts and are invited to respond to those texts in a variety of ways, writing not only deepens their understanding of what they've read but also boosts their ability to craft their own texts.

How Reading Colors Writing

Creating an awareness of and an appreciation for an author's decision-making process is key as learners develop their own writing style. Reading like a writer invites student authors into the process by giving them an opportunity to learn from experienced writers. By learning from authors who have "mastered" the writing process, students can take the models that they see in these mentor texts and experiment with them in their own writing (Anderson 2005; Ray 1999). As classroom teachers, we observe on a daily basis the importance of sharing the expertise of published authors with our students whether it is through an interactive read-aloud experience or a side-by-side conference with a writer; we know the power of a mentor text.

As students experiment with their own writing *moves* that they've gleaned from mentor authors, they not only better understand how texts work but also grow as writers. It is through this reading, writing, and experimentation cycle that the literacy bonds are strengthened in our students and in our workshop time.

Over time, we observed that creating connections between reading and writing for our students helped to strengthen the bonds between their learning of the two. Building instruction around the *common threads* (shown in Figure 1.5 and in Appendix 1) gives us the opportunity to nurture and cement this important relationship between reading and writing. Even Maria's first graders begin to use the language from the common threads as they share their discoveries with her and with their classmates. Likewise, as Karen's learners grow and develop, she notices them using the common threads terms as they converse with each other and create their goals during literacy workshop. In this way, literacy workshop is a win-win for you as a teacher as it helps to streamline your literacy instruction and empowers your learners at the same time!

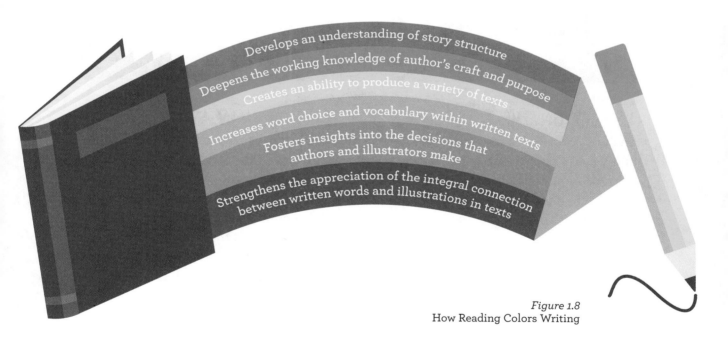

Develops an understanding of story structure

Deepens the working knowledge of author's craft and purpose

Creates an ability to produce a variety of texts

Increases word choice and vocabulary within written texts

Fosters insights into the decisions that authors and illustrators make

Strengthens the appreciation of the integral connection between written words and illustrations in texts

Figure 1.8
How Reading Colors Writing

TEXTS THAT HAVE SHAPED OUR THINKING ABOUT AN INTEGRATED LITERACY WORKSHOP

Our study of the connections between reading and writing has slowly developed over the years as we've written and read professionally, discussed our thoughts, and learned with and from our students. The following are some of the books that we've written and read that served as springboards and helped shape our thinking about blurring the lines between reading and writing:

- *Mentor Texts: Teaching Writing Through Children's Literature*, 2nd ed. (Dorfman and Cappelli 2017)

- *Transforming Literacy Instruction in the Era of Higher Standards (K–2)* (Walther 2016)

- *Transforming Literacy Instruction in the Era of Higher Standards (3–5)* (Biggs-Tucker and Tucker 2015)

- *Wondrous Words: Writers and Writing in the Elementary Classroom* (Ray 1999)

- *Writers ARE Readers: Flipping Reading Instruction into Writing Opportunities* (Laminack and Wadsworth 2015)

- *Writers Read Better: Nonfiction* (Cruz 2018)

- *Writers Read Better: Narrative* (Cruz 2019)

- *Writing About Reading: From Book Talk to Literary Essays, Grades 3–8* (Angelillo 2003)

REFLECT ON THE FOUNDATION: PONDERING A NEW VIEW

In this book, we'll share various paths we took on our journey to figure out the most effective ways to engage our learners and prepare them to be literate citizens through an integrated literacy workshop. We embarked on this quest not only with our students, but also with each other. If possible, we encourage you to find a colleague or two (educators you can chat with in person or those with whom you might connect virtually via social media) to join you in this new collaboration as you trek alongside us. At the end of each chapter, we'll share a few of the thoughts and questions that have shaped our exploration along the way with hopes that they'll help guide your conversations as you move forward in your thinking about literacy workshop:

- What are some of the similarities between what your students do in both reading and writing workshop? Think about the various ways your students' literacy learning behaviors in the two workshops have common threads.

- If you're a risk taker, have a conversation with your students about what literacy workshop might look like in your classroom. Even if it is something you do one day a week, explore the possibilities of integrating reading and writing during literacy workshop. Let your students show you what they already know about how reading and writing overlap. When you let your learners lead the way, it might be easier than you think!

- If you prefer to color within the lines, continue reading. In Chapter 2, we'll talk about how to plan a literacy workshop, in Chapter 3, we'll share how to launch the workshop, and in Chapter 4, you'll discover what we've learned so far about increasing students' engagement and independence.

Our classrooms should be places of inquiry, joy, trial and error, exploration, success and failure, and fascinations revealed—where the process of discovery matters as much as (if not more than) the destination.

Ruth Culham, *Teach Writing Well: How to Assess Writing, Invigorate Instruction, and Rethink Revision*

CHAPTER 2

Planning for Literacy Workshop—Behind the Scenes

The picture book *Same, Same but Different* by Jenny Sue Kostecki-Shaw (2011) tells the story of an American boy named Elliot and his pen pal, Kailash, who lives halfway around the world in India. By exchanging letters and drawings, the two boys discover that their lives are alike in some ways and different in others. When we read this book with our students, it sparks conversations about the similarities and differences in the texts they are reading and among the learners in our classrooms. The theme of the story has also helped us shape what we call a *literacy workshop mindset*. We're guessing that, after reading Chapter 1, you're starting to see how an integrated workshop structure is *same, same but different* from what you may already be doing in your classroom. If so,

Figure 2.1 The book *Same, Same but Different* helps frame the concept of literacy workshop.

you are already on your way to developing your literacy workshop mindset. As we describe how to plan for blending your workshops together, we'll use this notion of *same, same but different* to help you expand your frame of mind regarding literacy workshop.

REFLECT ON TEACHING:
PLANNING FROM A LITERACY WORKSHOP MINDSET

From the outset, we want you to know that planning for literacy workshop will take on some of the same characteristics that Ruth Culham uses to describe classrooms in this chapter's opening epigraph. There will be trial and error, successes and challenges, but the fascinations that your children reveal will make it worth the effort. We promise! Before we dive into the nitty-gritty of planning, we thought you would appreciate it if we spent a bit of time answering the two burning questions that might be on your mind at this point: *How will my teaching moves during literacy workshop look the same, yet different from my current practices?* and *How will I decide when to do literacy workshop?* To help guide our thinking, we reflected on Lucy Calkins's oft-quoted advice, reminding us to cultivate learning environments that are "deliberately kept simple so as to support the complexities of the work-in-progress" and, at the same time, are "deliberately kept predictable so the unpredictable can happen" (1983, 32). To sustain the creative environment of literacy workshop, our goal is to keep components of our instruction as predictable as possible so that we can all (teachers and learners) let the unpredictable happen. With this aim in mind, when defining the components of literacy workshop, we separate them into two distinct categories: *teacher actions* and *learner actions*. You'll notice that the teacher actions outlined in Figure 2.2 might look familiar, as they closely mirror the instructional practices that may already take place in your separate workshops. Thus, they are the *same, same but different*. Since the purpose of this chapter is to guide you in planning for literacy workshop, we will detail the teacher actions on pages 39-53. Then, in Chapter 3, you'll learn more about what your children will be doing, or what we refer to as learner actions.

TEACHER ACTIONS DURING LITERACY WORKSHOP

Over time, we noticed that our interactions with students in literacy workshop often consisted of similar strategies, or teaching techniques, that we were already using in our separate reading and writing workshops. Eventually, as we started focusing on these commonalities, we identified nine teacher actions that work in harmony to move students toward uncovering deep understandings:

- Teach Demonstration Lessons
  - ⊙ Anchor Learning in Literature
  - ⊙ Converse to Grow Thinkers and Learners
  - ⊙ Demonstrate the Strategies and Habits of Literate Citizens
  - ⊙ Record Thinking and Learning

- Let Them Go! Application in Practice
- Sit Among Learners: Small-Group Support
- Sit Beside Learners: Individual Conferences
- Share and Celebrate

Figure 2.2

Before we tackle your second burning question, it is important to acknowledge a well-established truth about teaching children—there is no one-size-fits-all approach (Figure 2.3). If there were, we could take a vacation each summer instead of attending conferences and reading the latest research-guided thinking found on Twitter, on education blogs, and in the professional books that teeter on the top of our to-be-read stacks. The fact that our approach to teaching reflects the needs of the students in our classrooms is one of the many reasons that teaching children is unpredictable. We've all spent hours planning what we believe is going to be an awe-inspiring learning experience, and then one compelling question from a student steers the lesson in a vastly different direction. Like teaching, in general, inviting children to learn in a literacy

Figure 2.3   There is no one-size-fits-all approach to teaching children.

workshop is an ever-changing venture, and you'll want to keep this in mind as you continue to read this chapter. As we discuss the teacher actions and structures to support your planning for literacy workshop, note that these understandings are based on our research-led experiences and current learning contexts. We encourage you to view our ideas as catalysts for innovation as you reenvision and adjust them to make sense for your students, your learning environment, and your unique teaching style. That's what accomplished teachers, like you, do!

REFLECT ON TEACHING:
NOTICING THE CUES THAT LEAD TO LITERACY WORKSHOP

Now to address your second question. How often do you choose to do literacy workshop, and how do you decide when it is most helpful for your students? In our first- and fifth-grade classrooms, integrated literacy workshop might happen once or twice a week or several days in a row based on the needs of our students and big ideas of our ELA (English Language Arts) curriculum. Of course, there are times during the year that our learners need targeted learning experiences in either reading workshop or writing workshop. During these times, we separate our workshop times, as usual. Thus, across a week or month our workshop times may look the *same, same but different.*

What are the cues that help us choose to blur the lines between our reading and writing workshops and move our students into literacy workshop? First and foremost, we consider the needs of our students and how we can create the optimal learning environment for them to dig deeper into their literacy learning. Then, we examine our English Language Arts (ELA) standards and curriculum, searching for the common threads. Next, we weigh the ever-present factor of time (Figure 2.4). In essence, the decision involves thinking about what our students already know and need to learn more about (big ideas), considering what they are ready to do independently (learning targets), and organizing the time and support (teacher actions) so that they can most effectively apply new knowledge (learner actions).

Imagine it is the beginning of the school year. As you get to know your students, you've noticed that your writers are having difficulty coming up with ideas for writing, and a few of your readers aren't using their background knowledge to help them make meaning from the texts they are reading. In both workshops, they need a bit more support with *ideas* (big idea). So, you decide to merge your workshops for a few days so that you can pause and further explore ideas. You craft a demonstration lesson (teacher action) with this goal in mind: *How does what I already know help me as a reader and writer?* (learning target). Following the demonstration lesson (for the complete demonstration lesson, see Online Resources for What's Inside My Idea Jar?), as learners are either reading or writing (learner actions), you bring a small group of kids together (those who are often without ideas for writing and have difficulty connecting with the texts they are reading) to revisit

CUES FOR ENGAGING IN LITERACY WORKSHOP

The following are a few reasons you might choose to engage in literacy workshop with your students:

- Strengthen students' understanding of the reciprocal nature of reading and writing
- Capitalize on optimal opportunities to blend the processes of reading and writing or *common threads* (see Appendix 1 in the Online Resources)
- Exceed curricular expectations
- Focus on integrated learning standards

- Dig deeper into a topic or question
- Highlight the habits and behaviors of literate citizens
- Build future-ready learning skills
- Meet the diverse needs of students
- Provide choice within structure
- Increase student engagement
- Make the most of precious instructional minutes

Figure 2.4

the book *Idea Jar* (Lehrhaupt 2018). For this group, you're hoping a quick focused review of how accessing background knowledge or schema is a helpful tool when searching for writing ideas *and* when trying to deepen their understanding of a text will reinforce this concept. Supporting these students as they revisit the words and phrases already in their "jar" to help them view the ideas through both their writers' and their readers' lenses may spark a new idea for a writing piece or reframe their reading stances. If you're lucky, it will do both! Once this group is back to learning, you confer with the students you've targeted to see whether your demonstration lesson resonated with them or if they, too, may need more guidance (teacher actions). Notice how the teacher actions in this example are the *same, same but different* from if you were to focus on background knowledge at one time with writers and, again, at a separate time with readers.

In Figure 2.5, we've included some questions that we use to guide our decision-making process. While this list offers a starting place, we encourage you to trust your professional judgment. We've found that our most successful literacy workshop experiences were the ones that happened organically—the teachable moments that surfaced when we listened to our students and focused on *the process of discovery*.

QUESTIONS TO GUIDE YOUR DECISION-MAKING PROCESS

- What do your students already know and need to know more about? (big ideas)

- What is your learning target for this literacy workshop time?

- Which text could you read aloud to illuminate the learning target?

- How might you demonstrate the habit, behavior, strategy, or skill?

- Will you co-create an anchor chart, or will your students record their own wonderings and discoveries?

- What integrated strategies/skills might students apply during literacy workshop learning time? (learner actions)

- How will you support learners as they gather or apply new knowledge? (teacher actions)

Figure 2.5

Before we take a close-up look at the practicalities of preparing for literacy workshop, it's important to examine its underpinnings, specifically the workshop approach to teaching and the *support and send out* model of instruction. Since the workshop approach can be interpreted differently, depending on whom you consult, we'll take a few moments here to define and describe what we will call a traditional workshop approach.

IN THE BACKGROUND: THE WORKSHOP APPROACH TO TEACHING

Both of us have been using the workshop approach for teaching readers and writers for decades. The beauty of this instructional practice is that it scaffolds learning for children in a way that nudges them toward independence. In addition, the components and structure that provide the foundation for the approach also nurture the development of students' reading and writing identities. Grown out of the gradual release of responsibility model of teaching, the workshop begins with the teacher leading the learning and gradually shifts the choices and responsibility to the students. The goal of a workshop over time is to provide students with the skills and strategies they need to independently navigate the text they are reading or the piece of writing they are crafting. More importantly, a workshop builds a vibrant community of independent learners (Figure 2.6).

Figure 2.6   The workshop approach builds a vibrant community of independent learners.

The components and structure of a traditional workshop lay the groundwork for authentic reading and writing experiences (Figure 2.7), so we mirror that format during literacy workshop. Typically, a reading or writing workshop begins with the teacher sharing a piece of text. Then, using that text, she highlights either a reading strategy or a writing craft move by teaching a minilesson. Following the minilesson, students engage in either independent reading or writing (depending on the type of workshop). To support students in applying their learning, the teacher confers with individuals or meets with students in small groups as the other students work independently. Finally, the class gathers together to share new learning and to celebrate successes. For additional professional resources about reading and writing workshop see Figure 2.8.

Interactive Read-Aloud

Minilesson

Supported Independent Reading or Writing

Conferring

Meeting with Small Groups

Sharing and Celebrating

Figure 2.7   The Components and Structure of a Traditional Workshop

As the term *workshop* implies, students are applying their accumulated knowledge to create meaning from the words in a text or to craft words to share their thoughts with others. The students' independent creation or crafting guided by the intentional nudging of the teacher mirrors the mentoring relationship in an apprentice-type workshop. Of course, the complexities of this relationship are the crux of the workshop, and that is where the support and send out model of instruction fits in.

PROFESSIONAL RESOURCES ABOUT READING AND WRITING WORKSHOP

If you're not yet familiar with the traditional workshop approach and/or want to learn more about its application in the classroom, here are a few of our favorite go-to professional resources.

About the Authors: Writing Workshop with Our Youngest Writers (Ray and Cleaveland 2004)

In the Middle: A Lifetime of Learning About Writing, Reading, and Adolescents (Atwell 2015)

Reading with Meaning: Teaching Comprehension in the Primary Grades (Miller 2013)

What's the Best That Could Happen? (Miller 2018)

The Writing Teacher's Companion (Fletcher 2017)

Writing Workshop (Fletcher and Portalupi 2001)

Figure 2.8

IN THE BACKGROUND:
THE SUPPORT AND SEND OUT MODEL OF INSTRUCTION

As previously mentioned, the workshop approach grew out of the *gradual release of responsibility* model of teaching (Pearson and Gallagher 1983). Like many teachers, when we first learned about the gradual release framework, we viewed the three stages of instruction as occurring in a linear fashion. In other words, progressing from *modeling (I do)*, to *guided practice (We do)*, and concluding with *independence (You do)*. Over the years, and as we began dabbling with literacy workshop, our view of the gradual release model has evolved as we were nudged by other experts in the field to think about it in a more flexible and student-focused manner.

During literacy workshop, we use the gradual release model work of Debbie Miller (2013), Keene and Zimmerman (2011), and others as we consider ways to release responsibility to students that best meet the needs of our learners. So, instead of following the linear progression from modeling to independence, we might choose to send students to apply their knowledge independently first. Then, as students are working, we use our kid-watching skills to observe, assess, and provide support as needed. Based on these informal observations, we *support* learners, either individually, in small groups, or as a whole class, who may need additional guidance. To do this, we invite them over for more targeted scaffolding. This support may take the form of a quick, focused conversation, demonstration, or shared reading experience. After the instruction, we *send* them back *out* to pick up where they left off equipped with the strategies or knowledge needed to work independently again. This type of intentional coaching is identified by Nell Duke (2018) and her colleagues as one of the techniques practiced by exemplary literacy teachers, citing the importance of remaining "present as a 'guide on the side' during the early stages of students' application, providing crucial prompting and other supports to scaffold students to independence" (2018, 399).

While you certainly can apply the *support and send out* model to traditional reading and writing workshops, we've found that it is tailor made for literacy workshop (Figure 2.9) because it offers flexibility in your teacher actions and opportunities to check in with students to reteach or redirect at the point of need. As we're sure you've noticed, a quick comment, leading question, or gentle nudge can give a student a renewed sense of purpose and confidence as they continue their work during literacy workshop. Students thrive in classrooms where they know you care about them, their interests, and their effort. For instance, when you spot Arden with a dolphin book using the diagram to help her write about what dolphins look like, you pause and say, "I notice you are using this nonfiction book to help you write facts in your own book. You're doing some research. That's what literacy workshop learners do!" You've now *supported* Arden in the act of using classroom resources, taken a brief moment to name what she was doing, and *sent* her back *out* to research. In essence, you've given Arden the *feedforward* (Johnston 2012, 48) she needs to do this again on another day.

Figure 2.9   The support and send out model is tailor made for literacy workshop.

FIND A MIDDLE GROUND:
USING TEACHER ACTIONS TO STRUCTURE LITERACY WORKSHOP

With the workshop approach and the support and send out model of instruction framing literacy workshop, let's explore some specific and intentional teacher actions that set the tone and work behind the scenes to support a successful literacy workshop. These teacher actions during literacy workshop are designed to be responsive to students' needs and to provide just enough guidance to nudge them toward independence. As we observed our learners naturally blurring the lines between reading and writing workshop, we quickly realized that, in order for this to continue, we needed to provide a predictable structure. Taking a look at the structures in the separate workshops students were already familiar with, we recognized that the answer was right there in front of us—we would build on the common threads in our existing reading and writing workshops to create a predictable structure through our teacher actions (see Figure 2.10).

READING WORKSHOP	LITERACY WORKSHOP	WRITING WORKSHOP
	Common Threads: Teacher Actions	
	Teach Demonstration Lessons	
Plan and teach reading-focused minilessons	Plan and teach demonstration lessons focused on integrated big literacy ideas	Plan and teach writing-focused minilessons
	Anchor Learning in Literature and Converse to Grow Thinkers and Learners	
Read aloud carefully selected texts to apply, demonstrate, or discuss skills, strategies, or behaviors	Engage in interactive read-alouds that provide a catalyst for collaborative conversations and inquiry	Read aloud and discuss mentor texts to showcase intentional craft moves
	Demonstrate the Strategies and Habits of Literate Citizens	
Model the strategies, skills, habits, and behaviors of proficient readers	Demonstrate the interplay among the strategies, skills, habits, and behaviors of readers and writers that help them become literate citizens	Model the strategies, skills, habits, and behaviors of skilled writers
	Record Thinking and Learning	
Invite students to record learning in a reader's notebook or work collaboratively to create an anchor chart	Invite students to record learning in a literacy notebook or work collaboratively to create an anchor chart	Invite students to record learning in a writer's notebook or work collaboratively to create an anchor chart

Figure 2.10   Using Teacher Actions to Structure Literacy Workshop *(continues)*

READING WORKSHOP	LITERACY WORKSHOP Common Threads: Teacher Actions	WRITING WORKSHOP
	Let Them Go!	
Provide ample time for students to engage in independent reading	Create an environment where students have ample time to choose to read, write, or research based on their line of inquiry, individual needs, or ongoing projects	Provide ample time for students to engage in independent writing
	Sit Among Learners	
Guide readers through small-group instruction	Guide students to help them apply their integrated literacy learning by meeting with them in small groups	Guide writers through small-group instruction
	Sit Beside Learners	
Guide readers through conferring	Guide students to help them apply their integrated literacy learning by conferring with them individually	Guide writers through conferring
	Share and Celebrate	
Celebrate students' new learning that occurred during independent reading	Celebrate students' new understandings of the integrated big ideas as they share and learn from each other	Celebrate students' written work and craft move attempts as they share and learn from each other

Figure 2.10   Using Teacher Actions to Structure Literacy Workshop *(continued)*

Teach Demonstration Lessons: Target Integrated Big Ideas

The integrated demonstration lessons in Part II of this book will serve as exemplars as you blend the teaching of reading, writing, and researching in a meaningful context. Similar to a traditional minilesson in either reading or writing workshop, literacy workshop demonstration lessons have a singular focus. The difference is that the focus, or big idea, weaves together the common threads from reading and writing so that your students get a multilayered understanding of the concept. For instance, if your big idea is *point of view*, an integrated demonstration lesson might begin with you demonstrating how to orally retell a personal *missing pet* story (speaking and listening) and asking students to notice who is telling the story. Following your oral retelling, you might engage in a shared reading of *Alfie* (Heder 2017), the tale of a missing turtle told both from the owner, Nia's, point of view and from the turtle's perspective. After discussing the author's use of point of view, you could return to your missing pet tale and let the children help you rewrite it from your pet's point of view. Something to note here: this demonstration may occur over a few literacy workshop sessions to allow ample time for students to explore this concept on their own. (See Look Who's Talking demonstration lesson in its entirety in the Online Resources.) This demonstration lesson, and others like it, develop the skill of comparing and contrasting, an underlying proficiency that leads to a lifelong habit of weighing different viewpoints and perspectives. The demonstration lessons found in Part II of this book include the following teacher actions:

- Anchor Learning in Literature
- Converse to Grow Thinkers and Learners
- Demonstrate Strategies and Habits of Literate Citizens
- Record Thinking and Learning

As you read through their descriptions in the next few pages, notice how these four components of the demonstration lessons work in unison to move students toward a deeper understanding of the integrated big ideas.

ANCHOR LEARNING IN LITERATURE

If you're like us, you can't teach a reading or writing minilesson without a carefully selected piece of text. In both of our classrooms, children's literature is a focal point for instruction. Books color our conversations and shed light on the particulars of author's purpose and craft. Certainly, the idea of using mentor texts during reading and writing workshops isn't new. Nearly two decades ago, Stephanie Harvey and Anne Goudvis encouraged us to read aloud and think aloud during reading workshop because "the sky is the limit on thinking and learning when readers are compelled by text" (2000, 53). During literacy workshop, with big ideas guiding the way, you can change the think-aloud conversation that surrounds the text to highlight the relationship between separate reading or writing skills or strategies or, better yet, a combined concept like character. Listen to Karen's think-aloud as she confers with a group of readers who are all interested in reading *Raymie Nightingale* (DiCamillo 2016). Notice how it is the *same, same but different* from a separate reading or writing conference: "What I loved about reading *Raymie Nightingale* is that as I read, the characters were becoming my friends and I wanted to learn more about them. I think it is because of the way Kate writes. So, as you're reading, I want you to see if you feel the same way about her characters. Since Kate is a mentor author I rely on when I create my own characters, I've jotted some sentences, words, or phrases from *Raymie* [showing her notebook] that helped me to understand the characters' actions and reactions. I'll reread these pages in my notebook next time I'm trying to develop my own unforgettable character."

Here, Karen used DiCamillo's text to demonstrate something that her students can use to move them forward in both understanding and creating characters. Like *Raymie Nightingale*, "Every single text we encounter represents a whole chunk of curriculum, a whole set of things to know about writing" (Ray 2002, 92), and we would argue reading, too!

During literacy workshop, we recommend thinking of the interactive read-aloud as an opportunity to shift the focal point away from you, as the teacher, and instead let the book and students' conversations do the work (Figure 2.11). Your role is to offer an open-ended question here and there to keep the conversations lively. To help with this, we'll recommend some classroom-tested titles throughout this book—and specifically in Part II's demonstration lessons—that we trust to serve as catalysts for deep literacy-based conversations. (For more about our selection criteria see Chapter 3, pages 48–51).

Figure 2.11   Books color our conversations and shed light on the inner workings of author's purpose and craft.

CONVERSE TO GROW THINKERS AND LEARNERS

Research shows that collaborative classroom conversations are essential to the growth of literacy learners (Zwiers and Crawford 2011) and that these interactions should focus on metacognitive and higher-level thinking (Duke, Cervetti, and Wise 2018). With mentors like Peter Johnston, author of *Choice Words* (2004) and *Opening Minds* (2012), spurring us on, we've learned a great deal about using language to impact student learning. Johnston stresses the need for us to create dialogic classrooms, cultures where teachers ask open-ended questions and learners engage in thought-provoking conversations. Embedding these types of discussions in the literacy workshop demonstration lessons encourages students to consider multiple viewpoints, challenge one another's thinking, and focus on meaning making (2012, 52). When you teach children to listen to one another, they learn to focus their energy and attention on the person speaking so that they can better appreciate, without judgment, their classmates' questions, concerns, and viewpoints (Routman 2018).

Another benefit of these collaborative conversations is that they nurture students' well-being by providing opportunities to talk about their feelings while empathizing with book characters. This emotion-rich language is just one of the many benefits that talking about books together provides (Cunningham and Zibulsky 2014). With a well-chosen book as your teaching partner, your high-level questions will guide learners to a deeper understanding of the big idea and also encourage a healthy dialogue among their peers.

DEMONSTRATE THE STRATEGIES AND HABITS OF LITERATE CITIZENS

A key teacher action during literacy workshop is intentional demonstration of the habits and behaviors you want your students to emulate. A demonstration lesson is similar to a minilesson that might take place in reading or writing workshop. The difference is that your instructional focus is centered on an integrated big idea. In other words, you are stressing the reciprocal relationship between reading and writing. The overarching goal is to inspire learners who will read and write beyond the walls of our classrooms. When we read and write along with our students we give them "a rare gift" (Fletcher 2017, 19). They get to see us engaged in the same learning processes that they are wrestling with, such as pondering, drafting, revising, wondering, discussing, debating, and much more. You can demonstrate these habits and strategies through shared literacy experiences and by thinking aloud in front of your students.

Shared Literacy Experiences. You may be familiar with the terms *shared reading* and *shared writing*. Shared reading typically occurs in a whole-class setting with the teacher and students reading the text together. Similarly, during shared writing, the teacher and children compose a text together with the teacher as a scribe. During shared literacy events, we blur the lines between shared reading and writing as we collaborate with our learners to explore the how and why of the reciprocal processes of reading and writing. For example, if our integrated big idea is *relationships*, while doing a shared reading of Minh Lê's *Drawn Together* (2018) about the evolving relationship between a boy and his grandfather, we would discuss the following questions:

- How did the relationship between the boy and his grandpa change throughout the book?
- What techniques did the author and illustrator use to highlight the changes?
- What role did the creation of art play in the change?
- What are your thoughts about the relationship between art and communication?

(For the complete demonstration lesson, see Chapter 7, pages 182–184.)

Learning events like these help students better understand how a writer's decision-making process impacts the reader's understanding and appreciation of the text. Moreover, we're developing the literacy behavior of considering why the bond between author and audience is essential.

Teacher Demonstration and Think-Aloud. We want to make sure our demonstrations are "always explicit and intentional" (Routman 2003, 45). To do this, show children exactly how to carry out a literacy skill, strategy, habit, or behavior through modeling, explaining, and thinking aloud. For instance, when thinking aloud to show literacy learners how authors use font size and punctuation to signal the reader's use of expression, Maria shares the book *OUT!* by Arree Chung (2017). She ponders aloud, "I'm noticing that the title is inside a speech bubble and it's written in all capital letters. Those clues are signals that I need to read the title loudly like a baby screaming that he wants to get out of his crib." Continuing in this fashion throughout the book, Maria intentionally thinks aloud to show children how, as readers, punctuation is key to reading with expression. On the flip side, she is also demonstrating how, as writers, they can use punctuation marks to signal their readers. When, over time, learners benefit from hearing you, as their mentor, demonstrate the integrated nature of literacy skills and strategies, they are building a deep understanding of the competencies that they will use long into the future.

RECORD THINKING AND LEARNING

Creating meaningful ways for students to record their thoughts and questions not only engages readers and writers but also provides avenues for children to reflect on their learning or capture their thinking. During literacy workshop, you can offer students a variety of resources to respond to and reflect on their learning in preparation for upcoming challenges or to revisit literacy goals. When students record their responses to literature, "they can express, reflect upon and clarify their thoughts and understandings, gaining self-confidence and motivation as they realize different interpretations of text are acceptable" (Pantaleo 1995,

89). Some of the ways you might choose to have students record their developing knowledge include the following:

- **Literacy Anchor Charts:** Co-created classroom charts where an integrated literacy skill or strategy is defined, described, explored, or reflected upon. Anchor charts might include, but are not limited to, children's reflections on a demonstration lesson, recent discoveries, mentor sentences from or reflections about a book, a list of ideas, thoughts, or questions. Learners use these charts as a reference as they independently apply the skill or strategy to their reading or writing (Figures 2.12 and 2.13).

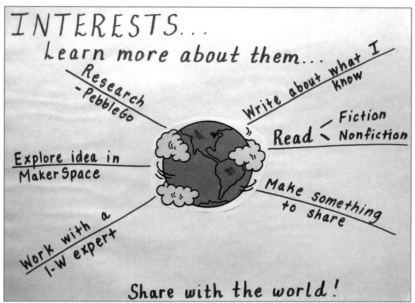

Figure 2.12   Anchor charts serve as a reference for literacy workshop learners.

- **Literacy Notebook:** We've built on Flitterman-King's (1988) definition of a response journal as "a repository for wanderings and wonderings, speculations, questionings . . . a place to explore thoughts, discover reactions, let the mind ramble . . . a place to make room for the unexpected" (5) to create our vision of a literacy notebook. A literacy notebook is simply a place in which learners capture reading, writing, research, and other thinking that may occur during literacy workshop time; it may include a combination of student and teacher-directed entries. Depending on the age and ability of your learners, you might choose to have students create their literacy notebook using a composition notebook, teacher-created notebook, three-ring binder, online resource, or anything you think will work best in your classroom. (See Chapter 4, pages 97–98, for more information about literacy notebooks.)

Figure 2.13   This fifth-grade learner writes her thinking after reading
She Made a Monster: How Mary Shelley Created Frankenstein (Fulton 2018).

- **Goal-Setting and Reflection Resources:** To build students' self-awareness and ability to set and strive for goals, we've created reproducible resources for response, goal setting, and self-reflection (see the Online Resources). As our learners' understanding of literacy workshop evolved, they helped guide us to revise and refine these resources. We encourage you to ask your learners for input and suggestions as you help them record responses and keep track of their goals. Depending on the age and experience of your learners, a goal-setting sheet could simply be a drawing or a phrase written on a sticky note. Another option might include students' oral responses to the Status of the Class. (See Chapter 4, pages 79–80 for more information on using Status of the Class during literacy workshop.) When using written resources stay mindful of the time they take learners to complete. We avoid having students spending more time completing the goal-setting sheet than working toward meeting the goal.

Facilitate Learner Actions: Independent Application

Up to this point, the teacher actions we've shared have been mainly whole-class practices, with you, as the teacher, guiding the learning. When you're ready to differentiate your instruction more intentionally, you can focus on the next three actions: *letting them go, sitting among learners,* and *sitting beside learners.* These instructional practices help boost students' independence through intentional scaffolding and support. Our aim is to help you facilitate learning experiences where children tackle big ideas by critically reading, writing, thinking, and discussing among multiple texts. When we do this well, we are, as Maria Nichols writes, "asking them to use what they learn to construct larger understanding about their world" (2009, 18). Using the *support and send out* model we described earlier, we exercise these teacher actions based on the ever-changing needs of our learners. For instance, we may choose to launch a literacy workshop with a text, a demonstration lesson, or a notebook entry. Then, when needed, we can gather the class back together to reteach or clarify with a text or demonstration.

LET THEM GO! APPLICATION IN PRACTICE

During literacy workshop, you'll create a predictable structure that offers your learners uninterrupted time to dive into reading, writing, or research. The selections they make during literacy workshop learning time will be based on their line of inquiry, their unique needs, or their ongoing projects. Giving children more time for goal-driven independent practice was one of the many reasons we started experimenting with literacy workshop. If we provide a firm foundation through demonstration lessons and consistent support, we are giving students a leg up on becoming literate citizens.

Debbie Miller and Barbara Moss (2013) affirm the importance of letting children go to engage in productive practice: "For children to develop the habits and identity of thoughtful, strategic, proficient readers, they need to practice, and to make their practice productive, they need the tools that we can provide through instruction. This extensive independent reading practice framed by instruction needs to happen in classrooms every day" (1–2). It's hard to argue with the importance of extensive reading practice every day, and the same holds true for writing. That's why, when our students are engaged in literacy workshop, we check in to make sure they are keeping up with their reading and writing. In Chapter 4, we will share strategies to help you do just that. In the end, you will know that your teacher actions have been effective if students display agency and independence when you let them go to learn on their own. There is nothing more gratifying than taking a moment to sit back and survey your classroom during literacy workshop learning time. This is an ideal time to note the smart things you observe your students doing so you can point them out when you sit among or beside your learners.

SIT AMONG LEARNERS: SMALL-GROUP SUPPORT

To build relationships and nudge students closer to independence, we sometimes boost our whole-group demonstration lessons with small-group guided-learning experiences. In this case, we gather learners together with similar needs or interests and then, based on our integrated big idea and learning target, share an additional experience with them that will move them forward.

SIT BESIDE LEARNERS: INDIVIDUAL CONFERENCES

Carving out a few moments to confer with a reader or writer is another way to guide learners toward independence and confidence. In Chapter 4, we'll share practical strategies to integrate conferring into your literacy workshop and make it a treasured time of day for both you and students alike.

Share and Celebrate: Synthesize New Understandings

One of the most rewarding times during literacy workshop is when your learners share and celebrate. It is the time when students show others what they have read, written, or learned together. In traditional workshops, sharing is centered on either reading or writing. The difference in literacy workshop is that your questions lead students to ponder how those two processes are interrelated. To keep sharing fresh and engaging, you might choose to alternate among different sharing structures, such as whole-group share, small-group sharing circles, or *team up and talk*, where students stand up, find a partner, share an idea or two, and then continue in the same fashion with a few more classmates. Regardless of which structure works best for your learning context, you can connect students sharing back to the overall purpose of literacy workshop by asking a question or two from Figure 2.14.

POSSIBLE QUESTIONS TO FOCUS LITERACY WORKSHOP SHARING

- What did you notice as a reader and writer today?
- Did you discover any connections or similarities between your reading and writing?
- What did you learn as a reader today that might help you with your writing?
- What did you learn as a writer today that might help you with your reading?
- How does recording your new learning help you better understand and remember?
- How might the similarities you've noticed between reading and writing help you as a learner?
- How did talking with and listening to others help you understand what you read or strengthen your writing?
- How do your literacy habits, skills, and strategies help you as you learn in other parts of your day?

Figure 2.14

IN THE FOREGROUND: LITERACY WORKSHOP PLANNING TEMPLATE

Now that you have an understanding of the roots of literacy workshop, the overarching framework, and your role as a teacher, you are ready to start planning. We have included exemplar demonstration lessons in Part II and in the Online Resources, but you can also chart your own path by using the planning template described here. We designed the Literacy Workshop Planning Template found in Figure 2.15 as a guide to help you plan your own literacy workshop experiences. As you look at the template, you'll see it is divided into three main sections. At the top of the template, there is a place for you to jot down your integrated big idea, or common thread, along with your selected learning targets and mentor texts. The middle section of the template has room for you to sketch out your whole-class demonstration lesson (knowing that students' thoughts and comments may take you in a different direction), and at the bottom, you'll find the learner actions your students will choose, surrounded by the teacher actions you can draw from to support them as they work toward their goals. For an example of how the template works, we take you step-by-step through this planning process in Figure 2.15. You'll find a reproducible version of the template in Appendix 2 in the Online Resources.

INTEGRATED BIG IDEA

Together, with colleagues, review your standards and curricular expectations. Identify the big ideas that are best explored during literacy workshop. (See Appendix 1 in the Online Resources for some ideas.) In this space, record the integrated big idea for the demonstration lesson(s). Certainly, we do not intend to imply that it takes only one literacy workshop experience to master a big idea. Plan to revisit big ideas over and over with increasing levels of complexity throughout the year.

LEARNING TARGET(S)/FOCUS PHRASE(S)

Using the big idea as the goal for students, determine the underlying concepts that they will have to understand and apply to have a working knowledge of the big idea. For each literacy workshop experience, we suggest selecting one or two learning targets. Then, to anchor your students' learning and goal setting, write these learning targets in kid-friendly focus phrases. We learned the term *focus phrase* from Terry Thompson's book *The Construction Zone* (2015). He defines a focus phrase as "a short, student-friendly statement of the goal that you and the learner repeat throughout the scaffolding process" (23). When students internalize the focus phrase, it provides a clear goal for their independent learning.

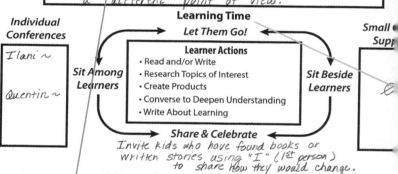

Literacy Workshop Integrated Big Idea
Point of View

Focus Phrase(s):
• I notice who is talking in the story.
• I decide who will talk in my stories.

Mentor Text(s):
Alfie by Thyra Heder

Demonstration Lesson

Anchor Learning in Literature
Converse to Grow Thinkers and Learners
• Discuss & define point of view
• Explain first-person point of view

Demonstrate Strategies and Habits
• Explain how the author's choice to tell the story from 2 different points of view helped me see the same events in different ways.

Record Thinking and Learning
Explore books or their own stories to think about how they would change if told from a different point of view.

Learning Time
Let Them Go!

Individual Conferences
Ilani ~
Quentin ~

Sit Among Learners

Learner Actions
• Read and/or Write
• Research Topics of Interest
• Create Products
• Converse to Deepen Understanding
• Write About Learning

Sit Beside Learners

Small Supp

Share & Celebrate
Invite kids who have found books or written stories using "I" (1st person) to share how they would change.

RECORD THINKING AND LEARNING

Plan how you want to record students' thinking and learning here. Will you co-create an anchor chart, have students record ideas in their literacy notebook, or use digital media to collect their thinking and learning?

ANCHOR LEARNING IN LITERATURE

Use this box to make a few quick notes to indicate whether you plan to read the whole mentor text, highlight certain passages, reread and revisit specific sections, or book talk the title as a possible independent reading book. If we are planning to read the whole text, we typically jot down a few key questions we might ask before, during, and after reading in this section.

DEMONSTRATE STRATEGIES AND HABITS

To complete this part of the planning template, revisit the integrated big idea and learning targets. Then, ask yourself, *What strategies or habits do my students need to build an understanding of the big idea or meet the learning targets?* Jot down how you might go about demonstrating this habit or strategy in this space.

INDEPENDENT LEARNING TIME

Although the decisions for how to guide students during learning time will mainly be based on informal assessments of their understanding and application (think back to the *support and send out* model we discussed earlier), use this space to plan your possible teacher actions. Circle your planned teacher actions (Sit Among Learners, Sit Beside Learners, Let Them Go!) and make note of any students to touch base with along the way.

SHARE AND CELEBRATE

Jot down how you'll share and celebrate during this experience and maybe some general ideas of what learner actions, habits, or behaviors to look for and highlight when the time comes.

Figure 2.15 Completed Literacy Workshop Planning Template

COMPONENTS AND STRUCTURE IN A PRIMARY-GRADE CLASSROOM

As the first snow falls in December (leading to quite a bit of excitement), Maria gathers her learners around her to enjoy the book *Jabari Jumps* (Cornwall 2017). Her purpose for selecting this text is for students to focus on how Gaia Cornwall created such a relatable character whose emotions change throughout the story.

TEACHER ACTION:
Anchor Learning in Literature

Before reading, she sets the stage by saying, "Today during literacy workshop, let's zoom in on one story element—characters. Together, we're going to investigate and learn more about how thinking about characters can help us as readers and writers." Behind her on the whiteboard, the word *Characters* is printed in the middle of an oval. As she reads, Maria engages her students in collaborative conversations by posing the following questions:

TEACHER ACTION:
Converse to Grow Thinkers and Learners

BEFORE READING
- Turn and talk to your neighbor about what you predict this story might be about.

DURING READING
- What do you know about Jabari so far?
- Are the main characters of books always kids?
- Let's think about the character Jabari. What did you notice about his mood at the beginning of the story? How was he feeling in the middle of the story?

AFTER READING
- Did you notice how in just one story the author created a character whose feelings change quite a bit?
- What do you suppose was the turning point in the story?

Students discuss these questions with their classmates to build an understanding of the text and of the creation of characters. As she reads, Maria says things like, "Now I'm going to show you my favorite illustration!" showcasing her enjoyment of reading and rereading.

TEACHER ACTION:
Demonstrate Strategies and Habits of Literate Citizens

After reading, she poses this question: "What are you wondering about how authors create characters?" Then she says, "I'm wondering how Gaia Cornwall made Jabari a character that changed. What are you wondering?" Students respond with questions like the following as Maria records them on the whiteboard:

- How do I show how a character feels?
- How do authors pick names for their characters?
- How do authors pick the right setting for their characters?

To guide students who are at the beginning stages of independence, Maria adds the question "How do you make a character funny?" She is bank-

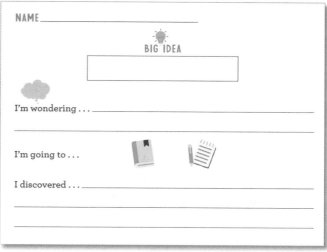

Figure 2.16 Literacy Workshop Goal-Setting Sheet: Primary

ing on the fact that students will identify Elephant and Piggie as funny characters and study Mo Willems's books to build their understanding. Students complete a goal-setting sheet (see Figure 2.16) that will double as a place to record their thinking and learning, and off they go!

TEACHER ACTION:
Sit Beside Learners

Knowing that most students will need guidance, Maria chooses to "honey-bee" confer (Farris 2005), meaning she buzzes from one child to the next, touching base with as many children as possible. As she checks in with learners, she helps guide their inquiry by making suggestions, asking questions, and celebrating their findings. Some students are skimming the books in their book boxes and writing down characters' names. Others are rereading an Elephant and Piggie book to try and figure out how Willems makes them so funny. Still others are writing their own little books to create their own characters.

TEACHER ACTION:
Let Them Go!

When there is a lull in the action and it is clear students need a break, Maria invites them over to share. Some of their findings include the following:

HOW DO AUTHORS MAKE CHARACTERS FUNNY?
- They used funny words. (Gabriela)
- He [Mo Willems] used onomatopoeia.
- He [Elephant] did funny things. (Braiden)

HOW DO AUTHORS PICK CHARACTER NAMES?
- Mr. Mosquito [from Ricky Ricotta's Mighty Robot series by Dav Pilkey (2000–2016)] is evil because mosquitoes are a pain. Sometimes they [the character] look and act like their name. (Andrew)
- Sometimes the characters can be the names of animals, like Elephant and Piggie.

In tomorrow's literacy workshop the students will build on their new understandings and add to their bank of questions to see what else they can discover. Since the components and structure of literacy workshop are similar to those of their reading and writing workshops, Maria's first graders are able to flow seamlessly from one to another.

THE VIEW FROM HERE:
COMPONENTS AND STRUCTURE IN AN INTERMEDIATE-GRADE CLASSROOM

It is midway through the first trimester and Karen's fifth graders are beginning to embrace the routines of literacy workshop. They are making choices about their reading and writing each day, as well as having conversations about the behaviors of literacy learners. The students have set goals for themselves and have begun to think about what they are doing in workshop to move them toward those goals. Now it is time for the next foundational piece in building the structure in literacy workshop: recording the "work" of workshop.

While displaying the cover of the picture book *Windows* (Denos 2017), Karen calls her students to join her on the carpet. As they gather around her, they start chatting about the book cover. She begins their conversation with the question that she often asks when they begin a shared read-aloud experience, "What do you notice and what are you thinking?" Because this is a predictable question, the students immerse themselves in conversation, and after a minute or two, she has them share their thinking. As they launch into reading and sharing together, Karen focuses their conversation on a few guiding questions:

TEACHER ACTION:
Anchor Learning in Literature

TEACHER ACTION:
Converse to Grow Thinkers and Learners

- What are windows and what purpose do they serve in the story?
- What are some of the things that the boy sees as he is walking in the neighborhood?
- Think about a time that you have looked into a window and what you saw.

As they move through the book, students discuss these questions with each other, creating an understanding of the text and how a window creates a way for someone to take a look inside at what is going on in someone else's world.

After a brief discussion, Karen transitions into thinking about how readers and writers record thinking about their literacy lives. She says, "I record what I am reading and writing in my literacy notebook because it helps me set and then evaluate my goals." She knows that it is important to model the behaviors that she wants her students to have not only while they are with her in her classroom but also beyond in the "real world" of reading and writing.

TEACHER ACTION:
Demonstrate Strategies of Literate Citizens

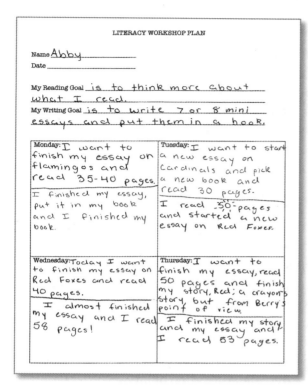

LITERACY WORKSHOP PLAN

Name Abby

Date

My Reading Goal is to think more about what I read.

My Writing Goal is to write 7 or 8 mini essays and put them in a book.

Monday: I want to finish my essay on flamingos and read 35-40 pages.

I finished my essay, put it in my book and I finished my book.

Tuesday: I want to start a new essay on Cardinals and pick a new book and read 30 pages.

I read 50 pages and started a new essay on Red Foxes.

Wednesday: Today I want to finish my essay on Red Foxes and read 40 pages.

I almost finished my essay and I read 58 pages!

Thursday: I want to finish my essay, read 50 pages and finish my story, Red; a crayon's story but from Berry's point of view.

I finished my story and my essay and I read 53 pages.

This is how my reading and writing helped me grow as a literacy learner this week: I have written 2 more essays and added more facts I have talked to my mom about how I feel about my book and sometimes I write it down.

I'm making progress on my reading goal by writing and thinking about what I read.

I'm making progress on my writing goal by writing more of my essays to add to the book.

Right now, I'm reading The Sun is Also a star and I'm thinking that people very diffrent can also be the same in many ways.

Right now, I'm writing about Red Foxes and I'm thinking that I didn't know they burrowed underground!

A literacy celebration I have from my work this week is: I have added to the length of my essays.

Next week, I'm planning on writing 1 more essay and then write some poetry.

Figure 2.17 Literacy Workshop Plan Sheet: Intermediate

Karen then invites her students into the conversation by sharing the Literacy Workshop Plan Sheet (Figure 2.17 and Appendix 4 in the Online Resources for the reproducible), explaining that they'll keep track of what they are doing during workshop time by recording their daily reading and writing in "windows" on the plan sheet. At the end of the week, they'll step back and evaluate what they've done and how it supports their literacy goals. Karen explains to her learners that "the plan sheet will help you think about your literacy goals, but it will also give me a 'window' into your reading and writing lives, helping me get to know you better as a literacy learner. This will help guide our conversations at conference time as we work together to help you grow as a reader and writer."

As with any new tool in workshop, Karen knows that her students will need support as they begin to use it. She devotes time at the end of workshop each day for students to record their work and makes sure that she is available to provide assistance and to support their success in developing the habits of lifelong literacy learners. Karen may ask questions, provide guidance, or even give feedback related to what she sees students writing each day, differentiating feedback based on their individual needs. As students are just beginning to take on this responsibility, Karen will set aside time at the end of each week to have students share their plan sheets, discuss

TEACHER ACTION:
Sit Beside Learners

what they have learned, and pose questions before moving on to the next week's plan sheets.

TEACHER ACTION:
Let Them Go!

She knows that as they have more time and practice, they will better understand the purpose behind what they are doing and how it helps them plan their reading, writing, and goal setting. At this point, the ways you might go about planning for literacy workshop should be coming into focus. Before we continue to meander through the literacy workshop landscape together, take a moment to reflect, question, and think about what you've read thus far.

REFLECT ON PLANNING: PONDERING A NEW VIEW

Just as literacy workshop shifts the control from teacher to student, this book places the professional decision-making power in your capable hands. Rest assured, there is no one *right* way to design a literacy workshop. In fact, as you will see from the vignettes in each of the chapters that follow, literacy workshop varies depending on the time of year, the integrated big idea, your specific grade level or teaching context, and your students' needs and interests. Remember, there isn't *one and only one* way to run a literacy workshop. Our goal in this book is to highlight our thoughts and experiences in an effort to *show* you what's possible when you shift your mindset. As you move forward into this shift, consider the following ideas and questions to help guide your evolving understanding of literacy workshop:

- Think about some ways you might use the phrase *same, same but different* with your students to explore the connections between reading and writing.
- How has your literacy workshop mindset changed? What small moves might you make to integrate a literacy workshop perspective into your teaching context?
- Do you notice opportunities in your curriculum to collapse and combine your workshops? Make a list of the integrated big ideas you might address during literacy workshop.
- If you're a risk taker, select a demonstration lesson from Chapters 5–9 or the Online Resources and have a go. Your students will teach you everything else you need to know!
- If you feel like you need more support, continue reading as we share how we launch literacy workshop in Chapter 3 and use strategies for fostering independence and engagement in Chapter 4.

IDEAS TO PONDER

IDEAS TO TRY

We have to teach toward children who,
individually or collaboratively,
make meaning and do meaningful things.

—Peter Johnston, *Opening Minds: Using Language to Change Lives*

CHAPTER 3

Launching the Literacy Workshop—
Developing a Purposeful and Joyful Learning Community

Whew! The beginning of the school year. It sure is an exhausting and exhilarating time; the first months of school serve as a backdrop for all of the learning that follows. You carefully select books and plan learning experiences that communicate your beliefs and unite a few dozen (or more!) kids together toward a common goal—making meaning. This meaning making along with doing meaningful things, as Peter Johnston (2012) calls for, are the main goals of literacy workshop. In this chapter, we'll demonstrate how you can use the teacher actions detailed in Chapter 2 to establish a purposeful literacy workshop (Figure 3.1). Next, to help you further

see how literacy workshop differs from your separate reading or writing workshops, we'll introduce the *learner actions*, or the various ways students can choose to do important work either individually or collaboratively. To enhance this chapter, we've detailed a few exemplar demonstration lessons that target the big ideas necessary to support students as they begin to do meaningful things during literacy workshop in Chapter 5 and in the Online Resources.

Figure 3.1   Establish a purposeful literacy workshop.

ESTABLISH THE PURPOSE OF LITERACY WORKSHOP

Reading aloud the picture book *Everywhere Wonder* by Matthew Swanson (2017) is an ideal way to illuminate the purpose for literacy workshop (Figure 3.2). Upon opening the book, we meet a young boy reading at his desk. His book transports him on adventures to faraway lands. Once back at home, he wanders outside to explore his neighborhood. There, too, he notices interesting and beautiful things. With all of these wonders filling his imagination, he pens his own story and encourages readers to do the same. The book *Everywhere Wonder* captures the importance of the relationship among book experiences, life experiences, and the written word. This synergy is emphasized in the grounding purpose of literacy workshop—that is, through reading, writing, researching, and experiences with others, students will develop a sense of wonder about their world and an understanding of themselves as literacy learners and their role as global citizens. And we communicate this purpose through intentional teacher actions that include the following:

- Strategically selecting texts and digital media that engage students' minds and hearts
- Filling children's imaginations with stories and experiences
- Providing uninterrupted time for learners to notice interesting and beautiful things as they read, write, research, and converse
- Promoting choice in *learner actions* so that students venture outside of their comfort zones
- Giving descriptive feedback that nudges learners to wonder and explore
- Celebrating students' attempts to share their stories with the world

Strategically selecting texts to match the big ideas that center your literacy workshop will help focus your learners' actions as they make deliberate choices during literacy workshop learning time.

Figure 3.2   Everywhere Wonder captures the importance of the relationship among book experiences, life experiences, and the written word.

SCAN THE STACKS: SELECTING CHILDREN'S LITERATURE FOR LITERACY WORKSHOP

A literacy workshop is brimming with texts. Sometimes during literacy workshop, you and your students reexamine, with fresh eyes, the books that you've read during reading and/or writing workshop. Other days, you choose new titles to help capture the essence of big ideas. The literacy workshop is buoyed by a constant flow of texts that learners listen to you read aloud, interact with during shared reading, read on their own, and discuss with their peers. Learners are encouraged to revisit these books during literacy workshop as they work independently or collaborate with their peers.

You don't have to be a children's literature expert to teach literacy workshop effectively, but you do have to know books (and love them). Research shows that teachers who read and share books with their students are more likely to have students who choose to read and *love* to read (Anderson 2005; Kittle 2012; Miller 2009). In the chart that follows, we expand our criteria for choosing books detailed in Figures 3.3 and 3.4 by sharing some exemplar titles along with our thinking behind each choice.

CRITERIA FOR SELECTING BOOKS FOR LITERACY WORKSHOP

- Highlights the behaviors needed to participate in community of caring learners
- Showcases the habits and behaviors of literate citizens
- Demonstrates the reading-writing connection
- Prompts learners to ponder, question, discuss, and debate the author's/illustrator's decisions and apply their findings to their own written pieces
- Serves as a *mirror, window,* or *sliding glass door* (Sims Bishop 1990)
- Illuminates a big idea

Figure 3.3

CRITERIA	EXEMPLAR TITLE	WHY WE CHOSE THIS BOOK
Highlights the behaviors needed to participate in community of caring learners	*Words and Your Heart* (Neal 2017)	Read Kate Jane Neal's debut picture book when launching literacy workshop to promote the use of kind words in conversations. Then, return to it later to discuss how a writer's choice of words impacts the reader. As Neal shares with readers, "Your words are amazing and powerful!" "The words that go into your ears . . . can actually affect your heart!" What a powerful message for your learners.
Showcases the habits and behaviors of literate citizens	*Detective Dog* (Donaldson 2016)	Literate citizens seek out opportunities to read, question, write, converse, and learn. In this tale, Detective Dog Nell, Peter, and the kids display many of the behaviors we want to foster in our students. Nell goes to school with Peter each Monday to hear children read. When a thief steals the books, Nell is on the case. She and the children discover Ted, the book thief, who only wants to borrow the books. So, Nell and the children take Ted to the library. On the last page, we see the children creating their own books.
Demonstrates the reading-writing connection	*The Word Collector* (Reynolds 2018)	Because Jerome uses words in a variety of ways, Reynolds's book captures the essence of literacy workshop. We see Jerome, the word collector, fill his scrapbooks with his favorite words. Then, when his words get jumbled, he strings them together to write poems and songs. In the end, he decides to share his word collection with others so that they can use words to make the world a better place.

Figure 3.4   Criteria for Book Selection *(continues)*

CRITERIA	EXEMPLAR TITLE	WHY WE CHOSE THIS BOOK
Prompts learners to ponder, question, discuss, and debate the author's/illustrator's decisions and apply their findings to their own written pieces	*The Long Island* (Beckmeyer 2018)	Intermediate-grade teachers, there is so much to notice and discuss in this book, making it ideal for intense study during a literacy workshop demonstration or for a group of students interested in learning more about themes—in this case man vs. nature. When five different members of the community set off to explore the other side of an island, they disappear one by one (readers can infer that many of the explorers have lost their lives). Once the remaining adventurers get to the other side of the island, they build a city. In the end, a lone explorer embarks to discover a new land.
Serves as a *mirror, window,* or *sliding glass door* (Sims Bishop 1990)	*Crown: An Ode to the Fresh Cut* (Barnes 2017)	When selecting books for literacy workshop, consider titles like this one that may either reflect or expand your students' worldview. In the author's words, "With this offering, I wanted to capture that moment when black and brown boys all over America visit 'the shop' and hop out of the chair filled with a higher self-esteem, with self-pride, with confidence, and an overall elevated view of who they are" (Barnes 2017, author's note).
Illuminates a big idea (For additional titles that illuminate big ideas, see Chapters 5–9.)	*The Wolf, the Duck and the Mouse* (Barnett 2017)	There are not many books set in a character's stomach; therefore, *The Wolf, the Duck and the Mouse* is ideal for a study of how a big idea like setting impacts a story and how to choose unusual settings as writers. With hints of Aesop and Grimm, this fable-like tale begins after a mouse is eaten by a wolf; he is surprised to find a duck living (in a fully furnished home) inside the wolf's stomach. After the duck convinces him how nice and safe it is in the wolf's stomach, the mouse decides to stay. But soon trouble finds the wolf, in the form of a hunter.

Figure 3.4   Criteria for Book Selection *(continued)*

You may notice that all of the titles in the chart are picture books. Whether you teach primary or intermediate grades, we are firm believers that picture books are an integral part of demonstration lessons during literacy workshop.

Importance of Picture Books in the Middle Grades

As you can see in Figure 3.5, picture books are abundantly available in Karen's fifth-grade classroom. You might be wondering why she chooses to spend her hard-earned money on *all* of these picture books when her students *should be* reading longer books. Karen's purchases (much to her husband's chagrin) are warranted because picture books are essential for middle-grade kids too (Figure 3.6)! Because there is such a discrepancy between what middle-grade students read and what they write, it may be more challenging for them to develop an awareness of the link between reading and writing. Their pieces of writing are usually one to three pages of narrative or informational text, yet most intermediate-grade learners are independently reading novels. The interrelationship between writing and reading is easier to internalize if students spend some of their time reading, studying, and listening to picture books, alphabet books, and poems (Calkins 1994). To this end, intermediate-grade learners and teachers benefit from having a wide variety of quality picture books and other shorter texts that they can use as mentor texts for writing (Anderson 2005; Fletcher and Portalupi 2001). In addition, picture books provide a low "effort-to-reward" ratio for those reluctant or striving readers, because unlike proficient readers, children who are striving "benefit from immediate gratification as they make their way into an unfamiliar text" (Harvey and Ward 2017, 96). With eye-catching illustrations, interesting characters, and page-turning plotlines, well-chosen picture books offer immediate rewards.

Figure 3.5   Picture books are abundantly available in Karen's fifth-grade classroom.

WHY PICTURE BOOKS ARE ESSENTIAL FOR INTERMEDIATE-GRADE LITERACY LEARNERS

- Provide engaging, short pieces of text for readers
- Serve as mentor texts for reading and writing strategies
- Contain vivid illustrations that support thinking about and beyond the text
- Include a wide range of topics, even for older readers
- Motivate vulnerable and reluctant readers because they are accessible
- Cement the connection between reading and writing

Figure 3.6

Reasons to Infuse Informational Text into Literacy Workshop

During literacy workshop, first graders study *Animals by the Numbers: A Book of Animal Infographics* (Jenkins 2016) to learn how to add infographics to their own animal posters. A group of Karen's fifth graders consider how Maria Gianferrari blends narrative with informational text in *Hawk Rising* (2018) and whether that craft move might work for a piece they are writing. Literacy workshop offers authentic opportunities for students to read and learn from informational texts.

When children read informational text with an eye toward writing their own texts, they read more strategically and pay closer attention to the nonfiction features (Duke 2004; see Figure 3.7). Moreover, as students study the diagrams, tables, and other graphic elements in order to gain information, they are strengthening their visual literacy skills. For demonstration lessons specifically targeting informational text, see Chapter 9. As teachers, we work to create a culture of literacy through rich and diverse book experiences. Literacy workshop learners build on these experiences as they do meaningful things during their independent learning time. With our purpose in mind and books by our sides, we collaborate with our students to create a shared definition of literacy workshop.

REASONS TO INFUSE INFORMATIONAL TEXTS INTO LITERACY WORKSHOP

- Builds a foundation for ongoing experiences with informational text
- Creates interest in topics and leads to questions and opportunities for inquiry
- Engages reluctant and/or dormant readers
- Demonstrates connections among life experiences, reading, and writing
- Bolsters students' ability to tackle content area reading and writing, which increases in importance as learners move from primary to intermediate grades and beyond

Figure 3.7

CREATE A SHARED DEFINITION OF LITERACY WORKSHOP

Our definition of literacy workshop (Figure 3.8) continues to evolve as we blend what we learn from professional reading with our observations and reflective conversations we have with students about their literacy workshop experiences. The more we read, notice, and discuss, the more we find connections and implications that go far beyond the relationship between reading and writing. In the end, what started out as a way to help our own learners better understand the reciprocity between

LITERACY WORKSHOP: OUR WORKING DEFINITION

An integrated workshop where students are independently and collaboratively applying the strategies, skills, habits, and behaviors of literacy learners while engaged in the reciprocal processes of reading and writing.

Figure 3.8

reading and writing has advanced our thinking about the power of blending our workshop times to further our students' development as literate citizens.

Once you begin dabbling with literacy workshop, you and your students will create your own evolving definition. Whatever direction you and your learners take it, the one aspect of the definition you'll want to keep consistent is that students clearly understand that reading will make them even better writers and that writing will make them more skilled at reading.

As we transition from separate reading and writing workshops to literacy workshop, it's important for students to understand the similarities between the work they've already been doing and the *learner actions* they'll maintain in literacy workshop. Creating this foundational, shared understanding emphasizes that they'll continue many of the routines they've already been using, just with the added *twist* of choice in their learner actions. This twist of choice in learner actions is one of the key ways that literacy workshop differs from the separate reading and writing workshops. As you read through a few examples of this process next, recall the many ways literacy workshop is *same, same but different* in relation to our characterizations of separate reading and writing workshops.

The View from Here:
A Shared Definition in a Primary-Grade Classroom

As Maria's students gather together in front of the morning message and schedule, she begins this conversation:

MARIA: *Does anyone notice anything new on our schedule today?*

PAUL: *There's a new schedule card.*

MARIA: *Smart detective work, Paul! Can you read what it says?*

PAUL: *It says literacy workshop. What's that? (By the way, Paul is an exceptional reader. Most first graders can't read the words* literacy workshop *at this point in the school year.)*

MARIA: *Hmm! Is anyone else wondering the same thing as Paul? (Many hands waving.) Let's see if we can figure it out together. I'm going to try to answer your question with a read-aloud called* In-Between Things *by Priscilla Tey.*

We chose Priscilla Tey's debut picture book because she uses rhyming text and engaging illustrations to explore things in the middle, both real and imagined. Since literacy workshop is an *in-between thing*, in other words, a blending of reading and writing workshops, we felt that this book would help young learners begin to understand the concept of literacy workshop. Later, we can return to this unique book to spark conversations or writing about in-between objects, animals, and other things in our world.

Reading Workshop Routines	"In-Between" Literacy Workshop Routines	Writing Workshop Routines
You read a book to us and we talk about it.	We read a book, notice, think, and talk about what readers and writers do.	You read and we notice things writers and illustrators do.
You show us how to do something to get even better at reading.	You show us how to read, write, or research to better understand or answer our questions.	You show us some of your writing or the writing of our classmates.
We read!	We read, write, and/or research.	We write!
You help us when we need it.	You help us when we need it.	You help us when we need it.
We share what we read and learned with our friends.	We share what we read, wrote, and/or learned with our friends.	We share what we wrote with our friends.

> At this point of the demonstration, Maria only fills in the columns for the familiar routines of reading and writing workshop. We've found that it is helpful to let students *dabble* with literacy workshop for a few days before adding their ideas to the middle of the In-Between chart.

Figure 3.9   The middle column of this In-Between anchor chart was created after children had time to *dabble* with literacy workshop.

After the book concludes, Maria begins building a shared definition: "For the past few weeks we've learned the routines of reading and writing workshop. Let's make a quick chart listing some of those routines" (Figure 3.9).

After jotting down the kids' ideas on the chart, Maria continues, "Notice there is a space in the middle of the chart *in-between* the reading and writing workshop. Today, we're going to do an in-between thing called literacy workshop. *Literacy* means being able to read *and* write. So, during literacy workshop you can choose to read *or* write. Some days you might even do a little of both. During literacy workshop we are going to explore the connections between reading and writing, see how reading and writing helps us answer questions, and think about how being even better literacy learners can help us understand big ideas."

Following this demonstration, Maria shares the focus of their supported independent time. "While you are reading or writing, I want you to think about these questions: 'What do you notice about yourself

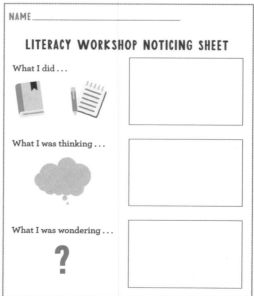

Figure 3.10   Literary Workshop Noticing Sheet

as a reader or writer? What are you doing, thinking, or wondering?' We'll share what we find out a bit later." To scaffold this type of reflective thinking for her first graders, Maria provides them with a noticing sheet (see Figure 3.10 and Appendix 5 in the Online Resources). Then, Maria invites the children to choose whether they would prefer to write, read, or a little of both.

After the students have had the opportunity to dabble with literacy workshop for a few days, they share their preliminary discoveries and Maria jots down their findings in the middle column of the chart (see Figure 3.9). By creating this shared definition of literacy workshop, learners take part in laying a foundation for future launching lessons (found in Chapter 5 and in the Online Resources) and the integrated learning that will follow.

The View from Here: A Shared Definition in an Intermediate-Grade Classroom

In the first days of literacy workshop, Karen reads aloud with students the picture book *What You Know First* (MacLachlan 1998), a story about a young girl who is saddened by a move to a new place but finds hope in the fact that she brings with her memories of her former home and an artifact or two that will help her as she begins her new life there.

> We chose this book because we want our learners to mimic what the girl did in the story by relating what they already know (or their memories) about reading and writing workshop to what they are learning about literacy workshop.

After reading the book aloud, she launches the literacy workshop conversation by reflecting on the experiences and routines that her students bring with them from their separate reading and writing workshops. Karen sets the stage for creating a shared definition by saying, "In *What You Know First*, the girl brings objects and memories from her old home to help her feel more comfortable in her new one. In the same way, we are going to bring what we know from our separate reading and writing workshops together to help

What Do Experienced Readers Do?
- Read more challenging books
- Understand the story and/or characters
- They know what reading level they are
- Read at least 20min. a day
- They can write summaries correctly
- They read lots of chapter books
- They understand the lesson in picture books
- They can understand big words
- They think about things in the book deeper
- They read when they don't nessasarly need to

Figure 3.11   A middle-grade learner's list of reading workshop routines.

What Do Experienced Writers Do?
- They write paragraphs
- They write in full sentences
- They write rough drafts and final copies
- They write with feeling
- They have someone else help them with spelling
- They try hard
- They start with lists of ideas
- They read it over many times
- They are creative
- They write about important things
- They write in all different genres

Figure 3.12   A middle-grade learner's list of writing workshop routines.

build an understanding and define a time that we're going to call literacy workshop." Then she asks, "What do you do as readers and writers during workshop time that makes you stronger readers and writers? Let's take a moment to jot down some of those routines that you will *carry with you* from reading and writing workshops" (Figures 3.11 and 3.12).

As her students are discussing their thinking with each other, she overhears a comment and asks Alyssa to share her thinking with the entire class. Alyssa smiles and says, "Well, it's like when you are reading a mentor text in reading workshop, then reading another mentor text in writing workshop. You're reading text and learning how to make your reading and writing better." Karen looks around and sees many heads nodding. She decides to dig a little deeper. She asks, "Are there other mentor texts that you might use during reading and writing workshop that strengthen your ability to read and write?" She waits as they ponder for a moment, and then many hands pop up. She calls on Rashesh. He answers proudly, "The books we read and the pieces that we write. Those are mentor texts too!" Sitting next to him, Aida hesitates, then says, "You know, if the books we write are mentor texts, then reading those can make me a better writer." Javier interjects, "And you're reading them, so you are also getting better at reading!" Karen returns to the chart they began and adds students' ideas to the routines for literacy workshop based on their conversation (Figure 3.13).

After adding student thinking to the chart, Karen invites the students to explore some learner actions during literacy workshop learning time. Karen says,

> The anchor chart in Figure 3.13 is evolving thinking, so they will be going back to it over the next couple of weeks as they work during literacy workshop time to add their thinking, but this gives them a starting place.

Today I'm going to invite you to try something that is *same, same but different* from what you have been doing in reading and writing workshop time. You notice on the chart and in our conversations, we've been calling this new time *literacy workshop*. During this time, you will have the choice to read, write, research, or a combination of any of these based on your goals. Think about what Aida and Javier said about how reading helps you get better at writing and how writing makes you a better reader. Literacy workshop is the time where we will explore when, how, and why this happens. Pay attention to yourself as a learner and ask yourself, "What am I doing as a reader that makes me a better writer? What am I doing as a writer that makes me a better at reading?" These questions will guide your work and will also help you set goals.

> Karen encourages students to read, write, or both during independent learning time over these few initial days, inviting them to process their choices and any connections they're beginning to see in the literacy work that they are doing.

The conversation defining literacy workshop starts by asking your learners to think about how reading and writing support their work as literate citizens. By zeroing in on this as your ultimate goal, you create a time where both of those things exist within the same space, which is what we want our integrated literacy workshop time to look like. With your guidance, students can identify the routines in both reading and writing workshop that have helped them flourish as readers and writers. Then, with your support, transfer and blend those practices during literacy workshop. As she wraps up the conversation, Karen discusses how this definition will be an ongoing one. But she knows this will be well worth the time and effort, because her learners are already excited to start integrating their reading and writing in this new, *repurposed* literacy workshop learning time. As your students are dabbling in literacy workshop and adding their insights to your shared definition, you will build on this energy by noticing, celebrating, and demonstrating the learner actions.

DEMONSTRATE AND PRACTICE LEARNER ACTIONS

Since the learner actions are one of the main ways an integrated literacy workshop differs from the two separate workshops, demonstrating and providing time for students to practice the actions is an essential element of the launch. To demonstrate and practice learner actions, we turn to picture books that high-

READING WORKSHOP	LITERACY WORKSHOP	WRITING WORKSHOP
Read independently or with friends	Read or write independently or with friends	Write independently or with friends
Read to research topics of interest	Read, write, and research to share new learning	Write to record information about topics of interest
Choose interesting books to read	Choose interesting topics to read, write about, or research	Write about interesting topics
Make connections between books and my life	Ponder connections among reading, writing, and life experiences	Make connections between written texts and my experiences
Think how reading impacts my writing	Consider how reading and writing are interconnected	Think how writing impacts my reading
Converse with others about the books I'm reading	Converse with others about the discoveries I've made while reading and writing	Converse with others about the writing I'm doing
Respond to the books I've read	Respond to the reading, writing, or research my friends share	Revise to the texts I'm writing and respond to texts others are writing

Figure 3.13
Literacy Workshop
Co-created Anchor Chart

light some of the actions we want our students to take. To introduce learner actions in the primary grades, try *I Do Not Like Books Anymore!* by Daisy Hirst (2018). In the book, Natalie and Alphonse enjoy the books their parents read aloud and the stories their grandmother tells them. But when Natalie tries to independently read her first book, it doesn't go quite the way she expected. Eventually, she decides that, rather than reading books written by others, she'll write her own (with the help of her family). The following actions that Natalie takes in the book mirror some of the actions we invite young learners to take during literacy workshop:

- Practice reading books again and again (reread)
- Make up your own stories
- Tell your stories to someone
- Write and draw your own stories

For older learners, we might choose the picture book *How to Read a Book* by Kwame Alexander (2019). As readers enjoy the poetic text and stunning collage illustrations, they experience the magic of being immersed in a book. They see readers in different places enjoying adventures that they hope will never end. *How to Read a Book* also gives you an opportunity to highlight the crafts of writing and illustrating. When students read the author's and illustrator's note, they learn about the thought and effort that both put into creating this celebration of the written word. In addition to sharing and discussing books such as these, you can begin a learner action conversation by posing one or more of the questions that appear in Figure 3.14.

QUESTION	CONNECTIONS TO LEARNER ACTIONS
What are your goals during literacy workshop learning time?	Goal-Setting Question: Invites students to set short- and long-term goals for their work.
Has something sparked your interest or caused you to ask questions? How can you learn more about that interest or go about answering those questions?	Planning Question: Prompts kids to make a plan for their learning time. They might initiate an inquiry experience or choose to do some self-directed reading, writing, and/or research.
How can you take the skills and strategies you've learned in reading and/or writing workshop and apply them to create a product during literacy workshop?	Product Question: Guides learners as they plan a literacy workshop end product. They will consider the integration of reading and writing along with ways to create the product, which may include, but not be limited to, verbally or visually representing content through creative use of format and structure.

How do people share their ideas and learning with others? What have you learned as a reader or writer that might help as you share?	Sharing Question: Asks students to consider different ways they might present their new learning or insights based on the work they've done during literacy workshop.
How has what you've noticed and discovered during literacy workshop helped you better understand yourself as a learner?	Reflective Question: Helps students to reflect on their learning preferences and consider what they've noticed in the relationship between reading and writing.

Figure 3.14   Questions to Spark Possible Learner Actions

BUILD ON LEARNERS' ROUTINES FROM READING AND WRITING WORKSHOPS

When launching literacy workshop in your classroom, building on the familiar routines your students are already practicing in reading and writing workshops will provide both you and your students with a sense of security. As you can see when you glance at Figure 3.14, each learner action comprises common threads from both reading and writing workshop, including the following broad categories your students will practice during literacy workshop learning time:

- Read and/or Write
- Research Topics of Interest
- Create Products
- Converse to Deepen Understanding
- Write About Learning

What do these actions look like in practice? As we walk through Karen's classroom during the first days of literacy workshop, you'll notice students trying out a variety of learner actions. They are deciding whether to read, write, or both based on their individual needs, interests, and questions (Figure 3.15). Looking around the room, we see Aarav and Brian at the bookshelf reading recommendations written by their peers to help them choose books to read, while other students are gathering the materials they need to work on writing projects. Learners may be working independently or with peers, collaboratively creating pieces to share with other students in their classroom, in school, or even in an online community. Grace and Ananya are quietly (but excitedly) chatting about a book that they have just finished reading and planning how they will create a product to recommend that book to others. On the carpet, a group of students are independently writing responses to the books that they are reading, pondering their connections to the texts, how those texts have changed them, and how they might apply their new understandings to the world in which they live. Many of the actions you see happening in Karen's classroom may be the *same* actions that are occurring in your separate workshops. The *difference* is that, during literacy workshop learning time, students are seamlessly (well, sometimes!) deciding what meaningful things *they* need to do in order to reach their goals and grow as learners and literate citizens.

Figure 3.15   During literacy workshop, learners decide whether to read, write, or do both, based on individual needs.

To further our shared understanding of literacy workshop learner actions, let's see what they might look like in a primary-grade classroom. It is the first official day of autumn; therefore, during literacy workshop, Maria's first graders are into all things fall. Ishaan, Ethan, and Christian are huddled around a laptop studying a PebbleGo article about how leaves change colors so they can explain it to their classmates. In the reading center, Luisa, Sarah, Kylie, and Ceci are spread out on brightly colored pillows rereading *Goodbye Summer, Hello Autumn* (Pak 2016), the book Maria read aloud that morning. A group of kids are gathered around a piece of bulletin board paper working on a poster of things to do in the fall. Children who prefer reading independently are tucked in small spaces with a stack of their favorite books, and those who are in the middle of making a book continue to write independently. With clipboard in hand, Maria circulates, jotting notes and observations to use when she confers or meets with small groups. She is focused on noticing children's learner actions and those who are using the habits and behaviors she has been teaching during the launching demonstration lessons (see Chapter 5 and in the Online Resources). What do all of these students have in common? They are all engaged with literacy in a very personal way (Figure 3.16).

As you reflect on these early moments of literacy workshop, you likely noticed some of the common threads that blend what our learners have practiced during their separate reading and writing workshops and provide them with focused opportunities to better understand how reading and writing are linked (Figure 3.17). When you're establishing these routines with your own classroom, it's helpful when the learner actions during literacy workshop make sense and are predictable. So, as you introduce them, build on the behaviors and routines you've already taught in your separate workshops, and your students will be on their way to making meaning in a literacy workshop.

Figure 3.16   Students are engaged with literacy in a very personal way.

READING WORKSHOP Learner Routines	COMMON THREADS: LITERACY WORKSHOP Learner Actions	WRITING WORKSHOP Learner Routines
Students engaged in independent and collaborative reading	**Read and/or Write** Learners choose to read or write based on their interests, questions, individual needs, or ongoing projects	Students engaged in independent and collaborative writing
Students read to answer questions	**Research Topics of Interest** Learners choose to research based on their interests, questions, or ongoing projects	Students write to share answers to their questions
Students create reading-related products	**Create Products** Learners work individually or with classmates to create shared products and deepen their understanding of the reciprocity of reading and writing behaviors	Students create written products
Students collaboratively read and discuss texts in book clubs	**Converse to Deepen Understanding as Readers and Writers** Students collaborate and converse to deepen their understanding of the reciprocity of reading and writing behaviors	Students collaborate to create written pieces and products
Students write about the books that they are reading	**Write About Learning** Learners write about their discoveries made while reading, writing, researching, or collaborating with others	Students write about topics that interest them

Figure 3.17   Common Threads: Learner Actions

Read and/or Write

Dick Allington and Rachel Gabriel (2012) assert that, in order for literacy learners to grow, they need to read and write every day. Devoting independent learning time for students to pursue their learner actions is an essential component of literacy workshop. Each time you choose to do literacy workshop, you invite your students to decide whether to independently or collaboratively read, write, research, or engage in a combination of them all. As Fountas and Pinnell (2018) remind us, "This repertoire of experiences and ideas acquired through texts enables students to understand their physical, social, and emotional world and their roles as informed global citizens" (8). In addition, the choice of learner actions provides students with an extended period of time to develop the habits, behaviors, and strategies of lifelong learners.

During literacy workshop, if learners choose to read, they will be reading for different purposes (Figure 3.18). Future-ready reading is much more than simply understanding the words. We want students to internalize the messages they get from reading and consider how their reading experiences might impact their life choices. To help readers with this work, we turn to mentors like Kylene Beers and Bob Probst who offer their Book, Head, Heart framework (2017, 63) asking readers to attend to the text, to their thoughts about the text, to their emotional reaction to the text, and to how they might be changed as a result of their reading experience. Similarly, Ellin Keene tells us that if we want students to be responsible for their own engagement they must "THINK–FEEL–BELIEVE–ACT" (2018, 65). The structure and routines of literacy workshop lend themselves to the type of thoughtful reading and reflective thinking that leads to forming beliefs and taking action. The advantage of literacy workshop is that students don't have to wait until another time of the day to prepare to take action. If their reading inspires action, they can get started right away by formulating and carrying out a plan.

Another key purpose for reading during literacy workshop is to read like a writer. By transferring this foundational component of writing workshop to literacy workshop (Fletcher and Portalupi 2001), learners can clearly see that reading is one way to enhance their writing. When reading like a writer, children discover that studying mentor texts is a way authors make their writing better (Ray 1999). As they read with a writer's stance and transfer the moves they learn from experienced authors into their own writing, another bridge between reading and writing is built. Mentor text experts Lynne Dorfman and Rose Cappelli (2007) share the benefits of reading like a writer during writing workshop:

- Invites writers to notice authors' and illustrators' unique choices
- Moves writers forward as they imitate the mentor text and find new ways to grow
- Ignites writers' imagination and determination to create high-quality texts
- Helps learners envision the kind of writer they can become
- Nudges writers to continually reinvent themselves
- Empowers writers to try something new

We've seen similar benefits during literacy workshop. In fact, as students independently read mentor texts during literacy workshop, they marinate in literature that will help improve their writing skills (Fletcher 1993). Reading like a writer is *same, same but different* in literacy workshop because learners can immediately integrate and apply their writerly knowledge into the pieces they choose to write.

Speaking of writing, the extended learning time that literacy workshop offers your students will help their writing flourish. As Ruth Culham (2018) points out, "Writing is a highly creative process that requires time, effort, and trial-and-error decisions" (96). Providing the time and space for students to work with each other is an important classroom ritual that leads to increased student engagement (Keene 2018). By building on and expanding the routines from writing workshop, you are giving students time to deeply engage in and mesh the creative processes that are essential for them to do meaningful work. In addition to reading and writing, literacy workshop learners can work independently or cooperatively to research topics of interest and create products, all the while having opportunities to converse in order to deepen their understanding as readers and writers. To help you better envision the choices your students might make during literacy workshop time, we compiled them in Figure 3.19. This chart is meant to be a starting place for you and your students. The creative learners in your teaching context will expand these choices as they gain experience with literacy workshop.

Figure 3.18   During literacy workshop, learners work collaboratively to research topics of interest.

LEARNER ACTIONS AND POSSIBLE CHOICES DURING LITERACY WORKSHOP

Read	• Select texts that interest and engage them. • Choose texts that challenge their thinking and offer multiple perspectives. • Engage with self-selected texts by attending to their thoughts and emotions. • Consider how the texts they read change them or prompt them to act. • Study texts from mentor authors who use craft moves that they can apply to their own writing. • Record mentor words or sentences in literacy notebooks or on anchor charts.
Write	• Choose topics that interest them as writers. • Write texts that help them grow as writers. • Deepen their understanding of the writing process. • Apply learning from mentor texts to revise pieces. • Understand how reading and writing are reciprocal processes. • Share and celebrate their written pieces.
Research Topics of Interest	• Choose research topics of interest or collaborate to select an interesting research topic. • Generate questions to guide individual or group research. • Use a variety of sources, including digital media, to research topics. • Decide how to present findings to others. • Reflect on how their research might make a difference to themselves and to others in their classroom, school, and beyond.
Create Products	• Create images, texts, or other evidence of learning for themselves. • Create images, texts, or other evidence of learning to share with others. • Share research findings in an innovative way with others in their school community and beyond. • Integrate reading and writing, understanding that they are reciprocal processes.
Converse to Deepen Understanding as Readers and Writers	• Converse with another reader to better understand a text (may or may not have been the same text read by both readers). • Offer feedback to one another to improve a written text. • Collaborate with another writer (or writers) to create a piece of text together.

Figure 3.19   Learner Actions and Possible Choices During Literacy Workshop *(continues)*

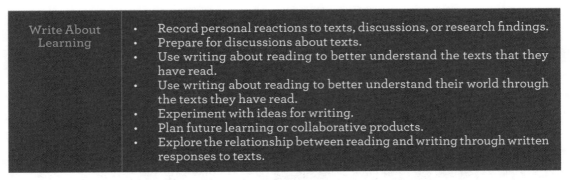

Write About Learning	• Record personal reactions to texts, discussions, or research findings. • Prepare for discussions about texts. • Use writing about reading to better understand the texts that they have read. • Use writing about reading to better understand their world through the texts they have read. • Experiment with ideas for writing. • Plan future learning or collaborative products. • Explore the relationship between reading and writing through written responses to texts.

Figure 3.19   Learner Actions and Possible Choices During Literacy Workshop *(continued)*

Research Topics of Interest

Why are there so many ladybugs on the playground slide? How many people died in the Civil War? We're sure you hear questions such as these in your classrooms all the time. When these questions are voiced, we often hear ourselves saying, "I don't know. We'll have to research that later." Then, the day breezes by without time for kids to explore their curiosities. Blurring the lines between your workshops will give kids the extra time they need to follow their own lines of inquiry. Conducting research engages learners and integrates reading and writing with their natural interest in the world around them (Lehman 2012). When students choose to do research during literacy workshop, they are

- engaging in authentic inquiry about relevant topics,
- motivated to investigate new ideas that fuel intellectual curiosity,
- using language and literacy for meaningful purposes, and
- acting as agents of their own learning (Fountas and Pinnell 2018).

When students are independently or collaboratively researching topics of interest, they find information in a variety of sources, including

- texts,
- online resources,
- interviews,
- conversations with experts, and
- observations.

Then, they decide how they will record their findings and share their new discoveries with others. Kids' interests are sparked by many things. After exploring the wordless book *Wolf in the Snow* (Cordell 2017), Kimora and her friends want to learn more about wolves. The field trip to a rock museum has Paul crazy about fossils. Spending a day or two in literacy workshop delving into these topics is the perfect invitation for students to apply their literacy skills. As an added bonus, conducting research helps them build content knowledge, and, as Nell Duke (2014) writes, "Knowledge matters to comprehension. It matters a lot" (75). When students are collaboratively researching topics of interest, you will find them making the learner choices listed in Figure 3.19.

At this point, you may be thinking that you usually provide time for your students to research during science or social studies. Why, then, do we choose to include research as a learner action during literacy workshop? We encourage students to research because it provides another avenue for them to apply their interest-driven literacy learning. In fact, you might consider weaving some of your science and social studies topics into literacy workshop. Integrating your content-area studies into literacy workshop is yet another way to broaden students' choices and deepen their understanding of the integral role reading and writing play in learning new things.

Create Products

As learners begin to understand how reading, writing, and research are interwoven, invite them to create products that demonstrate their new understandings. Whether they're writing a piece that will only be seen by a group of friends or researching a project because several students share the same passion for a topic, the time you provide during literacy workshop to collaboratively create products that integrate reading, writing, research, and technology will further expand their knowledge. Once the products are complete, encourage students to share their learning with an audience beyond the walls of their classroom via social media or other interactive platforms.

For example, Joe and Gino, Karen's fifth graders, were avid graphic novel enthusiasts who were beginning to incorporate what they learned from them into their written pieces. In addition to their conversations with each other, Karen spent time conferring with them to help them understand how graphic novels present content differently than other texts and how graphic novel authors make intentional design decisions to engage readers. At the same time, during social studies, their class was learning about the civil rights movement. Sparked by an interest in the time period, the boys wanted to learn more about civil rights activists so they could teach their peers about them. They decided to use their time during literacy workshop to create their own graphic novel about several civil rights activists and then share it with their classmates. Combining what they had learned during reading workshop and writing workshops about the structure of graphic novels with their research about these famous individuals, they created the graphic novel you see in Figure 3.20. In this example, you can see how the students set their own goal to teach others and used the extended independent learning time to collaborate and create. Because the topic was engaging to them, the resulting product demonstrated a much higher level of understanding than perhaps a written answer to the prompt, *Tell about a civil rights activist who inspired you and why.* When we let students take the lead in developing ideas for possible products they want to create, they often come up with something far better than we ever imagined (Figure 3.21)!

Figure 3.20   A collaborative literacy workshop product.

Converse to Deepen Understanding as Readers and Writers

Conversation breathes life into literacy workshop, so working with each other is always an option for students, especially if it helps them improve their own reading or writing. Allowing learners the opportunity to collaborate, whether it's a conversation about a book or a chance to write together, gives them a chance to experience how two heads are better than one.

As we look around Karen's literacy workshop, we see heads gathered together for a variety of

Figure 3.21   Literacy workshop learners collaboratively create products that integrate reading, writing, research, and technology.

purposes. Anna and Jackie have just finished reading *Ghost Boys* by Jewel Parker Rhodes (2018) and are discussing how it compares to other texts that they have read. They are also brainstorming questions after finishing the book and creating a plan to research them, hoping to learn more about gun violence and Emmett Till, both topics that are central to this powerful middle-grade novel. At a table, two writers are looking at pieces that they have written, taking turns reading them aloud to get each other's feedback on the character development in their writing. From their examination of characters in literacy workshop, they know how mentor authors develop characters in texts and are comparing their writing to their independent reading books—*The Crossover* by Kwame Alexander (2014) and *Garvey's Choice* by Nikki Grimes (2016).

If you were to listen in on these students as they work together, their conversations would sound very similar to the ones that happen in the demonstration lessons that Karen teaches and the conferences with her learners (Figure 3.22). Teacher modeling helps students learn the language to use with each other when talking about texts, supporting them as they begin to take ownership of their conversations and practice them within the framework of literacy workshop.

Write About Learning

Writing about learning is a way that readers develop a deeper understanding about the texts that they have read while also offering a meaningful context to practice the skills that they are developing as writers (Hansen 2001). As students write, they process what they have read, heard, discovered, or learned. Because writing is a thinking process, the act of writing (or drawing) helps students reflect on their internal thought processes, synthesize knowledge, and know themselves as individuals and learners.

Students better understand what they have learned when they write about it. Many times, in the beginning stages of literacy workshop, we support students with a prompt or an idea to get them started with a reading response. As students become more versed in

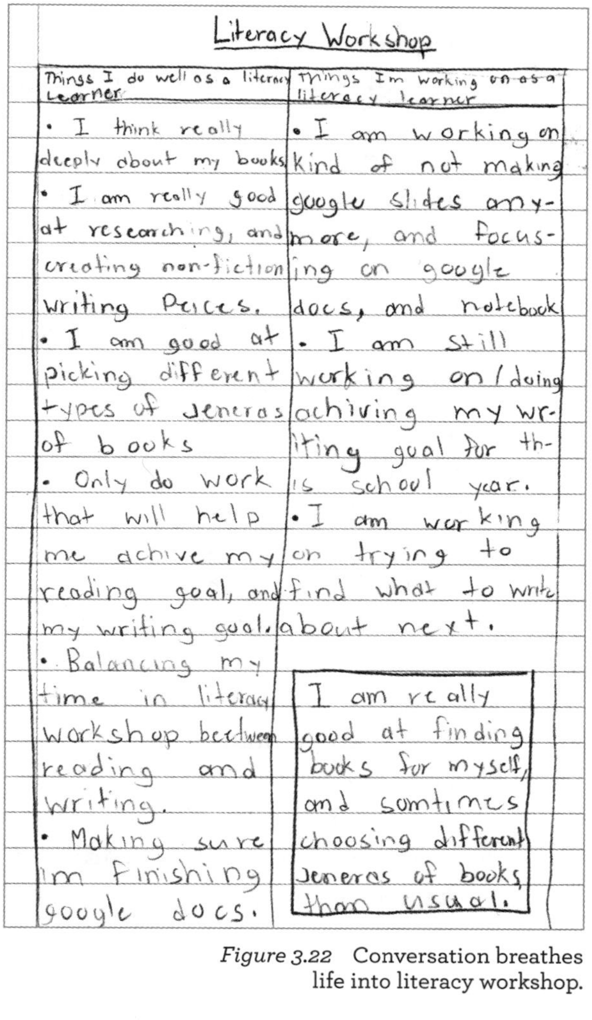

Literacy Workshop

Things I do well as a literacy learner	Things I'm working on as a literacy learner
• I think really deeply about my books • I am really good at researching, and creating non-fiction writing Peices. • I am good at picking different types of jeneras of books • Only do work that will help me achive my reading goal, and my writing goal. • Balancing my time in literacy workshop beetween reading and writing. • Making sure Im Finishing google docs.	• I am working on kind of not making google slides any-more, and focus-ing on google docs, and notebook • I am still working on/doing achiving my wr-iting goal for th-is school year. • I am working on trying to find what to write about next. I am really good at finding books for myself, and somtimes choosing different jeneras of books than usual.

Figure 3.22 Conversation breathes life into literacy workshop.

reading response, we allow them to choose how they might want to respond to the books that they are reading. Their responses are written in their literacy notebook—a place to gather thoughts on what they've read and even play around with some of their own writing pieces.

We introduce the literacy notebook as a place for recording written responses about reading, for noting favorite words or lines from mentor texts, or for anything else that learners choose to document from their literacy work (Figure 3.23). The notebook also becomes the place to gather anchor charts or other resources that we provide during demonstration lessons. (See Chapter 4 for more information about the literacy notebook.) When children regularly record their thinking in notebooks, they have a safe place to do the following (Robb 2017):

- Write open-ended and personal reactions
- Experiment with ideas
- Fine-tune thinking
- Discover what they think or know about a text or topic
- Express feelings or opinions toward characters or topics
- Record new learning and understandings

To further guide your students' use of a literacy notebook, each demonstration lesson found in Part II of this book contains a section entitled "Record Thinking and Learning." Here you will find more detailed ideas for learners to write the types of entries in the previous list.

REFLECT ON INSTRUCTION: **PONDERING A NEW VIEW**

Blending routines from reading and writing workshop lay a foundation for students to begin making choices about their literacy learning. Generating a shared definition builds on that foundation by providing a collective vision of what will happen during literacy workshop. Layering high-quality, diverse mentor texts on top of the foundation helps to illustrate concepts and spark conversations. And weaving the common threads for instruction among the books and the learner actions streamlines planning and provides meaningful, integrated learning opportunities for your students.

As you reflect on what you've learned in this chapter and consider how it might help you implement your unique version of an integrated workshop with your own students, here are a few guiding questions and suggestions to consider as you prepare to make the leap into literacy workshop:

- Scan your children's literature collection or visit the school or public library. Can you find texts that you enjoy sharing with children to match the criteria we've outlined in this chapter?

- You've read our definition of literacy workshop. Are there aspects of that definition that you would change? How will you create a shared definition with your learners?
- Reflect on the learner actions you read about in this chapter. How are they the *same, same but different* from what your students are already doing in your separate reading and writing workshops?
- If you're ready to launch literacy workshop, turn to Chapter 5 for some demonstration lessons we've found helpful for our students.
- If you feel like you need a few more strategies to support your students, then turn to Chapter 4, where we'll share what we've learned about fostering independence and engagement during literacy workshop.

Figure 3.23   The literacy notebook is a place for students to reflect on their internal thought processes, synthesize knowledge, and get to know themselves as learners.

An engaged learner isn't only interested in herself; she ponders how a topic or issue impacts others, and she considers how her thinking, emotions, beliefs, and/or actions might affect those around her. An engaged learner has a sense of *purpose*. There is something to be learned that reaches far beyond the words on the page or the immediate experience.

—Ellin Keene, *Engaging Children: Igniting a Drive for Deeper Learning K–8*

CHAPTER 4

Fostering Independence and Engagement During Literacy Workshop

A SENSE OF PURPOSE: THE KEY TO INDEPENDENCE AND ENGAGEMENT

In 1930, nearly a decade before ballpoint pens were invented, two men named Otis and Will plunged into the unexplored deep ocean in the first manned diving tank. Their story is chronicled in Barb Rosenstock's picture book *Otis and Will Discovered the Deep: The Record-Setting Dive of the Bathysphere* (2018). Growing up in different decades they each questioned, experimented, planned, and innovated in order to learn more about their individual topics of interest. They were *engaged* in learning; they had a sense of *purpose*. Once they met, this pair of scientists applied their combined skills to work collaboratively to create a diving tank—or what they dubbed the Bathysphere. Together, they risked their lives in the Bathysphere because they were certain that there was something more to learn, information that reached far beyond the words that appeared on the pages they had studied. Otis and Will's independent spirit, drive, and bravery embody what we are hoping for our literacy workshop learners and is the essence of what we share with you in this chapter.

As we dive into (pun intended) fostering students' independent spirits, we'll share some instructional habits for you to hone as you carry out your teacher actions. Then, we'll follow up with practical strategies that you can teach your students to further develop their sense of agency. To frame this chapter, we'll turn to the five big ideas Otis and Will used throughout their lives: question, plan, investigate, innovate, and reflect (see Figure 4.1).

INSTRUCTIONAL HABITS	STRATEGIES TO TEACH STUDENTS
Question	Teach Questioning Stances
Plan	Promote Proactive Planning
Investigate	Invite Investigation
Innovate	Inspire Innovation
Reflect	Encourage Reflection

Figure 4.1 Instructional Habits and Strategies to Teach Students to Foster Independence During Literacy Workshop

Because literacy workshop may be a new venture, we encourage risk taking for both you and your students. Like Otis and Will, you may be the first of your colleagues to experiment with literacy workshop, and that might feel a bit scary. Our purpose here is to help ease some of those jitters by filling in the details for ideas we mentioned in Chapters 1–3. In Chapter 6 and in the Online Resources, you'll find a sampling of demonstration lessons that also center on the five big ideas and extend the strategies you'll learn about in this chapter. We'll use the first big idea we learned from Otis and Will—question—to launch our conversation about teaching habits you can embrace to help lead learners on the path toward independence.

Question

Peter Johnston's work around student mindset and teacher language has drastically changed the way we question and respond to our students. Both of his books, *Choice Words* (2004) and *Opening Minds* (2012), have helped us, with a lot of practice, to shift our interactions with our students to a more dynamic learning stance. Essentially this type of language encourages children to see themselves as people who get smarter every day and their learning as a fluid and ongoing process. While engaging in teacher actions, ask questions or offer comments like those found in Figure 4.2 to help students recognize that purposeful learning is nurtured through mistake making, rethinking, revising, and persistence.

LITERACY WORKSHOP: DYNAMIC LEARNING STANCE QUESTIONS AND COMMENTS

During Read-Aloud
- What did you notice?
- What are you wondering?
- Why would the author/illustrator choose to do it that way?
- How might you use what you discovered today when you go out to learn?

While Conferring
- What are you doing as a literacy learner today?
- How are you planning to go about this?
- Tell me more about . . .
- Perhaps you could try . . .
- How does it feel to have accomplished your goal?
- What would you like to learn next?

During Sharing and Celebrating
- Did anyone innovate or try something new today?
- What challenges did you come across today? How did you go about solving them?
- How did the questions or comments of others support or change your thinking?

Figure 4.2

When the use of dynamic learning stance language becomes a habit, you'll start hearing your students use the same types of questions. The next step is teaching them how to ask questions effectively that will lead to meaningful dialogue among their peers. In *Building Bigger Ideas*, Maria Nichols (2019) offers characteristics and samples of effective questions or comments like those found in Figure 4.3. With these ideas as a jumping-off point, you can transfer the question-asking responsibility to your students. As their independence increases, they will, over time, become more adept at engaging in purposeful, collaborative conversations with their peers to build knowledge and ideas.

CHARACTERISTICS OF EFFECTIVE QUESTIONS TO PROMOTE COLLABORATIVE CONVERSATIONS	SAMPLES OF QUESTIONS TO PROMOTE COLLABORATIVE CONVERSATIONS
Explore new possibilities	• Is there a different way to think about that? How can you find out?
Focus on learners' wonderings	• Are you curious or wondering what your friends think? How might you ask them?
Respond to students' thinking	• Look around at your friends' faces. Can you infer what they're thinking? What could you ask them to find out?
Invite open-ended responses	• What are you thinking or wondering about that thought?
Seek out diverse perspectives	• Are you wondering about the differences in your friends' thinking? What could you ask them to find out more? • Is there anyone you might invite into the conversation?
Encourage reflection	• Are you curious to know if anyone thought about our ideas last night when they were at home? How might you ask?

Figure 4.3
Characteristics and Samples of Questions That Promote Collaborative Conversations

Refining teaching habits and behaviors takes time and practice. When it comes to changing our language, we find it helpful to keep a list of questions handy like those found in Figures 4.2 and 4.3 either on a clipboard or in our conferring notebook. That way we can refer to them when we find ourselves slipping back into the habit of asking "right answer" questions rather than those that promote students' independent thinking. Students in literacy workshop classrooms view learning as a question-answering process. To support students' independence as they move toward asking dialogic, idea-growing (Nichols 2019) queries, we can teach them a variety of questioning stances. By doing this, we show students how to ask even better questions to drive their learning and to engage in meaningful dialogue with their peers.

Teach Questioning Stances

Say your science unit about space systems is wrapping up, but you have that one student who is still curious and keeps asking questions about Earth's moon. During that same space unit, you read aloud *Mae Among the Stars* (Ahmed 2018) about Mae Jemison, the first African American female astronaut, and another learner wants to know more about her. When you build on the structures and routines you've already established, literacy workshop offers children time to explore lingering questions such as these and combine their abilities to read and write in order to seek answers.

Student-generated questions often require a higher thought process than when they simply answer the questions we ask. When we guide children to investigate their queries about themselves, the texts they're reading and writing, and the world around them, we set the stage for a purposeful learning environment. The questions your students ask will inevitably lead to more questions, and, oftentimes, they may not find every answer that they are seeking. When this happens, we remind them (and ourselves) that we are laying the groundwork to help students develop the habits of a curious questioner. How, then, might you go about teaching children to ask compelling questions? One of the ways we do this is to teach students six different perspectives, or stances, to frame their thinking and build on as they ask their questions (Figure 4.4). These viewpoints consist of the following:

- Individual's Stance
- Reader's Stance
- Writer/Illustrator's Stance
- Researcher's Stance
- Critic's Stance
- Literate Citizen's Stance

WRITER/ILLUSTRATOR'S STANCE
- What do I notice?
- Why did the author/illustrator choose to do it that way?
- How might I do this in my own work?

LITERATE CITIZEN'S STANCE
- How can I apply what I've learned to impact those around me?
- How can I take action based on what I've learned?

READER'S STANCE
- Does this text touch my heart and mind?
- What am I thinking or learning about?
- How does it connect to what I already think or know?

LITERACY WORKSHOP QUESTIONING STANCES

RESEARCHER'S STANCE
- What do I want to know?
- How might I attempt to figure it out?

INDIVIDUAL'S STANCE
- Does this book or learning experience speak to me?
- What can I take from it to apply to my own life?
- Who am I as a literacy learner?

CRITIC'S STANCE
- Is this text or idea worth thinking, talking, researching, or writing about?
- What information or whose perspective is missing?

Figure 4.4
Questioning Stances for
Literacy Workshop Learners

You can familiarize students with these questioning stances early in the year by naturally weaving them into the conversations that surround your read-aloud and shared-reading experiences. To further acquaint students, use the different types of questions when you confer or guide readers in small groups. As you ask these questions, label them by simply saying, for example, "I'm using my reader's stance right now."

In Figure 4.5, we offer a brief example of how you might introduce the questioning stances during a read-aloud. To preserve the joyful read-aloud experience, we suggest focusing on no more than one or two stances at a time. For this demonstration, we chose the book *Petra* (Coppo 2018) about a smooth, gray, egg-shaped rock whose optimism shines through as her circumstances change. Listen in to a bit of this demonstration lesson to find out more about Petra and about how you can easily introduce questioning stances:

INTRODUCING QUESTION STANCES DURING A READ-ALOUD EXPERIENCE

Today, we are going to read a book called *Petra* by Marianna Coppo. As we read, we're going to do what we always do—listen, think, notice, and ask questions. Today, I'm going to think aloud to help you see how people ask questions from different points of view, or stances.

When the dog picks up Petra and put her in his mouth, I have a question from a *writer's/illustrator's stance*. I want to know how the author made me believe that Petra was a gigantic rock at the beginning of the story. I'm going to research this by going back to look at the illustrations again. I see here that she showed a close-up view of Petra.

I have another question from that same stance. Why did Marianna Coppo choose to do this? I think I'll have to keep reading to find out. Now Petra imagines she's an egg? It seems like Marianna Coppo is helping me to see what Petra imagines by showing me that image in the illustrations.

I'm noticing that every time Petra gets moved, she thinks she's something new. I also notice that she is never upset. I have a question from an *individual's stance*. That means I'm wondering how I can use what I learned from this book in my own life. Hmm! I'm thinking that the author might be telling me that no matter what happens, stay positive.

Figure 4.5

Once you've introduced the questioning stances, continue to connect them to independence and engagement in the following ways:

- Post the different stances in the places in your room where it makes the most sense. For example, you might post the reading stances near your classroom library for students to refer to when selecting books.
- Copy stances and invite students to glue them into their literacy notebook to reference when reading, talking, or writing about text.
- Create an ongoing anchor chart where students can add their own questions to the various stances.

Teaching students how to question from different points of view shifts their mindsets from passive consumers of information to active producers who synthesize discoveries. Considering a text or experiences from various stances underscores the overarching goal of literacy workshop—the integration rather than the separation of learning. Following their own line of inquiry gives students clear purpose for their reading or writing. To support students as they make decisions about how to maximize their learning time, instructional habits in planning can be used to monitor and support their efforts.

Plan

In Chapter 2, we shared the cues we use to determine optimal times for engaging in literacy workshop and took you through the practicalities of planning. We also gave you a glimpse into the *literacy workshop mindset*, or how your planning will be the *same, same but different* from when you plan your separate workshops. Here, we will share some helpful habits to help you support students as they plan and to guide your future literacy workshop planning.

To monitor students' planning and progress and guide her teacher actions, Karen checks in with students on the Status of the Class Sheet (Figure 4.6 and Appendix 6 in the Online Resources). Periodic check-ins give you a glimpse of

January 28–
February 4

Literacy Workshop: Status of the Class

Student's Name:	Monday:	Tuesday:	Wednesday:	Thursday:	Friday:
1. Vinnie A.					
2. Everette A.					
3. Michael A.					
4. Lucy A.					
5. Maddie B.					
6. Ethan C.					
7. Josh D.					
8. Aubrey E.					
9. Leah H.					
10. Kylee H.					
11. Kai L.					
12. Leah M.					

January 28–
February 4

Literacy Workshop: Status of the Class

Student's Name	Monday:	Tuesday:	Wednesday:	Thursday:	Friday:
13. Abby P.					
14. Jack R.					
15. Wylder S.					
16. Bobby S.					
17. Molly S.					
18. Devin S.					
19. Brody T.					
20. Ashland W.					
21. Jayden W.					
22. Kayla W.					
23. Geovanni J.					
24.					

Figure 4.6 Sample of Karen's Status of Class Sheet

what students are doing and alert you to who might need additional support and guidance. To take the Status of the Class, quickly read each student's name and ask a question or two from the list that appears in Figure 4.7. Invite learners to tell you their progress from the previous day and plan for their independent work. The goal for each learning time is that students apply the understandings they've gained along the way from your demonstration lessons as they read, write, or research to answer their own questions. Getting in the habit of taking the Status of the Class will help you plan your teacher actions. In addition, you are communicating to students that you view them as readers and writers who can guide their own learning. When you invite literacy learners to check in on their own learning, they get a more in-depth look at the incremental progress they are making toward reaching their long-term goals.

Because primary-grade children have shorter attention spans, Maria finds that it is more efficient to check in with students during learning time, rather than before. Using a class observation grid (see Figure 4.8 and Appendix 7 in the Online Resources), you can quickly jot down what students are working on and whether they need support. Some questions you might ask yourself to help you plan your teacher actions include the following:

- Is the child reading, writing, or both?
- Are they working independently or collaboratively?
- If working collaboratively, how is it going?
- Are they engaged, or do they need additional support?
- Do they have a clear plan?

STATUS OF THE CLASS
GUIDING QUESTIONS

- What are you planning to work on as a literacy learner?
- Talk a little about what you will be doing.
- How will this help you reach your goals?
- Do you need any resources for your work today?
- Do you need any support from me or from your friends to move forward?

Figure 4.7

Literacy Workshop Class Observation Grid   1/28/19 - 2/1/19

1. Luke	2. Charani	3. Rohith	4. William
♡ Elephant + Piggie / Needs a goal-setting conference	♡ to write + draw / ✓ in to make sure she's reading	♡ Biographies / Reading + writing about Gandhi	♡ Dinosaurs / Reading + Writing / Working w/ Quentin
5. Shreya	6. Eli	7. Aarav	8. Anthony
Working w/Chloe to learn about baby animals / * Find resources	Mainly reading Otto books / Robot diagrams?	♡ Pokémon / Graphic Format books?	Small group conference / Focus: Read or Write?
9. Morgan	10. Rishav	11. Ava	12. Fatima
♡ Varied interests / Needs a goal setting conf.	Small group Conference / Focus: Read or Write?	Share her reading / writing plan w/ class	Small group conference / Focus: Read or Write
13. Abby	14. Crosby	15. Srikar M.	16. Nikhila
♡ to write + draw / ✓ in to make sure she's reading	♡ Hockey / Find more hockey books / How to book?	Hooked on Press Start series / Making own version w/ Srikar P.	(Gone on vacation)
17. Srikar P.	18. Rylan	18. Sabrina	20. Quentin
♡ Press Start series / Writing w/ Srikar M.	Videotape her working w/ Sabrina as model of collaboration	Co-authoring book about dolphins	Working with William / * Need to find more dinosaur resource
21. Chloe	22. Lexi	23. Nikita	24. Kaeden
Working w/ Shreya (baby animals) / * Find resources	Small group Conference / Focus: Read or Write	♡ Unicorns / See if she wants to work w/ Olivia	Confer w/ Kaeden + Christian / Focus: Teamwork
25. Paul	26. Olivia	27. Christian	28. Joshika
♡ Nonfiction Steve Jenkins	♡ Unicorns / See if she wants to work w/ Nikita	Working w/ Kaeden on shark research	♡ Biscuit Books / ✓ in to encourage some writing

Figure 4.8   A Sample of Maria's Class Observation Grid

In your literacy workshop classroom, students are creating individualized learning plans and you are making learner-focused decisions about your teacher actions. With students' interest and questions guiding your journey, you'll have time to enjoy the sights of your students' learning in their own ways.

Promote Purposeful Planning

Have you ever been on a guided tour when the guide is moving on to the next room and you still need time to linger and learn? What happens to your interest and engagement when the leader's purpose and plan is vastly different from yours? Like this tour guide and with best intentions, sometimes we have our own plan and quickly lead children in one direction rather than letting them wander from here to there. We acknowledge that there are times during our days, weeks, and year that we, too, find ourselves marching forward without looking back to see who's following. Luckily, literacy workshop has helped us to slow down and engage in student-focused planning. We hope it does the same for you. When students participate in, or take the lead in, planning their learning path, they clearly see the purpose for their learner actions and, in turn, are more engaged.

To illustrate our point, we turn to the humorous picture book *Two Problems for Sophia* (Averbeck 2018), where Sophia has to figure out how to stop her new pet giraffe's snores from waking up the whole house. When her family insists that she find a permanent solution to her problem, she carries out the following plan:

STEP ONE: Research
STEP TWO: Apply What You've Learned from the Research
STEP THREE: If That Doesn't Work—Think of a Better Solution
STEP FOUR: Build a Prototype
STEP FIVE: If the Prototype Doesn't Work—Consider a Fresh Approach
STEP SIX: Create a Blueprint

While Sophia's plan is unique to her situation, we can adapt what we've learned from her to guide literacy workshop learners as they scope out a plan to effectively use their learning time (Figure 4.9).

SOPHIA'S PLAN	TIPS FOR LITERACY WORKSHOP PLANNERS
Step One: Research	Reread your long-term goal; reflect on what you accomplished yesterday. What questions will guide your learning today? If you need ideas or help, talk with your friends or your teacher.
Step Two: Apply What You've Learned from the Research	Based on what you learned from your research, formulate a plan for today's work.
Step Three: If That Doesn't Work—Think of a Better Solution	Are you getting closer to accomplishing your long-term goal? If you notice that, at the end of literacy workshop learning time, you didn't quite meet your goal, reflect and make a new plan for tomorrow.
Step Four: Build a Prototype	Do you need to adjust or rethink your plan based on your new thinking? Don't forget—your plan might look different from everyone else's, and that's okay.
Step Five: If the Prototype Doesn't Work—Consider a Fresh Approach	Are you getting closer to accomplishing your goal? If you notice that, at the end of literacy workshop learning time, you didn't quite meet your goal, reflect and make a new plan for tomorrow. You are building your own knowledge to answer your unique questions.
Step Six: Create a Blueprint	How would you like to share the answers to your questions with others? Create a blueprint or rough idea to share with your teacher.

Figure 4.9   Tips for Literacy Workshop Planners

The example in Figure 4.9 is just one of the many ways you might choose to guide learners in their planning. In Chapter 6, we offer demonstration lessons to gradually release the responsibility of planning to your students. The eventual goal is that students will be able to map out a clear learning path and articulate their reasons for following that particular plan, like Wylder, who chose to use Google Slides when writing a piece entitled "Everything You Wanted to Know About Digimon Monsters." When Karen asked Wylder why he made this plan, he pondered her question for a moment and then shared that he was a more successful writer when using this digital tool because he was able to easily insert images and add text to multiple slides each day. As Karen listened to him explain his reasoning, she discovered that writing on paper was still overwhelming and creating his piece digitally was helping him meet his goals and find his voice. Whether your students are reading, researching, crafting texts, or creating other products, they are more engaged in their literacy workshop investigations when their learner actions are driven by their own goals and carried out through self-paced learning plans.

Each year, Karen asks her students to set long-term literacy goals (Figure 4.10). After her students set their first long-term goals, she settled in to confer with Vinnie. When she asked why he chose the goal *to identify the main idea in the text I am reading*, he shared, "At my last school that's what we had to do each time we read a book." She told him that she trusted that he could read a book, comprehend, and identify the main idea. She then invited him to take a day or two to think of a goal that would be more meaningful and personal to him. After a few days of literacy workshop, Karen returned to touch base with Vinnie. During the conference, he said he was ready to revise his goal based on what he had learned so far during literacy workshop. His new goal became *to choose books that will challenge me as a reader and help me become a better writer*. This example illustrates the different levels of support your students may need with goal setting.

Depending on your students' previous experiences with setting their own learning targets, you might consider two strategies that we learned from Gravity Goldberg's book *Mindsets and Moves* (2016)—creating a list of class goals or dividing goals into categories. When students are just beginning with goal setting, create an anchor chart with class goals. To connect these goals to students' independence, use the focus phrases from your demonstration lessons. For example, when Maria launched literacy workshop, her three class goals were

1. I read, write, or learn more about the things I like.
2. I keep trying even when it is challenging.
3. I listen and respond to my friends' ideas and thinking.

The first two goals are designed to get students to read and/or write for a little bit longer each day, and the third goal is to help them understand the importance of their collaborative conversations. Once the goals are posted and you've demonstrated what each goal means, invite your learners to post a sticky note under the goal that will help them the most. To make it easy to remember, Maria writes the goal number under the child's name on her Class Observation Grid (see Appendix 7 in the Online Resources) and then uses this information to guide her observations and interactions with learners.

You might try an alternative to this by offering students categories from which to choose when setting their goals. To do this, you could use the common threads listed before every demonstration lesson. For instance, if students are reading and writing fiction texts, your goal categories might be learning about characters, thinking about themes, and noticing style. Then, like the example presented, write the goals in a place where students can put a sticky note under their goal or record it in their literacy notebook. Eventually, you want students to be able to identify their own goals, because when children set their own short- and long-term goals, it helps them to better articulate what they've done during learning time. During sharing and celebrating time, you'll hear goal-oriented celebrations like Kylee's: "I read past my goal for today, and according to Aubrey, I'm at the good part!" Kylee's self-awareness, engagement, and connection to her peers clearly demonstrate the benefits of encouraging goal setting and proactive planning during literacy workshop. Next, we'll share some helpful teaching habits that guide your investigations into students' learning progress.

Figure 4.10   Literacy Learner's Long-Term Goals

Investigate

You probably have a lot of questions about the learners in your class. The teacher action that we find the most helpful when seeking answers to our student-related queries is sitting beside a learner to engage in a conference. Conferring with learners is an action that takes time and patience (mostly with yourself). When conferring, it is helpful if you view yourself as an admirer (Goldberg 2016), noticing what students are doing and building on that potential to help them set goals. When you view children this way, you see them as unique individuals and are able to encourage their agency and independence.

To direct our attention in conferences, we find it helpful to ground our interactions in a specific focal point for each conference. To help you do this, you can use the four purposes Karen and her husband, Brian, set out in their book *Transforming Literacy Teaching in the Era of Higher Standards* (Biggs-Tucker and Tucker 2015). When sitting beside students, try to focus on one of the following purposes:

- **Assessing:** Collecting formative data to plan your next steps. Some examples include surveying students about their literacy habits and preferences, taking a running record on a text they've chosen, noticing a child's style choices in their writing, or determining whether they are making steps toward reaching their literacy workshop goals. Your aim is to leave an assessing conference with insights that answer some of your questions.

- **Teaching:** Following up on information gleaned from an assessing conference or from kid watching. A teaching conference gives you the opportunity to review and help students apply the integrated big ideas you've highlighted during your demonstration lessons. A learner will often walk away from a teaching conference with a focus phrase or strategy-focused goal to work on while reading or writing.

- **Goal Setting:** Supporting students as they set and monitor their own progress toward goals. For less experienced goal setters, a goal-setting conference is supportive as they transition from using whole-class goals or category goals to setting their own personal goals. Students will usually go back to work after a goal-setting conference with a record of their personal goal either in their literacy notebook or on a planning or goal-setting sheet.

- **Sharing and Celebrating:** Applauding a student's accomplishment or discovery. During a sharing and celebrating conference, you and the student might swap new book titles, share a piece of writing, marvel at a discovery they made when researching, or anything else that engages the learner and encourages them to continue their personal quest for new knowledge.

With your purpose in mind, begin a conference by referring to the student's goal or something that you have taught during a demonstration lesson. For example, you might ask, "How has your reading or writing been going? What have you noticed about yourself as a learner?" For additional conferring tips, see Figure 4.11. As you listen, let the learner's thoughts and questions guide your responses. To determine the next steps for your small-group or whole-class demonstration lessons, look for patterns of similar needs or next steps on the road toward independence.

TIPS FOR CONFERRING DURING LITERACY WORKSHOP

- Try to listen more than you talk.

- Begin with an open-ended question like, "How's it going?" or "Tell me about your reading or writing today."

- Keep the conference conversational; refrain from asking a series of test-like questions.

- Focus on getting to know learners rather than the book they're reading or text they're writing. If it helps you to be present, consider taking notes after the conference is over.

- Relax and enjoy having conversations with your students about their reading and writing!

Figure 4.11

Capturing the answers to your questions and the things you discover during a conference can take on different forms. Karen prefers to keep her notes in a three-ring conferring notebook with one page for each child. Maria chooses to keep everything on a clipboard using the Class Observation Grid (see Figure 4.7 and Appendix 7 in the Online Resources). The notes you choose to record relate to the purpose of the conference (Figure 4.12).

TIPS FOR KEEPING CONFERRING NOTES MEANINGFUL AND MANAGEABLE

- Determine the focus of the conference.

- Based on your purpose, record the most essential takeaways.

- Assessing: Key findings from assessment.

- Teaching: Focus phrase or strategy you taught.

- Goal Setting: Student goal and/or progress toward meeting that goal.

- Sharing and Celebrating: Take a photo of the child and their accomplishment or mark the date on your notes.

- Plan next steps: What will the student work on after leaving the conference? What do you need to do or prepare to help your reader or writer move forward in their work?

Figure 4.12

Conferring is teacher action that will help you study your learners so that you can engage in student-focused planning. Sitting beside a child gives you a window into their literacy learning. You'll learn how they select or progress through a book, how a writing piece is coming along, and what literacy behaviors might need additional support. Spending a few minutes admiring each student cultivates a trusting relationship that pays off as you recommend book titles, negotiate literacy goals, or nudge learners to take the risks necessary to learn. At the same time you are learning about your students through investigation, they will be developing the ability to study topics of interest by reading and/or writing.

Invite Investigation

When you invite investigation into your literacy workshop classroom, engagement and independence follow closely behind. Children are driven when learning new things about preferred topics. While researching, learners discover real reasons to read, write, converse, collaborate, and share their learning. As researchers, they learn how to find information efficiently and share their new learning in meaningful ways (Hoyt 2002). In Chapter 9, we offer demonstration lessons for four elements of nonfiction—topic, structure, author's purpose, and style. Here we will take a quick look at additional strategies you can teach as students ask questions, seek information, and share their newfound knowledge with others.

GROW STUDENTS' KNOWLEDGE ABOUT TOPICS OF INTEREST

To scaffold your primary-grade investigators as they begin to explore topics of interest, consider providing students with an overarching category under which they can choose a particular topic (Figure 4.13). For example, to weave science into literacy workshop, Maria gives her students the overarching category of *animals*. Then, each of her students decides which animal they would like to investigate during their learning time. To incorporate social studies, Maria invites children

SCIENCE	SOCIAL STUDIES
Weather	Friendship
Space	Our Earth
Animals	Our Customs and Traditions
Bugs	Inspiring Individuals

Figure 4.13   Examples of Overarching Categories to Guide Primary-Grade Students' Investigations

to investigate *inspiring individuals*. Then, she goes to the school and public libraries and checks out as many accessible biographies as she can find. When researching, her students also have access to digital resources, such as PebbleGo, to enhance the books she has in her classroom library.

Two strategies that are helpful in increasing the independence of budding investigators are gathering information from the visual images and writing facts in their own words. The best way we've found to teach researchers to strategically interpret visual information is a method we learned from Tony Stead's book *Is That a Fact? Teaching Nonfiction Writing K–3* (2002) (Figure 4.14). When you show your beginning readers how to use images as their primary source of information, they will be less likely to rely on you for help or to copy words directly from the page. It is equally important to give researchers a strategy to use when recording the facts they've learned from reading. A helpful approach for primary-grade note takers is collecting what JoAnn Portalupi and Ralph Fletcher call "Dash Facts" (2001, 24) (Figure 4.15). Because we spend so much time teaching students how to write a sentence, it seems counterintuitive to teach them *not* to write one, but this is exactly what we want them to do when taking notes. So, we show them how to write the main idea that they want to remember in a word or a phrase preceded by a dash. Hence, the name *dash fact*. So, when recording information, they simply make a dash, record a fact, make a dash, record a fact, and so on.

TEACHING CHILDREN HOW TO INTERPRET INFORMATION FROM VISUAL IMAGES

Preparation

- Select a page from a nonfiction book, classroom magazine, or other resource that includes visual images and a small amount of text. You can also use a poster on a specific topic such as the life cycle of a butterfly.

- Cover up the text.

- Display the page so everyone can see it.

Demonstration

- Invite children to tell you what they see. Record their findings.

- Draw their attention to a specific aspect of the image. Ask them to zoom in and tell you what else they notice. Record their additional findings.

- Separate fact from opinion. For example, if using the poster of a life cycle of a butterfly and a child says, "Butterflies are my favorite bug," help your students understand that their statement is an opinion because they cannot prove it by pointing at something in the visual image.

- Uncover the text. Notice and celebrate how much more information they found in the visual images than was present in the text.

Adapted from Stead (2002), 52–54

Figure 4.14

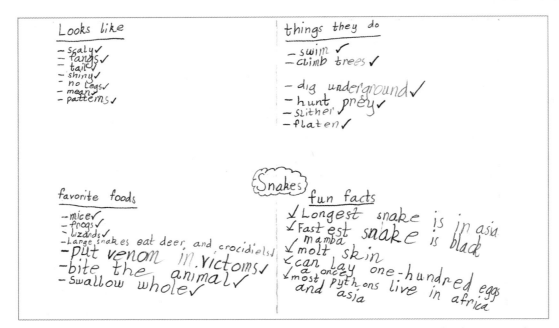

Figure 4.15   Literacy Notebook Entry: Dash Facts

For middle-grade learners who have experience gathering information from resources, your focus shifts to teaching them strategies for collecting research from multiple sources and for considering the reliability of these sources. To teach students how to research using multiple sources, use the process outlined in Figure 4.16. This process came in handy when Karen's class wanted to research giraffes after her students' curiosity was piqued by watching the YouTube video about April, the giraffe who gave birth to a calf at the Animal Adventure Park in New York. Of course, the class was instantly curious: How tall was the baby giraffe when it was born? What is the gestation period for a giraffe? How far is it to the Animal Adventure Park? The questions continued. Karen used this teachable moment to demonstrate how, together, they could find the answers to their questions using multiple sources. As with this example, you'll find that students' literacy workshop investigations might connect to your science or social studies topics (Figure 4.17), showcasing the inter-disciplinary use of reading and writing.

TEACHING RESEARCHERS HOW TO GATHER INFORMATION FROM MULTIPLE SOURCES

Demonstration 1

- Select a topic of interest.
- Invite your students to brainstorm a list of possible sources, including, but not limited to, print, visual images, primary sources, and digital resources.

Demonstration 2

- Demonstrate where you find or who you contact to gather multiple sources about a topic of interest.

Demonstration 3

- Start with one source. In your literacy notebook, on an interactive whiteboard document, or chart paper, jot a few notes using a colored pencil, pen, or marker.

Demonstration 4

- Using a different source and a different color, take more notes containing new facts. Continue in the same fashion for another source or two.

Reflection

- When your notes are complete, invite students to notice how you learned different facts from different sources, and together, they create a more complete picture of your topic.

Figure 4.16

SCIENCE	SOCIAL STUDIES
Scientists and Their Contributions to the Field	Making a Difference in the World
Earth and Space	Places, Regions, and Cultures
Ecology/Taking Care of the Earth	People Who Shaped History
Health and Wellness	Events That Impacted History
Animals and Their Ecosystems	Informed Citizenship

Figure 4.17   Science and Social Studies Connections
for Middle-Grade Students' Investigations

Middle-grade learners often believe that if they read information on the Internet, it must be true. Giving students a strategy for critically judging the reliability of online sources is important as they begin to realize that not all sites are created equal. The approach that we've found helpful for our students is the "WWWDOT" approach for evaluating websites (Zhang, Duke, and Jiménez 2011, 152) outlined in Figure 4.18. If you teach learners these questions, post them in your classroom and model asking them yourself. You will be helping to build critically literate citizens.

As students expand their knowledge about topics of interest, they see the direct connection between literacy and learning. This link provides a purpose for the work they choose to do and helps them see that the learner actions they use in school are the same actions adults use at home or in their places of work.

Who wrote this? What are their qualifications?

What was their purpose?

When was it written?

Does this information answer your questions? How?

Organization of information. Is the organization helpful?

To Do. How can I verify this information?

Figure 4.18   Adapted from Zhang, Duke, and Jimenez (2011, 152)

SHOWCASE REAL-WORLD PURPOSES FOR READING, WRITING, RESEARCHING, AND SHARING

Student-driven investigations create real-world applications for literacy learning. When investigating, students are engaged in asking questions about topics of interest, looking for answers, solving problems, and then choosing how to share this information with a wide range of audiences. In his book *Energize Research Reading and Writing*, Chris Lehman (2012) encourages us to provide students with a variety of these types of experiences because this is the work of literate citizens. Informed people hear or see something that makes them wonder and then seek out resources to answer their questions. Once they have that information, they decide what to do with it. Will their findings prompt action, or did finding the answer to their question satisfy their curiosity? When we translate the actions of informed citizens to literacy workshop, students find practical ways to share their knowledge. For example, we might see a group of third graders who are fascinated by germs and how they are spread. After collaboratively researching this topic, they decide to create posters on the importance of handwashing to post in the school's bathrooms. To design the poster to meet the needs of the different audiences in their school, they consider their words and pictures. They debate about the language and images that will be most helpful for the kindergarten bathrooms and how the posters for the fifth-grade bathrooms will differ. As they consider vocabulary, illustrations, and even appropriate content, they are demonstrating a highly developed level of understanding much more advanced than what would be expected on a multiple-choice test or fill-in-the-blank quiz on the topic of germs. This literacy workshop learning experience strengthens not only students' understanding of the content but also their awareness of a real-world purpose for their reading and writing.

As students conduct their investigations, focus on their *process* rather than on a final product or project. Trust that the time learners spend reading, writing, and researching not only will build their content-area knowledge but also will reinforce their understanding of the interrelatedness of the language arts. That may mean that sometimes learners will investigate a topic or a question but choose not to create a final product. The focus is on using resources and gathering information to answer questions. Viewing your students' learning this way is habit forming. The more you can focus on their process, the more willing students will be to take risks and innovate. The same is true for you, as their teacher!

Innovate

If you are willing to try literacy workshop in your classroom, we would argue that you already have what George Couros (2015) calls an "Innovator's Mindset." Approaching your interactions with students with this mindset helps them to see firsthand what it looks like to believe in yourself and your abilities. We believe the characteristics that embody an innovator's mindset, many of which we've already discussed, are essential for literacy workshop teachers. To get in the habit of being innovative during literacy workshop:

- Be empathetic: When considering students, actions, get in the habit of stepping back and putting yourself in their shoes.
- Accept approximations: Notice the small strides they are making toward their goals.
- Question and solve problems: When literacy workshop isn't going well, ask your students or colleagues what they think and invite them to offer solutions.
- Take risks: The most student-focused teaching happens when you follow your learners' lead (even though it might not always be what you had planned!).

- Invite other professionals into your conversations and literacy workshop journey: Processing your teaching trials and triumphs with others strengthens your practice.
- Step back and observe: Before you get busy conferring, take a moment to scan the entire class and notice their level of engagement.
- Create your own version of literacy workshop: We've offered our version of literacy workshop today (which will probably change by the time this book is published); we encourage you to do it the way that works best in your teaching context.
- Don't give up: Teaching isn't picture perfect. Keep going, even when it gets messy.
- Be reflective: Keep a notebook or digital file to jot your ideas and thinking as you experiment with literacy workshop.

When you approach teaching with an innovative mindset, it naturally inspires students to become more inventive. With that goal in mind, here are a few strategies you might try to inspire innovation.

Inspire Innovation

Being innovative, or creative, is one of the 4Cs identified by the National Education Association (2011). Literacy workshop is an ideal setting for learners to be innovative in their thinking and in their work with their peers. Innovation can happen without the latest technology tool in a child's hand. In fact, the technology tools our students are using today probably won't exist when they're adults. By its nature, literacy workshop promotes innovation because it offers students choice in the way they think, act, and learn. For strategies to use to inspire innovation, see Figure 4.19. If we prescribe every move our students make, they will come

STRATEGIES FOR INSPIRING INNOVATION
- Make supplies easily available
- Focus on process rather than on product
- Celebrate all ideas
- Model innovation

Figure 4.19

to rely on us to solve their problems. They won't learn that creativity and innovation are a recurring process of small successes and frequent mistakes. To demonstrate this process, you can use books that promote innovation or highlight innovative characters as your teaching partners (Figure 4.20).

> ### BOOKS TO PROMOTE INNOVATIVE THINKING
> - *Charlotte the Scientist Finds a Cure* (Andros 2019)
> - *Doll-E 1.0* (S. McCloskey 2018) (see demonstration lesson in Chapter 6)
> - *Going Places* (Reynolds and Reynolds 2014)
> - *How to Build a Hug: Temple Grandin and Her Amazing Hug Machine* (Guglielmo and Tourville 2018) (see demonstration lesson in Chapter 6)
> - *Made by Maxine* (Spiro 2018)
> - *The Most Magnificent Thing* (Spires 2014)
> - *Rosie Revere, Engineer* (Beaty 2013)
> - *What to Do with a Box* (Yolen 2016)

Figure 4.20

By inspiring innovation, you create time for students to follow their passions and use their newly acquired knowledge to spark original thinking, ideas, or ways to share. Finally, when encouraging independence and engagement we believe reflection—a characteristic of individuals with an innovator's mindset—is essential for both ourselves and for literacy workshop learners.

Reflect

In his seminal book *Writing: Teachers and Children at Work,* Don Graves (1983) reminds us that teaching is a craft that "demand[s] constant revision, constant reseeing of what is being revealed by the information in hand" (6). Reflective practitioners are continuously teaching and learning at the same time. They do this by questioning, gathering more information, and revising their pedagogy based on their new discoveries. Isn't this exactly what we want our students to do—ask questions, gather information, and revise or add to their schema based on their new learning? Literacy workshop learners deserve innovative teachers, like you, who are willing to take risks, think outside of the box, and trust their research-guided instincts. When you integrate reading, writing, speaking, and listening into your workshop time, you not only prepare students for the challenges of an ever-changing world but also continually prepare yourself for the ever-changing horizon of the education profession. Follow the needs of the class and trust your teaching wisdom. Refine your workshop practices as you learn from and reflect on what you've discovered about and with your students. Two habits that help us as reflective practitioners are periodically checking our students' literacy notebooks and listening carefully during sharing and celebrating conversations.

Flipping through the pages of your students' literacy notebooks gives you some quiet time to reflect on their progress. Developing this habit is a personal choice, so you'll want to think about how and when to collect and read through their notebook entries. Your decision will be based on your purpose, the time you have available, and the number of students you have. As a result, there isn't a one-size-fits-all approach for admiring student notebooks, so try for something that makes sense for you and for your learners. At first, it may be helpful to *peek* at a few of them at a time once or twice a week. Another option is to collect them all every couple of weeks and spend a bit more time *poring* over them. Whatever you decide to do, you'll find evidence of your students' literacy lives waiting inside the pages. Reflecting on the contents will help guide your instruction and give you specific topics, skills, or strategies to discuss with your learners, their families, and other interested colleagues. As you reflect on the contents of students' literacy notebooks, look for the following:

- Evidence of thinking and reflection during and after demonstration lessons
- Demonstration of the habits and behaviors of literacy learners
- Exploration of self-awareness and independent thinking
- Goal setting and self-assessment of goals
- Insightful responses to text
- Growth in writing ability
- Questions about topics of interest
- Exploratory research
- Proof of planning
- Projects in progress
- Personal reflections on learning and life

The literacy notebook is a place for learners to explore their literacy identities. Blending the responses to their reading and writing in one notebook helps students weave together the common threads of literacy. As their understanding of integrated big ideas becomes clearer, they are able to put the pieces together and celebrate their literacy growth in more meaningful ways. Another habit to help you reflect on students' progress toward independence is to actively listen during sharing and celebrating time.

Literacy workshop celebrations further connect and cement the learning that happens during whole-group demonstration lessons, small-group or one-to-one teaching, and self-guided learning time. In addition, it spreads the wealth as students learn from each other. The share-and-celebrate conversations are another ideal time to collect anecdotal observations and reflect on your literacy workshop learners' progress. For some questions to prompt reflective sharing, see Figure 4.21. During share and celebrate time, notice your students' ability to do the following:

- Clearly communicate their progress or problems
- Actively listen to each other
- Build on the thinking or learning of others
- Consider the thoughts and feelings of others
- Learn from mistakes
- Celebrate each other's successes
- Ask for help

QUESTIONS TO GUIDE LITERACY WORKSHOP SHARING CONVERSATIONS

- What did you learn or do today that you want to celebrate?
- What did you learn today that you didn't know yesterday?
- How do you prefer learning? On your own or with your friends?
- What have you learned from or with a classmate?
- What is your favorite thing to do during literacy workshop? Why?
- How are you balancing your time between reading and writing?

- Are you working toward your goals? What's helping you or getting in the way?
- Have you been investigating anything interesting? If so, tell us one fascinating fact you learned.
- What did you learn as a reader that you can teach us?
- What did you learn as a writer that you can teach us?
- Based on what you did today, what do you plan to do tomorrow?

Figure 4.21

Protecting time (two to three minutes at the end of literacy workshop) to share your students' celebrations boosts their engagement. When they have the opportunity to share, learners see the purpose of their hard work. As their teacher, you have the chance to stand alongside them in their moments of joy and independence. Together, you see the fruits of your shared labor, which is especially important on those days when we wonder whether we are making a difference in their literacy lives. Taking a moment at the end of workshop to reflect on those successes gives everyone in the community a chance to stop, think, and say, "Hooray, I learned something new as a reader or writer today!"

If you find yourself running out of time to share at the end of literacy workshop, be innovative and begin the lesson block with a share or stop halfway through to make time for celebrations. It doesn't matter *when* you do it, it does matter *that* you do it because you are promoting literate conversations, where children analyze, comment, and compare what they've read and learned, increasing their reflective thinking. Additionally, fostering this type of collaborative learning environment as your learners switch between writing, speaking, reading, and listening helps solidify connections among these processes and strengthen the skills they use in each separate area of literacy (Allington and Gabriel 2012).

Encourage Reflection

Effective thinkers, writers, problem solvers, readers, and researchers are continually self-monitoring and self-evaluating (Daniels 1994); therefore, we encourage these meta-cognitive processes during literacy workshop because they lead to engagement and independence. In Shawna Coppola's inspiring book *Renew!* she challenges us to revise how we teach the writing process in three ways (2017). Jumping off from there, we borrowed from her three ways to teach the writing process to help us better model reflection during literacy workshop. Building on Coppola's thinking, in order to help students become more reflective learners, it's important to

1. be transparent about your own learning processes during demonstration lessons and interactions with your students.
2. invite students to reflect on and share their unique learning processes in their literacy notebook, with each other, and with you during conferences.
3. examine and reflect on the learning processes of others through mentor texts like the ones you'll find in Chapter 6.

Reflection is essential to learning, independence, and engagement. Asking reflective questions, such as those found in Figure 4.22, invites students to pause and contemplate their learning. When you begin asking reflective questions, you'll find it helpful to be patient and provide scaffolds. For instance, when Karen asks Kayla, "How are you growing as a literacy learner?" Kayla responds with silence. Knowing that silence means Kayla is thinking, Karen refrains from interrupting or jumping in with a follow-up question. Instead she waits. After a couple of minutes of wait time, Kayla replies, "The books that I am reading are more challenging." Karen nudges her by scaffolding, "Tell me more." Kayla continues, "I've been reading more verse novels. I had never read verse novels before. I notice that I have to reread more often to understand what they're saying and think differently about the text. I also realized that because I've been reading verse novels, I've been writing more poetry." Karen smiles, appreciating Kayla's reflections and insightful connection about her reading and writing. This interaction underscored the importance of silent listening and scaffolding as you develop self-reflective learners.

> ### REFLECTIVE QUESTIONS TO ASK YOUR LITERACY LEARNERS
>
> - In what ways are you growing as a reader and/or writer?
> - How are the books you're reading helping to improve your writing?
> - How do the pieces you write help you choose books to read?
> - What are you doing as a literacy learner that makes you feel proud?
> - What are you doing as a literacy learner that is challenging?

Figure 4.22

In addition to modeling reflection and asking reflective questions, invite students to record their learning and reflections in their literacy notebook. Building on the ideas we shared on pages 69–70, the literacy notebook is a place where students

- document how they are doing in literacy workshop;
- detail reflective thinking during a read-aloud experience;
- record text-related reflections, ideas, and/or quotations to ponder;
- reflect on and ask questions about current events;
- experiment with seed ideas for future writing;
- play with language and reflect on how it might improve writing; and
- keep an organic record of their reflection on their growth as literacy learners.

Some strategies we use when setting up our literacy notebooks can be found in Figure 4.23. In the demonstration lessons in Chapters 5–9 and the Online Resources, you'll find additional ideas for students to record reflections along with their thinking and learning in their literacy notebooks. These ideas will help lead students toward developing a habit of documenting their learning so that they can revisit and reflect on it throughout the year.

SETTING UP A LITERACY NOTEBOOK

- Invite students to personalize the cover of a traditional composition notebook with various items like stickers, pictures of book covers, photos, or other decorations that showcase their reading and writing lives.

- Show learners how to begin recording their literacy workshop responses on the front side of page one in their notebooks.

- Provide students with a self-sticking colored tab to place on the first page and show them how to keep their place by moving it back one page after each response.

- Demonstrate how to glue an anchor chart or other resource on the back of the last page of the notebook. To help them easily locate these references, provide a different-colored self-sticking tab that they move backward with each collected resource.

- Since their written responses are always on the front of the pages and the resources are collected on the back side, it is not a problem when they meet in the middle. They simply keep going forward with their responses and backward with their resources until all pages are filled with a yearlong record of their thinking and learning.

- If they complete one literacy notebook before the year is over, we give them another.

Figure 4.23

Because it is impossible to sit beside your learners each day, a literacy notebook is a window into the work they're doing and will provide you with a wealth of information about their learning processes. Based on the insights you gain from your notebook check-ins, you can follow up with individual students, small groups, or even the whole class to reteach or reinforce an integrated big idea. With this concrete representation of your students' thinking in your hands you are better able to reflect on the choices you are making as a teacher and how they are impacting your literacy learners. Reflection. Integration. Connections. At this point in the book, you have read these words over and over. To support you as you move forward, we will take one final visit to Maria's and Karen's classrooms.

THE VIEW FROM HERE: INDEPENDENCE AND ENGAGEMENT IN A PRIMARY-GRADE CLASSROOM

It's the beginning of March, and spring is finally peeking out in Illinois. Maria and her first graders are using what they've learned from dipping in and out of literacy workshop to embark on a monthlong unit focused on the big ideas we learned from Otis and Will (and discussed in detail earlier in this chapter). Through demonstration lessons and literacy workshop learning time, her first graders will apply what they've discovered so far about questioning, planning, investigating, innovating, and reflecting to read and write about an animal of interest. Maria guides some children to form research teams based on their questions and shared interests while other students prefer to work independently. For her demonstration lesson, Maria reads aloud a few pages from the book *How to Swallow a Pig* (Jenkins 2015) to help kids see one way they might innovate when sharing their information. In this book on each two-page spread, Steve Jenkins has highlighted one distinctive animal behavior and provided step-by-step instructions on how a human might go about trying that behavior themselves. Maria chose this book because Jenkins's innovative way of sharing information is doable for most of her first graders as are the structures of many of Jenkins's other nonfiction books. Therefore, she has checked out a collection of his books from the library so that her investigators can read and learn from them.

As Maria walks around the room during literacy workshop learning time, she sees Ava, Abby, and Charani huddled around a book about dolphins, trying to answer their question, "Where do dolphins live?" Maria stops by to join them and notices that they are flipping through the book page by page. She asks them if they remember anything that they learned about nonfiction books that might help them find the information. Charani's eyes light up and she says, "The table of contents!" Then, Ava thinks back and replies, "We could also see if the book has an index." As if Maria was never there, the girls carry on with their investigation.

Next, Maria joins Eli and Liam, who have a collection of shark books in front of them (all closed) and are each drawing their own picture of a shark. Thinking perhaps they might need a visual model for the work they are doing, Maria asks, "What are you doing as investigators today?" Liam continues drawing and says, "We are learning more about sharks by drawing them." "Hmm," Maria responds. "Do you remember when we read *The Watcher* [Winter 2011] about Jane Goodall? What did Jane do before she drew in her notebook?" Eli stops drawing and thinks aloud, "She watched things." Maria continues, "I wonder if you have anything nearby that you could look at to help you draw your sharks." The light bulb goes off and the boys open the books and begin searching for a diagram to help them learn even more. With twenty-eight first graders, Maria is not able to check in with every group or individual every day. She trusts that she has fostered their independence by setting up clear expectations during her literacy workshop launch and continues to follow through with consistent strategies and structures. The sharing and celebrating time offers Maria another opportunity to gather anecdotal information about her learners and the progress they are making toward meeting their individual or group goals.

THE VIEW FROM HERE: INDEPENDENCE AND ENGAGEMENT IN AN INTERMEDIATE-GRADE CLASSROOM

It is a cloudy, freezing-rain, January day as fifth graders return from P.E. to Karen's classroom breathless and sweaty. On the screen, she has projected the cover of *The Book Tree* by Paul Czajak (2018). Karen's learners grab their literacy notebooks and a pencil before joining her on the carpet. Karen instructs them to divide the front of a fresh literacy notebook page into a T-chart with the words *What I Notice* on the left and *What It Means* on the right. Page by page they read, think about, and discuss the happenings in the book. When they reach the page where a book belonging to the main character, Arlo, falls on the mayor's head, Karen asks, "What is the mayor so upset about?" Aubrey responds, "He doesn't want the boy to be interested in the book." Karen interjects, "Agree or disagree? Why or why not?" Jack agrees but adds, "He [the mayor] doesn't want them to have any ideas or questions." Kylie builds on Jack's thinking and responds, "He wants to teach the kids what they have to learn." To keep this demonstration lesson brief, Karen stops the shared reading of *The Book Tree* in the middle of the book. Then, children prepare for their literacy workshop learning time. Around the room, students are focused on meeting their long-range goals posted on a bulletin board by accomplishing a small goal recorded on their Literacy Workshop Planning Sheet (Figure 4.24). Abby is researching and composing her third essay about an animal on a Chromebook. She has already written about a dog and a bird; today's animal is a whale (Figure 4.25). Molly and Ashland have a little paper book on which they're co-designing a graphic novel (Figure 4.26).

The strategies and structures that Karen has put in place since August support the learning that happens in her classroom in January and beyond. As students are reading, writing, and researching, Karen observes and confers with them individually or in small groups. During these interactions, she thinks about what they will need next to help them work productively during literacy workshop learning time. She also takes a moment in the middle of their learning time to assess the engagement of all her students. She notes who is focused and who might need a bit more support. Karen's purposeful kid watching and conferring helps her plan for her next demonstration lessons.

REFLECT ON INDEPENDENCE AND ENGAGEMENT: PONDERING A NEW VIEW

As you reflect on this chapter, we'd encourage you to transition to a literacy workshop in the same way Otis and Will approached their passions and projects—question, plan, investigate, innovate, and reflect. *Ask questions* like, *What will literacy workshop look like in my learning context?* Make plans but be flexible in executing them. We believe that some of our best teaching occurs in the unplanned moments or in those situations where we've made a teaching mistake and have to regroup. Let your students be your guide. As they are working during literacy workshop, *be an investigator* and collect anecdotal data about their thoughts and experiences. Based on what you learn from your students, rely on your professional decision-making power to *be an innovator*. There isn't a textbook publisher, teacher online, or colleague (including the two of us) who knows your students better than you do. Innovate to create demonstration lessons and literacy workshop learning experiences based on what you know from kid watching with your trained professional eyes. Finally, *take a moment to reflect* on the learning experiences you share with your students. Use your phone to capture photos and/or videoclips that record your students' learning so that you can go back and revisit them when you have a moment. We understand how hectic teaching days quickly turn into weeks and months. But we also know that anytime you are trying something new, it's helpful to celebrate your successes and consider how you might tweak your instructional moves to make them even better.

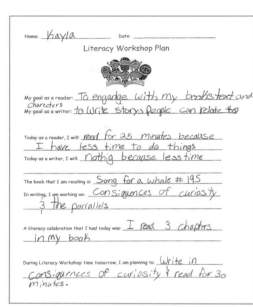

Figure 4.24   Literacy Workshop Planning Sheet

Figure 4.25   A fifth grader composes an animal essay during learning time.

At this point in the book, we'll shift our focus from building your foundational knowledge about literacy workshop to highlighting a sampling of demonstration lessons you might want to share with your students. As we make this transition, we offer these final questions to ponder:

- What are the teacher actions, strategies, and habits that you already have in place to build on as you embark on your literacy workshop journey?
- How can you use the strategies you've learned from this chapter to promote independence and engagement?
- Did you find a teaching habit that you want to focus on? What is your goal? How will you record and reflect on your progress?
- What are some ways you can show your students how you question, plan, investigate, innovate, and reflect outside of school?

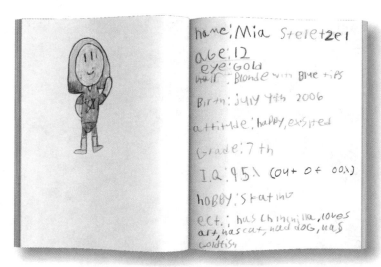
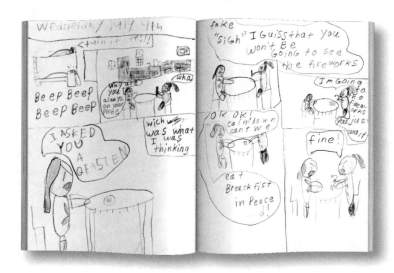

Figure 4.26   Co-created graphic novel

PART II

Zooming In—
Literacy Workshop
Demonstration Lessons

CHAPTER 5

Demonstration Lessons—
Launching Literacy Workshop

Helping learners make connections is one of the most beneficial teaching strategies we can use when introducing new information, and this also applies when we're preparing students to try something *same, same but different* in their instructional day. In the early days of literacy workshop, we set out to identify the common habits and behaviors of literacy learners that our students were already demonstrating in their separate reading and writing workshops to help them see how they would intermingle in literacy workshop.

Those *common threads* are the big ideas we use to launch literacy workshop and serve as a common language to help students relate what they were already doing as readers and writers to the blended actions they will practice during literacy workshop time. You will find the big ideas listed at the beginning of each demonstration lesson. For a complete chart of the big ideas found in Chapter 5 see Demonstration Lesson Big Idea Charts for Chapter 5 in the Online Resources. Above all, when you shift students' focus to integrated common threads, they come to realize that what they learn from reading helps them as writers and vice versa.

COMMON THREADS:
BIG IDEAS FOR LAUNCHING LITERACY WORKSHOP

To help you get started sharing the habits and behaviors of literacy learners with your students, this chapter contains exemplar demonstration lessons for primary- and middle-grade learners. You'll notice that the two lessons differ a bit in format. For example, the primary-grade lessons contain page-specific comments for you to use during your read-aloud experience, whereas the middle-grade lessons are a bit more open ended. In addition, in the middle-grade lessons, we've included big idea–focused questions to ponder. You can use these queries to guide your conferences, spark literacy notebook responses, or plan future demonstration lessons. To frame each integrated big idea, we've provided our research-based rationale for teaching each behavior as a way to support students' understanding of the reciprocal processes of reading and writing.

BIG IDEA: INTEREST

READING WORKSHOP	LITERACY WORKSHOP COMMON THREADS	WRITING WORKSHOP
	Interest	
What kinds of reading do I like to do?	What things, topics, and ideas interest me? How do I learn more about and share my interests with the world?	What do I want to write about?

What Experts Say About Interest

Learners' interests motivate them in a way that very few things can. When students identify their interests, they have an increased focus on their learning and more effectively apply the strategies that they have been taught (Paul 2013). So, as teachers, we find ways to incorporate student preferences into the framework of our literacy instruction and harness the energy that those interests provide our learners.

Setting aside time to learn about your students will help you focus and individualize your literacy workshop. Discovering students' curiosities develops relationships, shows students that you are invested in them as learners, and adds diversity to the literacy topics children might explore. Asking students to generate and pursue their own learning interests provides a wealth of topics for reading, writing, and research. More importantly, when students contribute to their own learning, it leads to authentic engagement (Keene 2018). Looking for ideas to help you get to know your learners' interests? Here are two demonstration lessons that might help. Use or modify these model lessons to launch an ongoing quest to better know your students.

L E S S O N PRIMARY

INTEREST: IT'S A MAGICAL LEARN-SOMETHING YEAR!

FOCUS PHRASES	MENTOR TEXT SUGGESTION	

- I am able to tell you what I like.

- I read, write, or learn more about the things I like.

On a Magical Do-Nothing Day
(Alemagna 2016)

Why We Chose This Book: We've noticed that many of our students spend their free time outside school immersed in a video game world, similar to the child in this book, who is destroying Martians on a video game while their mom is busy writing. In an effort to get the child to stop playing, Mom hides the game, but they find it. With the device in hand, the child ventures outside on a rainy day to explore the forest. After the game falls into the frigid pond, the child is drawn into a magical and mysterious forest world that has been right outside the cabin this whole time. If you ask primary-grade children about their interests (or things they like), it can be challenging for them to identify more than one or two things. This book serves as an ideal discussion starter about the topics, books, ideas, and people that children haven't experienced . . . yet.

Additional Mentor Text Suggestions for Interest

- *Bunny's Book Club Goes t School* (Silvestro 2019)

- *Unplugged* (Antony 2017

ANCHOR LEARNING IN LITERATURE/CONVERSE TO GROW THINKERS AND LEARNERS

BEFORE READING

- Set a Purpose: What do you like to do when you're not in school? [Listen to a few responses.] Things you like or like to do are called *interests*. As we're reading *On a Magical Do-Nothing Day,* notice what the child likes.
- Discuss the Book Cover: What do you think the child is doing on the cover? Where do you think they are?

DURING READING

- "She took the game out of my hands and hid it, as usual" page: How do you think the child is feeling right now? What do you predict the child is going to do when he goes outside?
- "I talked to a bird" page: Hmm! Something interesting happened on this page. I'm noticing that the child's attitude has changed. Turn and tell your neighbor how they were feeling at the beginning of the story, in the middle, and right now.

AFTER READING
- What did the the child like to do at the beginning of the story? [Play his video game.]
- How do their interests change?
- What do you think the child learned in the story?

DEMONSTRATE HABITS AND STRATEGIES

[For this demonstration, insert your own personal interest instead of swimming.] One of my interests is swimming. People who don't swim have a hard time understanding why I like it. Today, during literacy workshop, I'm going to draw and write to show my friends why I like swimming. What are you interested in writing or reading about today?

RECORD THINKING AND LEARNING

During and after independent time, ask children about their interests. Record on a chart like the one in Figure 5.1 for future reference.

It's a Magical Learn-Something Year!!		
First Grade Learners	I'm interested in...	I want to learn more about...
Keile	whales	how they make sounds
Ryan	hockey	my favorite players
Olive	space	the planets

Figure 5.1 Anchor Chart: It's a Magical Learn-Something Year!

WHAT'S NEXT?

Use the insights you gained from this demonstration lesson to guide students' book selections and choice of writing topics as you continue to build on and broaden their interests.

L E S S O N : INTERMEDIATE

INTEREST: HOW INTERESTS CAN MOTIVATE AND GUIDE MY LEARNING

FOCUS PHRASES	MENTOR TEXT SUGGESTION

- I identify my *interests* as a reader, a writer, and a learner.

- I record and refer to my interests to guide my learning.

The Brilliant Deep: Rebuilding the World's Coral Reefs (Messner 2018)

Why We Chose This Book: This book sets the scene for a conversation about how identifying interests can lead to a lifelong passion for learning. Ken Nedimyer learned that coral reefs were beginning to become extinct and decided that he wanted to do something. Although the job seemed daunting, he remembered that it only took one coral gamete to start a colony, so he was confident one person with an original idea could make a difference in the world—and he did.

Additional Mentor Text Suggestions for Interest

- *Count on me* (Tanco 2019)

- *Imagine* (Herrera 2018)

ANCHOR LEARNING IN LITERATURE/CONVERSE TO GROW THINKERS AND LEARNERS

BEFORE READING

- Set a Purpose: We are going to think about how our interests motivate us as learners. Our interests can also help us make a difference in our world. Isn't that what literate citizens do? Let's read a biography about someone who did just that. He had an interest, which led to a passion for learning and later became a project that made the world a better place.
- Discuss the Book Cover: Take a look at the subtitle, *Rebuilding the World's Coral Reefs*. Why do you suppose coral reefs would need rebuilding? What do you already know about coral reefs? Share with a partner.

DURING READING

- Even though Ken grew up around NASA, astronauts, and engineers, he wasn't interested in any of those things. Instead, he was interested in the ocean. Why do you think his interests may have been different from what everyone expected him to be interested in? What do you suppose influenced his interest? [As he was growing up, he loved the ocean and watching Jacques Cousteau.]
- As we continue to read, pay attention to the clues Ken noticed that led him to realize that the coral reefs were beginning to disappear.

- How might Ken have learned about coral reefs? How was that learning important to coming up with a plan for saving the reefs?
- How did Ken's interests guide him as a learner and a citizen?

AFTER READING
- How do your interests motivate you as readers and writers? How might you build on your interests to help you set purposes when you read and write?
- Questions for Learners to Ponder:
  » What am I interested in as a learner and a citizen?
  » How do my interests guide my choices during learning time?
  » Can I use my interests to challenge myself as a reader and writer?

DEMONSTRATE HABITS AND STRATEGIES

Learners use interests to keep them going as they are reading, writing, and researching. Interests are my go-to when I need an idea for a book to read or a writing topic. I'm going to take a minute to show you how I might brainstorm some of the things that I'm interested in. You'll see that my list includes things like favorite authors, topics that I enjoy researching, and people who are important to me.

RECORD THINKING AND LEARNING

There are many different ways to record your interests so that you can refer to them when you are looking for books or ideas for your writing. One way you might choose to record your interests is to use a heart map (Heard 2016). To start your heart map, ask yourself, "What do I carry in my heart that is important to me?" Some ideas might be family, friends, sports, places, authors, events, and so on. You can choose to do two separate heart maps for reading and writing (Figures 5.2a and 5.2b) or combine your interests together in one map (Figure 5.3). It's up to you! When you're done, glue your heart map(s) in your literacy notebook to refer to as you're looking for ideas to read, write, and research. Also, remember that the topics on your heart map may change over time, so feel free to add to or revise them as your interests evolve.

Figure 5.2a
Literacy Notebook Entry: A Writing Heart Map

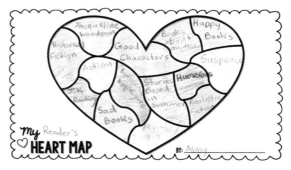

Figure 5.2b
Literacy Notebook Entry: A Reading Heart Map

(continues)

L E S S O N CONTINUED

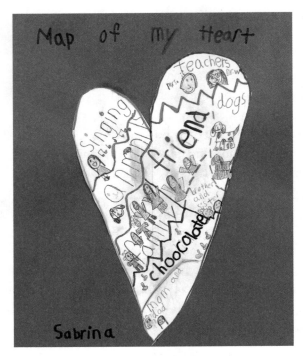

Figure 5.3   Literacy Notebook Entry:
A Literacy Workshop Heart Map

WHAT'S NEXT?

During literacy workshop learning time, confer with students about their interests. Use what you've learned to guide students as they make decisions about writing topics and to match them to books or other texts that they might want to read. The relationship and trust that you build when you ask, "What interests you?" goes a long way in creating the bond that readers, writers, and learners have with you as their literacy mentor.

BIG IDEA: PERSISTENCE

READING WORKSHOP	LITERACY WORKSHOP COMMON THREADS	WRITING WORKSHOP
How do I keep reading even when it's challenging?	Persistence What are the habits and behaviors of persistent people? How do I use these behaviors in school and in life?	How do I keep writing even when it's challenging?

What Experts Say About Persistence

Persistence. The ability to keep going when faced with challenging tasks. Clearly, the demands of today's higher standards and the expectations of tomorrow's employers require that our students develop a persistent mindset. In their book *Disrupting Thinking*, Kylene Beers and Bob Probst (2017) remind us that we are nurturing literacy learners who do more than simply answer our questions. They must be able to raise important questions that they, as future leaders, will need to answer. Thinking deeply enough to inquire requires the ability to follow a line of reasoning and stick with it for an extended period of time—the ability to persist.

Helping students develop the habits and behaviors of persistent people prepares them to tackle any learning challenges that might arise throughout their day. This is especially important for learners who tend to give up easily when the *work of learning* gets too hard. For them, fostering an *I can do this*! attitude starts with your in-the-moment comments and conversations and continues as you read aloud mentor texts, like those that follow, and discuss how persistent learners thrive during literacy workshop.

L E S S O N PRIMARY

PERSISTENCE: WHAT CAN I TRY?

FOCUS PHRASES   MENTOR TEXT SUGGESTION

- I keep trying even when it is challenging.

- I try different actions to reach my goals.

The Dreamer
(Na 2018)
Why We Chose This Book: Do you have students in your class who balk when faced with uncertainty or challenge? Depending on the demeanor of the student, this lack of persistence takes on different tones. Some children cry, others shut down, and a few angrily lash out at their peers. In *The Dreamer,* a pig dreams of flying. Instead of giving up or getting frustrated, he uses strategies such as planning, experimentation, listening, and persistence to finally achieve his goal.

Additional Mentor Text Suggestions for Persistence

- *The Little Red Fort* (Maier 2018)

- *Made by Maxine* (Spiro 2018)

ANCHOR LEARNING IN LITERATURE/CONVERSE TO GROW THINKERS AND LEARNERS

BEFORE READING

- Set a Purpose: I've dreamed of hiking across the Grand Canyon for a long time. Do you think I can do it tomorrow? [Discuss why that might be challenging.] You're right, I'm probably not ready yet—it is a big dream. What things might I have to do to get ready? We're going to read about another dreamer today to find out some different ways we can reach for our dreams.

- Discuss the Book Cover: The title of this book is called *The Dreamer.* What do you dream of doing someday? Turn and ask your neighbor about his or her dreams. [Pause and mingle among learners as they share.] Who can share what their neighbor is dreaming of doing someday?

DURING READING

- Let's read to find out what the pig is dreaming. [Read aloud text and pause to notice the actions the pig takes to accomplish his dreams such as admire, learn, try, ponder, hope, get help, listen, and modify.]

AFTER READING

- Did the pig fly? What steps did he take to help his dream come true?

DEMONSTRATE HABITS AND STRATEGIES

I'm going to project the book, so we can take a closer look at the words the author used to describe what the pig did to accomplish his dream. I'm wondering if there is anything we can learn from the pig that we can use during literacy workshop.

[In a shared-reading format, reread the book. As you are rereading, notice, jot down, and define (if needed) the actions the pig takes to accomplish his dream of flying (Figure 5.4).]

RECORD THINKING AND LEARNING

Wow! The pig did many different things. It might be a good idea to create a persistence chart using what we learned from the pig. Who would like to work with a partner to create this chart for our class? [Provide the partnership with the materials and support needed to create a chart. Post and refer to the chart as you see children displaying persistent actions.]

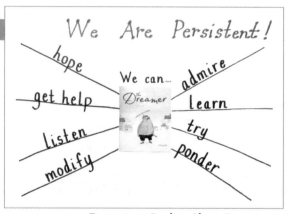

Figure 5.4 Anchor Chart: Persistence

WHAT'S NEXT?

Continue to draw attention to and celebrate persistent behaviors during literacy workshop and throughout your day. Provide constructive feedback when you observe persistent behaviors and invite children to share how they have powered through challenging tasks.

L E S S O N INTERMEDIATE

PERSISTENCE: HOW PERSISTENT PEOPLE SUCCEED AND MAKE A DIFFERENCE

FOCUS PHRASE	MENTOR TEXT SUGGESTION

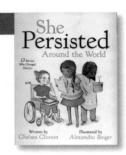

- I show *persistence* in my reading and writing even when it is challenging.

She Persisted Around the World: 13 Women Who Changed History (Clinton 2018)

Why We Chose This Book: This book is a celebration of women from around the world who persevered and succeeded in their own unique ways against all odds. Clinton offers thirteen brief biographies of women arranged in birth order. Because the book does not contain additional information about these women in the back matter, it can spark interest in further research. As a mentor text for literacy workshop, it serves as a reminder that people who persist, both in and out of school, achieve great things.

Additional Mentor Text Suggestions for Persistence

- *The Most Magnificent Thing* (Spires 2014)
- *Sparky & Spike: Charles Schulz and the Wildest, Smartest Dog Ever* (Lowell 2019)

ANCHOR LEARNING IN LITERATURE/CONVERSE TO GROW THINKERS AND LEARNERS

BEFORE READING

- Set a Purpose: Today's mentor text is a special one because it contains thirteen stories of thirteen remarkable women from around the world. We will read the biographies over several days and think about each woman's story. Their stories will be similar in some ways and different in other ways. Notice the traits these women all have in common. As we are reading, I'll give you time to jot down your thinking in your literacy notebook.
- Discuss the Book Cover: Why do you think the illustrator chose to portray children on the cover rather than grown women? How does that help you, as a reader, connect to the book? Look at the back cover, I'm wondering if, when we are done reading, we can name all of the women in the portraits.

DURING READING

- As we are reading, think about these women and how they changed the world. Notice how they faced challenges head-on and overcame them.
- What did they do when confronted with a challenge? What traits did these women possess?

- What motivated them to keep going even when things seemed to be overwhelming, difficult, and hopeless?

AFTER READING

- Think about one of the women in the book and how she showed persistence. What were her persistent actions? What was she able to accomplish because of her determination?
- Could you see yourself in any of these women (even if you don't identify as a woman)? How did you make that connection?
- All of these women demonstrated a habit of persistence that led to their success. This habit of persistence is one that also applies to us both in and out of school. How do you think persistence will help you continue your work during literacy workshop even when it is challenging?
- Were any of the women's stories compelling enough to spark your curiosity?
- Questions for Learners to Ponder:
  - » What is persistence?
  - » How do I demonstrate persistence?
  - » What are the characteristics of people who persist?
  - » Why is persistence important in my learning and my life outside of school?

DEMONSTRATE HABITS AND STRATEGIES

The biographies in this book inspired me to think about how being persistent has helped me in different situations. To do this, I'm going to chart a couple of examples of challenges that I have faced and how I have demonstrated persistence (Figure 5.5). Then, I'll reflect on what I learned that could help me in the future. I try to remind myself that just because I'm persistent doesn't mean I'll always be successful. Sometimes, I will work hard and fail. What I try to focus on each time I fail is that I am learning something new about the experience that I hope will help me when I attempt it again.

DR. BIGGS-TUCKER'S PERSISTENCE CHART

Challenge	How I Showed Persistence	What I Learned from the Challenge/Showing Persistence
Joining an Exercise Class	Kept going even when I didn't want to and it was hard for me	That I could do something new and difficult but good for me
Learning to Knit	Continued to try even when what I was making didn't look like it was supposed to	That I could learn something new and eventually I got better

Figure 5.5   Karen's Literacy Notebook Entry: Persistence Chart

(continues)

L E S S O N CONTINUED

RECORD THINKING AND LEARNING

- You can apply what you've learned from these women to literacy workshop by thinking about the characteristics of readers and writers who persist. How do readers and writers show persistence? In your literacy notebook, start a chart that shows your thinking (Figure 5.6). You might be writing down things that you already do or persistent habits that you want to set as goals for yourself. As you reflect on or share your chart of persistent behaviors, remember that you can add to it throughout the year. It will also be a great resource to use when you are setting literacy workshop goals!

- To further explore the characteristics of persistent people you are learning about as you read and research, you might consider making a T-chart like the one that Leah made in her literacy notebook. She chose a few women from the book *She Persisted Around the World: 13 Women Who Changed History*, and on the left side of the chart, she wrote what she learned *about* them and then on the right side she reflected on what she learned *from* them about being persistent (Figure 5.7). This helped her to better understand how their persistence helped them stay on course even when they were frustrated and wanted to give up. If you find other people who've demonstrated persistent habits, you can do the same thing and share it with us. Think about the lessons you can learn from influential people and how their mindsets helped them accomplish great things and positively influence the world around them.

Figure 5.6 Literacy Notebook Entr[y] Characteristics of Learners Who Persi[st]

Figure 5.7 Literacy Notebook Entry: A Reflection on *She Persisted Around the World*

WHAT'S NEXT?

As you continue to demonstrate and encourage the habit of persistence, naturally weave the language into your literacy workshop demonstrations and conferences. Continue to read aloud and book talk titles about persistent people. During sharing time, point out and celebrate examples of persistent behaviors that you've noticed while observing your learners and invite them to do the same. When students begin to recognize, reflect on, and share the habits of literate citizens, they develop ownership of these habits. Persistent-focused conversations will encourage your learners to take risks and see the rewards that come from working through the hard parts of a task.

BIG IDEA: CHOICE

READING WORKSHOP	LITERACY WORKSHOP COMMON THREADS	WRITING WORKSHOP
	Choice	
How do I make choices about when, where, what, and why I read?	How do I learn to make choices?	How do I make choices about when, where, what, and why I write?
How do my choices help me grow as a reader?	Why is it important to make choices about my reading and writing life?	How do my choices help me grow as a writer?
	Why are choices important in my everyday life?	

What Experts Say About Choice

Choice is one of the most important components of literacy learning. Earlier we discussed the big idea of *interest*. Building relationships with students and learning more about their interests is a key factor in promoting choice because learners' interests powerfully influence the choices they make (Paul 2013). In the reading realm, we know that students who choose their own books "develop elaborate strategies for selecting books and are more likely to become intrinsically motivated readers" (Fisher and Frey 2018, 91). When students leave your classroom with the ability to seek out books they *want* to read, you've given them a foothold on the climb to becoming a lifelong reader. Writers who know how to select a topic and write for a specific audience and purpose are exercising *true* choice; therefore, they "are empowered to make decisions throughout the writing process" (Fletcher 2017, 54). Finding ways to balance *true choice* and *choice within structure* (Routman 2018) is a challenge that we face daily, especially during reading, writing, and literacy workshop. Let's be honest: many of us in the education profession like to feel as if we are in control. Turning over control to students takes planning, practice, and patience, but the result is worth it for our literacy learners. We're hopeful that, as you develop your literacy workshop mindset, you are finding occasions during your school year where you can offer your students increasing amounts of choice. The following demonstration lessons will spark discussions about the choices your students might make during literacy workshop.

L E S S O N PRIMARY

CHOICE: HOW DO I LEARN?

FOCUS PHRASES	MENTOR TEXT SUGGESTION

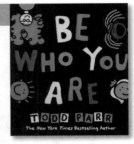

- I am a reader, writer, and learner.

- I learn in different ways.

Be Who You Are
(Parr 2016)

Why We Chose This Book: In Todd Parr's signature bold and colorful style, he broadens the idea he explored in *It's Okay to Be Different* (2001) by encouraging children to interact with the world in their own ways. This book can lead to a literacy workshop conversation about individual learning styles.

Additional Mentor Text Suggestions for Choice

- *Ogilvy* (Underwood 2019a)

- *Where Are You From?* (Méndez 2019)

ANCHOR LEARNING IN LITERATURE/CONVERSE TO GROW THINKERS AND LEARNERS

BEFORE READING

- Set a Purpose: During reading workshop, we read, think, and talk about our reading. During writing workshop, we write and learn more about being authors. Literacy workshop is going to be the *same, same but different* from reading or writing workshop. During literacy workshop, you are going to choose whether you want to read, write, or research during independent learning time. To get us started, I chose the book *Be Who You Are* to help us think about the different ways we like to learn.

- Discuss the Book Cover: Wow! Todd Parr's illustrations are bright and colorful, aren't they? What do you notice about the children on the cover? What do you think Todd Parr means by *Be Who You Are*? I'm going to read you the author's note to help answer this question.

- Author's Note page: In the author's note at the front of the book, Todd Parr explains why he wrote this book. Let's read it to find out. [He learned to be himself.]

- As a boy, what lesson did Todd learn?

- Let's read *Be Who You Are* to see how Todd uses what he learned from his childhood to write this book.

DURING READING

[Read the book aloud to your students, pausing when they have questions or comments.]

AFTER READING

- [Return to the page that reads, "Learn in your own way."]
- I'm thinking about what Todd taught me in this book. What do you think he means by "learn in your own way"?

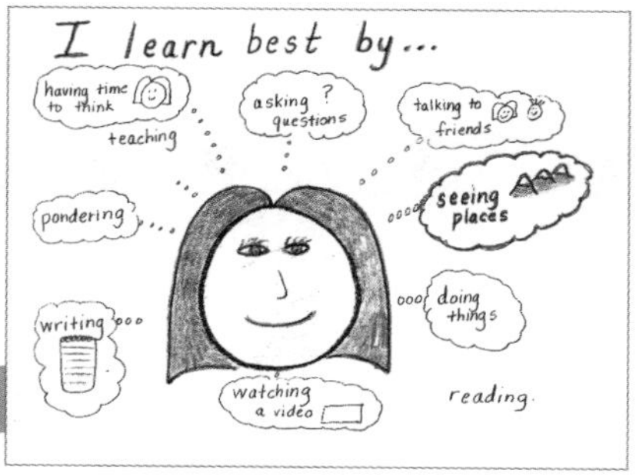

Figure 5.8
Maria's Demonstration Drawing

DEMONSTRATE HABITS AND STRATEGIES

To explore the idea of learning my own way, I'm going to draw a picture of myself and draw some ways I learn best (Figure 5.8). To better explain my thinking, I will label the different ways I like to learn.

RECORD THINKING AND LEARNING

Now it's your turn to think about how you like to learn. In your literacy notebook [or on a piece of paper], draw a picture of yourself learning (Figures 5.9a and b). Add labels to show the ways you learn best. This will help me better understand how to help you as you challenge yourself as a learner.

LITERACY NOTEBOOK ENTRIES: HOW I LEARN BEST

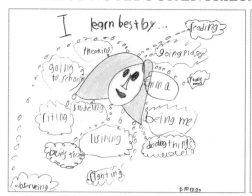

Figure 5.9a   Learn Best Emma

Figure 5.9b   Learn Best Kaeden

WHAT'S NEXT?

Use the insights that children share during this demonstration lesson to help them set goals and plan their literacy workshop learning experiences. As the year continues, you can build on this preliminary information to guide your students to better understand the ways in which they learn and how to capitalize on their strengths as literacy learners.

L E S S O N INTERMEDIATE

CHOICE: HOW DO CHOICES AFFECT MY LITERACY LEARNING?

FOCUS PHRASES   MENTOR TEXT SUGGESTION

- I make *choices* about my reading and writing.

- I think about how my choices impact my learning.

Green Pants
(Kraegel 2017)
Why We Chose This Book: The story *Green Pants* brings to light how choices are important to the people who make them and also how those choices may affect others. This story is about a boy named Jameson who *loves* his green pants and wears nothing else. When he wears his beloved pants, he feels like he can do anything! Then, Jameson is invited to stand up in his cousin's wedding, and he learns that he must wear a tuxedo, which has black pants—that means no green pants for Jameson! Now he must choose: wear his preferred green pants or wear the tuxedo pants and join in his cousin's special day.

Additional Mentor Text Suggestions for Persistence

- *I Can Write the World* (Sanders 2019)

- *When Aidan Became a Brother* (Lukoff 2019)

ANCHOR LEARNING IN LITERATURE/CONVERSE TO GROW THINKERS AND LEARNERS

BEFORE READING

- Set a Purpose: In our mentor text, Jameson has some choices to make. As we read, we'll think about Jameson's choices and how they affect him and the other people in his life. We'll also consider how this book relates to the work we're doing during literacy workshop.

- Discuss the Book Cover: Think about the title and look at the illustration. How you do think the boy feels about the green pants? What makes you think that?

DURING READING

- How do you think wearing green pants makes Jameson feel? [Special and empowered.] Think about how the choices you make help you feel special or in control. Because Jameson feels that he is powerful in his green pants, he believes he can do anything. We make choices each day—from what to wear in the morning, to what to eat for lunch, to what we want to read or write during literacy workshop. Why do you think choices are important to each of us?

- How do you think Jameson feels about being asked to be in the wedding? Does it seem like an easy choice to make?

- Why is wearing a tuxedo such a big deal for Jameson? [Now he has to decide whether to continue to choose what he wants to do or make another choice that could be better for his cousin's wedding.] Could there be another choice that Jameson hasn't thought of yet? Are there different kinds of choices?

AFTER READING

- What did you think of the ending of this story? What did you learn about making choices from *Green Pants*?
- Why do you think choice is important to your learning?
- How will the choices that you make as a reader and writer during workshop time help you grow as a learner?
- Questions for Learners to Ponder:
  » Why is choice important to me as a literacy learner?
  » How do I make choices about what I'm going to write?
  » What drives my book choices?
  » How do the choices I make during literacy workshop strengthen my reading and writing?

DEMONSTRATE HABITS AND STRATEGIES

When I get to make decisions about what I'm learning, it helps keep me motivated, focused, and interested in what I'm doing. To explore the different ways choice is helpful to me, I'm going to start a list of the choices I make as a learner in my literacy notebook (Figure 5.10). This list will help me to think about how making thoughtful decisions about my learning focuses my time and energy.

RECORD THINKING AND LEARNING

Figure 5.10 Karen's Literacy Notebook Entry: Literacy Learning Choices

Because making decisions will be a big part of what you do during literacy workshop, we're going to jot down some ideas about what we learned about making decisions from *Green Pants*, why choice is important to you, and how you will make smart choices during literacy workshop. In your literacy notebook, divide a page into four boxes and do the following (Figure 5.11):

- In the first box, write a brief one- to two-sentence summary of Jameson's story and the choices that he made in the book.

- In the second box, jot down what you were left thinking about after the book was over. This is often referred to as the theme/moral of the story.
- In the third box, write a bit about why choice is important to you as a reader, writer, and/or learner.
- In the fourth box, write a goal that is related to making choices during literacy workshop. What might you improve on as a literacy learner? Reflect on your book choices, preferred writing topics, and/or the questions you might research during literacy workshop.

As we share and discuss your notebook entries, we'll focus on answering these questions: When will you be making decisions during literacy workshop? What should you be thinking about when you choose to read, write, or research? How will you make wise decisions that lead you toward becoming an even better reader and writer?

WHAT'S NEXT?

Choice empowers learners. Conferring is one of your teacher actions that will be helpful in determining whether the decisions that your students are making are best suited for their learning needs and style. If a student needs assistance with making better choices, then this is a perfect opportunity to discuss the *why* behind the choice that they are making or provide a "negotiated" choice for them. Sometimes guiding their choices will help students begin to understand which choices are better for their reading and writing.

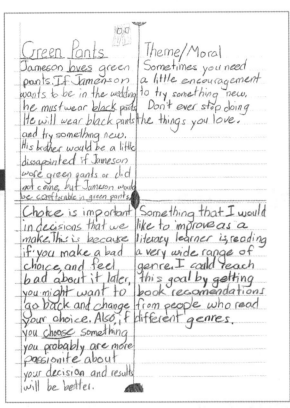

Figure 5.11 Literacy Notebook Entry: *Green Pants* and the Importance of Choice

BIG IDEA: CHALLENGE

READING WORKSHOP	LITERACY WORKSHOP COMMON THREADS	WRITING WORKSHOP
	Challenge	
How do I challenge myself as a reader?	What are the habits and behaviors of people who challenge themselves?	How do I challenge myself as a writer?
How do the challenges I face help me grow as a reader?	How do I challenge myself as a literacy learner?	How do the challenges I face help me grow as a writer?
	How do I challenge myself every day?	

What Experts Say About Challenge

Productive struggle leads to student progress. Students who embrace challenges learn more and often demonstrate increased enjoyment in the learning process. Keene (2018) encourages teachers to create a culture of engagement that includes ways to hook learners through thought-provoking conversations and interactions. During literacy workshop discussions, help students envision any struggles they might encounter and then brainstorm resources that could help them. To further create a culture of learning in literacy workshop, model and share your own learning challenges. Demonstrating the struggle as you narrow a topic for writing or share a book that has pushed your thinking are examples of behaviors you can model for students. As we share the learning experiences that we find tricky and discuss how challenge propels us as learners, our students begin to perform successfully as readers, writers, and researchers. When we have high expectations for students' learning and offer them compelling texts to read and thought-provoking topics to explore, we create a culture where challenge is valued and celebrated. We challenge you to try out the ideas in the demonstration lessons that follow to see whether they meet the needs of your literacy learners!

L E S S O N PRIMARY

CHALLENGE: I CAN DO THIS!

FOCUS PHRASES	MENTOR TEXT SUGGESTION

- I do challenging work.

- I tell myself, "You can do this!"

Off & Away
(Atkinson 2018)
Why We Chose This Book: Part of facing challenges is overcoming fears or uncertainties. Jo, the protagonist in *Off & Away,* has to face her fears to deliver messages in a bottle to creatures in the sea. Once out in the sea, she realizes a lot of what she feared was in her imagination.

Additional Mentor Text Suggestions for Challenge

- *Mighty Reader and the Big Freeze* (Hillenbrand 2019)

- *Saturday Is Swimming Day* (Yum 2018)

ANCHOR LEARNING IN LITERATURE/CONVERSE TO GROW THINKERS AND LEARNERS

BEFORE READING

- Set a Purpose: During literacy workshop, we are going to challenge ourselves. Sometimes we can learn lessons from books that help us in our lives. I picked the book *Off & Away* to read today because I thought we might learn something about facing our fears from the main character, Jo.
- Discuss the Book Cover: Turn and tell a friend what you notice on the cover. What do you predict this book might be about?

DURING READING

- "... a fear of what lurked below" page: What is stopping Jo from being an adventurer? [Her imagined fears of what is under the water.]
- "Taking a deep breath in ..." page: Can you read the words in the sky? Jo is saying, "I can do this" over and over again.

AFTER READING

- What do you think Jo learned from her adventures? How can what we learned from reading about Jo help us during literacy workshop?

DEMONSTRATE HABITS AND STRATEGIES

To demonstrate your ability to challenge yourself, you might share your own process like Maria did here: We all have challenging things to do in our lives, even adults. For me, going to exercise class after teaching all day is challenging. It's challenging because I'm tired and just want to go home and sit on the couch. So, when I don't want to go to class, I say words to myself, like Jo did, to help my brain feel better about going. I might say, "You can do this!" or "You'll feel better after you go!" That is called helpful or positive self-talk (because you say good things to yourself). Do you ever do that? What words do you say to yourself? Turn and whisper a few ideas with your neighbor.

RECORD THINKING AND LEARNING

After students have had time to discuss with their peers, invite them to share their ideas with the whole group. Record their positive self-talk on a chart or Google document to print and glue in their literacy workshop notebook (Figure 5.12).

Figure 5.12 Anchor Chart: Positive Self-Talk

WHAT'S NEXT?

Model using positive self-talk when you face a challenge in your classroom. For example, when demonstrating a written response say, "This response is challenging for me, but I know if I keep working hard I can do it!" Then, when you see students who are stuck, refer them to the story or the chart. Remind them how important positive self-talk is for everyone when they are faced with challenging tasks.

L E S S O N INTERMEDIATE

CHALLENGE: I CAN OVERCOME CHALLENGES!

FOCUS PHRASE	MENTOR TEXT SUGGESTION

- I *challenge* myself as a reader and writer, helping me grow as a literacy learner.

After the Fall: How Humpty Dumpty Got Back Up Again
(Santat 2017)

Why We Chose This Book: Dan Santat's inspiring book demonstrates how a character who is faced with a challenge makes the decision to overcome his fear of it. Humpty Dumpty was an avid bird-watcher who loved sitting on top of a high wall. One day, he falls and suffers injuries beyond the physical ones that everyone sees. After the fall, he is terrified of heights and isn't sure if life will ever be the same again.

Additional Mentor Text Suggestions for Challenge

- *Brave Molly* (Boynton-Hughes 2019)
- *Truman* (Reidy 2019)

ANCHOR LEARNING IN LITERATURE/CONVERSE TO GROW THINKERS AND LEARNERS

BEFORE READING

- Set a Purpose: Today, we are going to think about challenges and how when faced with them we can make a decision to either give up or face them head-on. In this book, we'll meet a familiar character, Humpty Dumpty. From the nursery rhyme, we know his story. But Dan Santat tells us what happens—after the fall. How do you think Humpty Dumpty will face life after he falls off of the wall and he is put back together? Turn and talk with someone about your prediction.
- Discuss the Book Cover: What do you think Humpty Dumpty is doing atop the wall? If we open the book, we can see that it has a wraparound cover. The back cover blurb might give us a clue to the lesson or theme of this book. It reads, "Life begins when you get back up." What are your thoughts about that statement?

DURING READING

- What parts of Humpty Dumpty couldn't be healed with bandages and glue? Do you think it is more challenging to overcome emotional or physical injuries?
- What convinced Humpty to climb the wall? [He was thinking about all of the things he missed.] What would you have done at this point? Would you have reacted the same way?
- How did Humpty feel when he reached the top of the wall? Have you ever overcome a challenge? How did that make you feel?

AFTER READING

- Let's think about how Humpty Dumpty's story relates to literacy workshop. What learning might you miss if you shy away from challenging work?
- Think of a learning challenge that you have faced. How did you overcome it?
- Questions for Learners to Ponder:
    - » What is challenging for me?
    - » How do I challenge myself as a reader?
    - » How do I challenge myself as a writer?
    - » Why is challenge important to my growth as a learner and as a person?
    - » What does it feel like when I'm challenged?
    - » How do I feel when I overcome challenges?

DEMONSTRATE HABITS AND STRATEGIES

Challenges have helped me grow as a learner and a person. Sometimes I enjoy facing challenges, and other times they are tough to get through. When they are difficult, I have to persist to be successful, just like Humpty Dumpty did. As a reader and a writer, I look for ways to challenge myself because those challenges help me learn new things and better understand myself. As a reader, one way I stretch myself is to read books with characters that are different than I am. They may live somewhere I've never visited or do things I've never done. When I read about people whose experiences are different from mine, I'm able to learn about the world and better understand others. Oftentimes, these books lead me to research people, places, or customs. I usually end up writing about these books in my literacy notebook because they challenge my thinking. By challenging myself to read more broadly, I expand my view of the world and my place in it.

RECORD THINKING AND LEARNING

In the book, Humpty Dumpty taught us that "life begins when you get back up." What do you think that statement means? In your literacy notebook, you could explore the many challenges that Humpty Dumpty faced and how he overcame them (Figure 5.13). By doing this, you will be able to reflect on what you learned from him that might help you as you face challenges. You could also read other books where characters face challenges and compare them to *After the Fall*. Another choice is to write about a time that you faced a challenge and what you learned from that experience.

(continues)

> After The Fall
>
> Challenge—It means that
> something is hard to do,
> therefore, it is a challenge
> Being challenged is a good
> thing.
> Humpty Dumpty is challenged
> because he can not un-
> remember the fall and he
> is afraid of heights.
> Humpty Dumpty is challenged
> because he looks really sad
> and all the good cereals
> are on the top, which he
> can't get to.
> He was challenged because
> he wants to make a
> paper airplane that looks
> like a bird so he could
> see his bird with the other
> ones.
> He started climbing the
> wall and he was challenged
> because he was scared.

> He is climbing up the
> ladder and the illustration
> shows him streching his
> arm, which means he is
> trying.
> Humpty Dumpty isn't
> afraid anymore and
> he hatched!
>
> The author leaves me
> thinking that even if
> you are challenged, you
> should keep trying.

Figure 5.13   Literacy Notebook Entry:
After the Fall Responses

WHAT'S NEXT?

As you work alongside your students, continue to demonstrate how you overcome challenges. Then, reinforce and encourage learners as they challenge themselves as readers and writers. Informal observations during whole-group and small-group instruction, as well as when you are observing students at work during learning time, will give you information to discuss with individual learners at conference time. While conferring, match learners to increasingly challenging books or teach a skill or strategy to overcome a challenge they may be having as a literacy learner.

BIG IDEA: SELF-AWARENESS

READING WORKSHOP	LITERACY WORKSHOP COMMON THREADS	WRITING WORKSHOP
	Self-Awareness	
How can becoming self-aware help me understand who I am as a reader?	Why is becoming self-aware important to my reading and writing life?	How can becoming self-aware help me understand who I am as a writer?
How can becoming self-aware help me set and accomplish my reading goals?	How can becoming self-aware help me reach my goals?	How can becoming self-aware help me set and accomplish my writing goals?

What Experts Say About Self-Awareness

In an interview with Leah Fessler (2018), Angela Duckworth, author of *Grit: The Power of Passion and Persistence,* said that she thinks happy and successful people have a meta-cognitive understanding of themselves. They can look at themselves honestly to better understand what they are doing well and what they are not. Eventually, self-aware people "will mediate their weaknesses and raise their strengths." Cultivating students who are self-aware and reflective of their strengths and weaknesses helps to equip them with the mindset they need to be the kind of learners who determine their own learning needs, set goals, evaluate their progress, and revise or recommit to meeting their goals. Self-awareness prepares students for learning independently far beyond our classroom walls. During literacy workshop, work to help children develop an accurate self-perception of their strengths and learning needs along with an optimistic outlook toward learning. In the upcoming two lessons, you will find books and ideas to help your learners begin to develop honest self-perceptions.

L E S S O N PRIMARY

SELF-AWARENESS: MY BRAIN GETS STRONGER EVERY DAY

FOCUS PHRASES   MENTOR TEXT SUGGESTION

- I notice what I do when things are challenging.

- I pay attention to my mind-set.

- I use the word *yet* when I have to change my mindset.

When Sophie Thinks She Can't...
(Bang 2018)

Why We Chose This Book: We choose to read *When Sophie Thinks She Can't...* when launching literacy workshop because it sets the stage for our developing conversation about being aware of your own mindset for learning and approaching tasks with an "I can do this!" attitude. In Molly Bang's third book about Sophie, readers enter when Sophie is at home and frustrated because she can't put together a tangram. The next day at school her teacher, Ms. Mulry, invites the children to exercise their brains by doing a math puzzle. Sophie, already discouraged from her experience at home, doesn't even try. Her friends encourage her, but soon they, too, are frustrated. Then, Ms. Mulry introduces students to the concept of YET. With persistence, collaboration, and effort, the children solve the problem in various ways. [Because this is a long read-aloud, you might consider splitting this demonstration lesson into two parts.]

Additional Mentor Text Suggestions for Self-Awareness,

- *Elbow Grease* (Cena 2018)

- *Linus the Little Yellow Pencil* (Magoon 2019)

ANCHOR LEARNING IN LITERATURE/CONVERSE TO GROW THINKERS AND LEARNERS

BEFORE READING

- Set a Purpose: In this book, Sophie's smart teacher shows the class how to change their *mindset,* or the way they think, about their brain and about learning. I can't wait to find out what she says.
- Discuss the Book Cover: Look at Sophie's face. Can you infer how she is feeling? If we read the title, we might be able to figure out why she is feeling that way. The title of this book is *When Sophie Thinks She Can't...* Think and share with a neighbor why you think Sophie is feeling sad or upset. What do you think is making her feel that way?

DURING READING

- "Sophie's sister walks by" page: Wow! Now I see why Sophie was feeling that way on the cover. [When she is unable to solve the tangram, her sister says she isn't smart.] Have you ever been in a similar situation?

- "'Flex those strong muscles of yours,' says Ms. Mulry" page: What is Ms. Mulry teaching the kids about their brains? Did you know that your brain is a muscle?
- "'Now's the time to use the Most Important Word. The word is . . . YET'" page: Hmm! Why do you think *YET* is the most important word?

AFTER READING

» What things do you do to exercise your brain?

» Sometimes your learning in literacy workshop might be a little like Sophie's puzzles—challenging. When that happens, we'll all try to remember what Sophie learned in this book—if you try and try again and help each other, you can solve any problem.

DEMONSTRATE HABITS AND STRATEGIES

[For this demonstration, think about something that you are still struggling to learn how to draw and use that as your focal point for this demonstration.] Sophie's teacher talks about exercising your brains. To exercise my brain, I'm going to write about the bunny who ate all of our flowers this summer. I usually don't write about bunnies because I'm not good at drawing them. After reading this book, I'm going to remember to tell myself that I'm not a bunny-drawing expert—yet. If you decide to challenge yourself like I did today, bring your work over when it is time to share.

RECORD THINKING AND LEARNING

Can you think about something that you are not good at doing *yet*? Let's record your ideas on this chart (Figure 5.14).

WHAT'S NEXT?

To further develop students' self-awareness during literacy workshop, use the power of the word *yet* as you discuss learning challenges and confer with students about the process of learning new things.

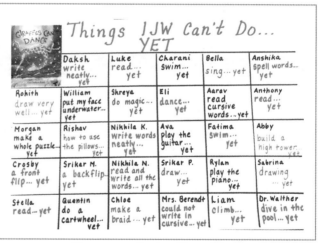

Figure 5.14   Anchor Chart: The Power of YET

L E S S O N : INTERMEDIATE

SELF-AWARENESS: WHO AM I AS A LITERACY LEARNER?

FOCUS PHRASES

- I notice my strengths and weaknesses.

- I am aware of how my thoughts and feelings impact my learning.

- I am self-aware, which helps me to better understand myself as a reader and writer.

MENTOR TEXT SUGGESTION

The Thing Lou Couldn't Do
(Spires 2017)

Why We Chose This Book: Meet Lou, a girl who spends her days creating make-believe adventures with her friends. When her friends decide to build a pirate ship in a tree, Lou tries to convince them to play a not-up-a-tree game. Unaware that she is afraid of climbing trees, her friends carry on without her. Lou has many reasons not to try even though her friends offer to help. She declines their help and tries to invent ways to reach the top without climbing. In the end, Lou convinces herself to try to climb but doesn't quite make it. Readers see that Lou clearly knows her strengths and weaknesses. They also learn that, although Lou failed the first time, she's going to try again.

Additional Mentor Text Suggestions for Self-Awareness

- *Crown: An Ode to the Fresh Cut* (Barnes 2017)

- *Rock What Ya Got* (Berger 2018b)

ANCHOR LEARNING IN LITERATURE/CONVERSE TO GROW THINKERS AND LEARNERS

BEFORE READING

- Set a Purpose: Today, we are going to think about how it is important to be *self-aware* of who we are as learners. Being self-aware means understanding what we can do well and what we still have left to learn. To start the conversation, we are going to read a book about a girl named Lou who can do many things well. However, there is one thing that she can't do, and she doesn't want her friends to find out.
- Discuss the Book Cover: Look at Ashley Spires's illustration on the cover of the book. What do you think Lou can't do? Why do you think that?

DURING READING

- Are Lou's thoughts and actions helping her get better at what she wants to learn to do? What could she do instead?
- How do her thoughts and actions change? What does she know about herself?

AFTER READING

- What has Lou learned about herself? Do you think she is more self-aware now than she was at the beginning of the story? What do you think that Lou might do next?
- What did you think about the ending? What did Lou learn that might help her next time? What does that teach us about learning new things?
- Questions for Learners to Ponder:
  » What does it mean to be self-aware?
  » How does self-awareness help me understand myself as a reader and a writer?
  » Why does knowing my strengths and weaknesses help me set goals?
  » How does striving for my goals help me grow as a learner?

DEMONSTRATE HABITS AND STRATEGIES

I know that being self-aware is an important first step in getting to know myself as a reader and a writer. Recognizing what I do well and the challenges I face will help me set goals and create an action plan to meet them. I'm going to think about my own literacy life and create a "self-portrait" of who I am as a literacy learner, but rather than drawing a picture of myself, I'm going to write my ideas in a chart. I will include the things that I do well and the things that challenge me (Figure 5.15).

RECORD THINKING AND LEARNING

Now it's your turn to think about who you are as a literacy learner. In your literacy notebook, you can either create a chart like I did or design a picture of yourself using an outline of a person that will help me get to know you as a literacy learner (Figure 5.16 and Appendix 9 in the Online Resources). Share your strengths, challenges, and anything else that you feel would help me get a better picture of your learning preferences. This self-portrait will become a tool to help you plan your learning time and also when you think about setting goals for yourself during literacy workshop.

My Literacy Learner Organizer

What I do well as a learner	What challenges me as a learner
• choose books to read	• getting started on a writing piece
• generating topics to write about	• sticking with a book that is challenging
• talking about my books w/others	• taking feedback on what I've written
• choose topics to research	• read different genres
• think about big ideas	• writing in different forms and for different purposes
• listen to others' book recomendations	• share research in a variety of ways
• I ♥ reading and writing!	

Figure 5.15 Karen's Literacy Notebook Entry: Who Am I As a Literacy Learner?

Figure 5.16   Literacy Notebook Entry:
Who Am I As a Literacy Learner?

WHAT'S NEXT?

- Facilitate a conversation with students about their strengths and challenges as literacy learners. Encourage students to notice the connections between reading and writing that they have made on their self-portraits.
- Discuss how what students have noticed about themselves as readers and writers can help them plan their independent learning time. For example, if they want to work on writing more complex pieces, they may want to spend more independent learning time focusing on their writing. On the other hand, if they want to read more informational text, they may want to spend some time working on a research project that could include reading some informational books with a specific purpose in mind.
- Think about how you might begin to incorporate goal setting into your conferences with students. Information on these portraits would be a great place to begin conversations with learners about what they might like to begin working on in their reading and writing.

BIG IDEA: COLLABORATION

READING WORKSHOP	LITERACY WORKSHOP COMMON THREADS	WRITING WORKSHOP
	Collaboration	
How can I collaborate with others about my reading?	What are the habits and behaviors of collaborative people?	How can I collaborate with others while I'm writing?
Why does collaborating with others help me better understand my reading?	Why is being collaborative important to my reading and writing life?	How does collaborating with others help me improve my writing?
	How does collaborating with others make me even smarter?	

What Experts Say About Collaboration

As students prepare for life in an ever-evolving world, one thing is certain: they will need to collaborate with others (Wagner 2012). Whether they collaborate with a partner or small group, in person or virtually, our students will benefit from learning collaborative behaviors. According to Ellin Keene (2018, 13) *true collaborators* display the following behaviors:

- Generate questions
- Wrestle with ideas
- Seek to influence or be influenced by others' perspectives
- Generate new ideas
- Fail frequently
- Revise, revise, revise

The good news is that literacy workshop is the ideal instructional context to develop collaborative behaviors. As facilitators of the workshop, your goal is to create authentic collaborative experiences for students where they are interdependent and learn from each other—the goal of *true collaboration* (Dillenbourg 1999). To get you started, we offer two demonstration lessons to use during literacy workshop that will introduce collaborative behaviors for students to try out as they work with each other to strengthen their reading, writing, and research.

L E S S O N PRIMARY

COLLABORATION: WE CAN DO IT TOGETHER!

FOCUS PHRASES

- When working in a group, I help make a group plan.

- I help my group decide who will do each part of the plan.

- I help my friends follow a group plan.

- I compromise (do a little of what my friend wants and a little of what I want).

MENTOR TEXT SUGGESTION

Box Meets Circle
(Hartline 2018)
Why We Chose This Book: Box and Circle want to do something together. Circle can jump, Box can't. Box can sit, Circle can't. Instead of giving up, they come up with an idea of something they can do as a team. This short and lively book illustrates the joy that comes from solving problems with a friend.

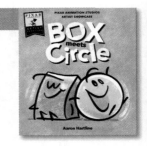

Additional Mentor Text Suggestions for Collaboration

- *Crab Cake: Turning the Tide Together* (Tsurumi 2019)

- *Penny and Penelope* (Richards 2019)

ANCHOR LEARNING IN LITERATURE/CONVERSE TO GROW THINKERS AND LEARNERS

BEFORE READING

- Set a Purpose: When I look around at all of us sitting here together, I'm thinking how lucky we are to have so many people to learn with this year. Did you know that when you work together, or *collaborate,* with your friends you can get even smarter? The word *collaborate* means working with other people to do something.
- Discuss the Book Cover: Look at the cover of *Box Meets Circle*. How do you think the two characters are feeling? [happy, proud, excited] I'm wondering what they did that made them feel that way. Let's read to find out!

DURING READING

- "We should do something together" page: Look at Box's face when Circle jumps. Have you ever felt that way? Share your story with your neighbor.
- "I know. Let's sit!" page: What do you notice on this page? [Now Circle is upset.]

AFTER READING

- How did Box and Circle solve their problem? [Weave words like *compromise* and *collaborate* into your conversation about the book.]

DEMONSTRATE HABITS AND STRATEGIES

Let's say that during literacy workshop Kayla and I were collaborating on a poster to teach everyone about the book *Box Meets Circle*. We both want to draw the pictures; neither of us want to write any words. What are some of the ways we could *compromise*? [Record students' ideas for future reference.]

RECORD THINKING AND LEARNING

The best way to record occurrences of collaboration and compromise is to catch children in the act. Notice and name what they are doing. Snapping a quick photo with your phone to add to a collaboration and compromise chart is another way to continue to celebrate these learner actions during literacy workshop.

WHAT'S NEXT?

Collaboration and compromise don't magically happen after one demonstration lesson. You will likely need to extend this conversation with additional read-alouds and demonstration lessons, as needed.

L E S S O N INTERMEDIATE

COLLABORATION: WORKING WITH OTHERS MAKES A DIFFERENCE!

FOCUS PHRASES   MENTOR TEXT SUGGESTION

- I *collaborate* with others to learn new things.

- I listen to suggestions from my classmates to improve my reading and writing.

Hidden Figures: The True Story of Four Black Women and the Space Race
(Shetterly 2018)
Why We Chose This Book: This book is a great example of teamwork and collaboration in the real world. Four African American mathematicians worked collaboratively alongside NASA scientists in a world where they were not often welcomed to provide accurate calculations for several of the Apollo missions.

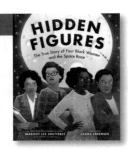

Additional Mentor Text Suggestions for Collaboration

- *The Case of the Missing Chalk Drawings* (Byrne 2018)

- *When Pencil Met Eraser* (Kilpatrick and Ramos 2019)

ANCHOR LEARNING IN LITERATURE/CONVERSE TO GROW THINKERS AND LEARNERS

BEFORE READING

- Set a Purpose: Today, we are going to think about working with others collaboratively. Our book is about a group of young women without whom the Apollo space missions may not have been successful. What do you think of when you hear the word *collaboration*? What do you think needs to happen for a group or a partnership to successfully collaborate? Discuss with your neighbor.

- Discuss the Book Cover: What do you notice about the women's clothing? Why do you suppose the illustrator chose to draw equations all over their clothing? Let's read to find out how math is important in this biography and what we can learn from these four women about collaboration.

DURING READING

- What did you notice about Katherine? [She was self-aware that she was good at math and persistent when asking her boss to invite her to the team meetings.] How did these traits help her to become part of the team?

- What did Dorothy do to help the other women in her group? [She taught them a new skill.] How did that action help the group as a whole?

- What happened after the moon landing? [They set new goals.]

AFTER READING

- What did you notice about these women? What traits did they possess that made them effective collaborators?
- Questions for Learners to Ponder:
  - » What does true collaboration look like and sound like?
  - » How and when do I collaborate?
  - » How does working collaboratively help me grow?

DEMONSTRATE HABITS AND STRATEGIES

We know that it is an important for people to work collaboratively. Throughout my life, there have been many times that I've worked with others to extend my learning or to achieve a goal. Sometimes, working collaboratively can be a challenge. To be proactive, or address the challenge ahead of time, what we usually do is create some norms. [If you have norms that you've used at your staff meetings or while serving on a committee, bring them in to show your students.] Norms are agreed-upon actions to use when working collaboratively. When contributing to this list, I think about what needs to happen when I'm working in a group. What do I bring to the group that is positive? What do I bring to the group that I need to be aware of that could be a challenge to working together?

RECORD THINKING AND LEARNING

- Let's work collaboratively to co-create a list of norms to use in our classroom during literacy workshop. I'll title our shared document Things to Remember When Working Together (Figure 5.17). Once we're finished, I'll give you a copy to glue into your literacy notebook so that you can refer to them as you learn from your collaborative working experiences.
- Reread our class norms or Things to Remember When Working Together. In your literacy notebook, create a list of your own personal norms. Record the specific things you think would help *you* the next time you are working collaboratively. As a group member, what are your strengths? What challenges do you have when working collaboratively? Keep your list handy to share the next time you are with a partner or small group. If you start your group work by sharing your norms, it helps everyone begin with similar expectations. It will also be interesting to see what the similarities and differences are when you compare your norms to your classmates'.

(continues)

Figure 5.17   Anchor Chart: Things to Remember When Working Together

WHAT'S NEXT?

Provide opportunities for students to discuss, reflect on, and revise their personal list of strengths and challenges of working collaboratively. In addition, view the class norms chart as an ongoing document. When issues arise, you may need to review or add to the norms as you *support and send out* students during collaborative work time.

IDEAS TO PONDER

IDEAS TO TRY

CHAPTER 6

Demonstration Lessons— Fostering Independence and Engagement

As you continue to build on what students are learning during literacy workshop, you may notice that you are highlighting habits, behaviors, and big ideas that will increase your learners' independence. Moreover, when your students are seeking answers to interesting questions, planning investigations, and sharing newfound knowledge in innovative ways, they are creating their own learning path. Because, during literacy workshop, you are offering learners time, community, access, and choice, along with clear goals and one-on-one conferring, you will see their agency grow (Miller 2018). As their agency grows, your students will become even more independent.

COMMON THREADS:
BIG IDEAS FOR FOSTERING INDEPENDENCE AND ENGAGEMENT

In this chapter, the demonstration lessons focus on the habits of inquisitive learners. These habits are loosely based on the method students use when conducting scientific research. We present these habits in the order that we typically introduce them, but we encourage you to adjust the sequence as needed to best fit your learners and learning context. Through your demonstrations and the students' self-directed learning, they will continue to increase their ability to question, plan, investigate, innovate, and reflect as literacy learners. All the while, they will be discovering how reading and writing are inherently connected. (The demonstration lessons that focus on the big idea of reflecting appear in the Online Resources.)

BIG IDEA: QUESTION

READING WORKSHOP	LITERACY WORKSHOP COMMON THREADS	WRITING WORKSHOP
	Question	
As I am reading, what do I wonder?	What are the habits and behaviors of people who question?	As I'm writing, what do I wonder?
How do I read to learn more about topics that fill me with wonder?	What kinds of experiences fill me with wonder?	How can I write to figure out more about topics that fill me with wonder?
How can I learn more about myself, others, and the world around me by reading?	How do I read, write, and research to learn more about myself, others, and the world?	How do I research and write to help me learn more about myself, others, and the world?
How does wondering while I read help me better understand the text and move me forward?	Why do the questions that I have about my learning help me grow as a literate citizen?	How does thinking about the questions of my readers help me move forward in my piece?
Why do the questions I ask myself as a reader help my knowledge grow?		Why do the questions I ask myself as a writer improve my craft?

What Experts Say About Questioning

Children are natural detectives. Many of them ask questions from the time they walk into the door until the time they leave at the end of the day. Harnessing the power of these questions is one way to help them become engaged literacy learners because queries "open up conversations, generate respect, accelerate learning, and build relationships" (Knight 2016, 92). Their questions give them purpose when they are writing, whether it is about a book they just read or something they learned from their research. They also propel readers through text as they wonder about what will happen next and how the characters' experiences relate to their own. Questions help guide learners to a deeper understanding about life, learning, and ultimately themselves (Keene and Zimmerman 2007). Helping students understand how their curiosities guide their reading, writing, or research empowers them as learners and gives them authentic purposes for their literacy work. Teaching students how to merge their reading and writing skills to ask and answer questions is the focus of the upcoming demonstration lessons.

L E S S O N PRIMARY

QUESTION: QUESTIONS LEAD TO MORE QUESTIONS

FOCUS PHRASES	MENTOR TEXT SUGGESTION	

- I know the difference between asking and telling.

- I ask questions about things I'm wondering.

Ada Twist, Scientist

(Beaty 2016)

Why We Chose This Book: Young Ada Twist's parents are worried. She is almost three years old and still hasn't made a sound. When she climbs to the top of a grandfather clock to investigate, her parents yell, "Stop!" Hearing this, Ada utters her first word, "Why?" From then on, she questions everything. Ada embodies the characteristics of a curious learner; therefore, this book is ideal for launching a discussion about questioning, observing, and fact finding.

Additional Mentor Text Suggestions for Questioning

- *Just Because* (Barnett 2019)

- *Why?* (Seeger 2019)

ANCHOR LEARNING IN LITERATURE/CONVERSE TO GROW THINKERS AND LEARNERS

BEFORE READING

- Set a Purpose: During literacy workshop you've been challenging yourselves to read or write about things that interest you. We've been practicing how to use strategies and persist when things get tricky. We are also learning how to collaborate, or work with our friends, to learn and solve problems. Now we're going to dig a little deeper and discover five habits that will help you during literacy workshop, in other subjects, and also when you are not in school. The first of these habits is *asking questions*. Let's read to find out how the character in *Ada Twist, Scientist* uses the habit of asking questions.
- Discuss the Book Cover: Look at the way Ada is holding her hands. What does it mean when someone holds their hands this way? [They are thinking or wondering.] I can't wait to find out what she's wondering about!

DURING READING

- "She started with Why? and then What? How? And When?" page: [Write the question words on a whiteboard or a piece of paper.] What do you notice about all of these words? What does it mean to be curious? What are you curious about? Turn and ask your friend what he or she is curious about.

- "Ada was busy that first day of spring" page: There are some words on this page I would like to ponder together—*mystery, riddle, puzzle,* and *quest.* What do all of those words have in common? [You have to do something to figure them out or discover the answer.] Why do you suppose Ada loves this moment the best?
- "And so Ada sat" page: What did you notice about Ada's questions on this page? [One question led to another and those questions led to more questions.]

AFTER READING

We can learn a lot from Ada. I'm going to go back through the book so we can write down some of her traits and things that she did (Figure 6.1).

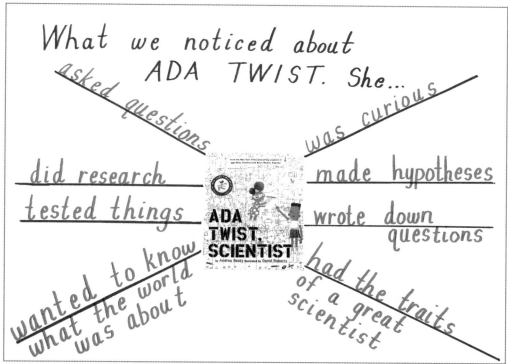

Figure 6.1   Anchor Chart: What We Noticed About Ada Twist

DEMONSTRATE HABITS AND STRATEGIES

I noticed that Ada Twist had a habit of asking a lot of questions. To help her remember her questions, she wrote them down. I think that is a smart idea, don't you? I'm going to do the same thing Ada Twist did and start recording my questions on this question sheet. (See Figure 6.2 and Question Mark reproducible, Appendix 10 in the Online

L E S S O N CONTINUED

Resources.) To help make sure that I'm writing a question, I'm going to use some of the question words we learned from the book like *why*, *what*, *how*, and *when*. Then I'm going to remember to end my questions with a question mark.

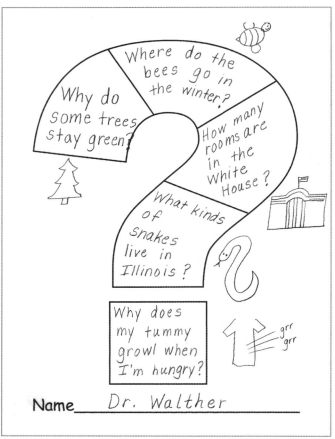

Figure 6.2
Maria's Literacy Notebook Entry: Questions

RECORD THINKING AND LEARNING

Are you ready to ask some questions? I would like you to take a few moments at the beginning of your learning time to write down a few questions on your question sheet (Figure 6.3). If you fill the sheet, there are extras right here. We will save these question sheets in our literacy notebook so that you can add to them and also so we can use them as we continue to learn the other habits that will help you during literacy workshop.

Figure 6.3   Literacy Notebook Entry: Questions

WHAT'S NEXT?

Encourage children to write as many questions as they are able. The more questions they generate, the better. Take some time to transcribe under your students' questions if they are written in developmental spelling so that the children can refer to them later. The goal here is to get learners in the habit of wondering and generating their own questions. The questions children generate will become authentic topics for them to investigate during literacy workshop.

L E S S O N INTERMEDIATE

QUESTION: ASKING QUESTIONS HELPS ME LEARN

FOCUS PHRASE	MENTOR TEXT SUGGESTION

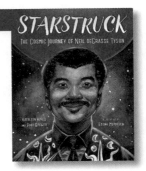

- I ask questions to guide my learning.

Starstruck: The Cosmic Journey of Neil deGrasse Tyson
(Krull and Brewer 2018)
Why We Chose This Book: From the time that he was a young boy, Neil deGrasse Tyson was inquisitive. He asked questions about the things he saw in the night sky. Those questions, and many others, helped guide his learning throughout his life until he ultimately became a famous astronomer and physicist. Neil's learning journey reflects the habit of questioning that we want to promote during literacy workshop and beyond.

Additional Mentor Text Suggestions for Questioning

- *The Sad Little Fact* (Winter 2019)

- *why am I me?* (Britt 2017)

ANCHOR LEARNING IN LITERATURE/CONVERSE TO GROW THINKERS AND LEARNERS

BEFORE READING

- Set a Purpose: During literacy workshop, we're going to be thinking about how *questions* guide learners. When we are studying a topic, questions help us set a purpose and create both short-term and long-term plans for finding the answers. In the biography *Starstruck: The Cosmic Journey of Neil deGrasse Tyson,* we'll meet a man who took a childhood interest and continued to ask questions about that topic throughout his life. Notice how Neil's questions influenced his lifelong learning path and helped him develop a passion for astronomy.
- Discuss the Book Cover: What do you notice about Neil on the cover of the book? Do the details on the cover help you predict what Neil might be asking questions about throughout his life?

DURING READING

- Notice how Neil asks questions throughout his life. How do his questions help guide his learning? How do his questions help motivate him to keep pursuing the answers even when things get challenging for him?

AFTER READING

- What did you learn from Neil's life at the end of the book? How can you apply that to your own life? How did Neil's questions help drive his learning? How do you know? What can you learn about the relationship between questions and learning from Neil?
- Questions for Learners to Ponder:
  » What does it mean to question?
  » How does asking questions help to guide my reading and writing?
  » How does asking questions about learning help me grow as a reader and a writer?
  » How does questioning help me meet my goals?

DEMONSTRATE HABITS AND STRATEGIES

As we were reading this biography, I was thinking about how important questions are to me as a learner. Questions help move my learning forward. When I'm reading, there are always things that make me wonder. Sometimes it is a puzzling word that I have to look up to understand. After reading a historical fiction book, I often want to learn more about that time period. I also wonder about the author's choices, and that helps me consider how I might borrow something to use in my own writing. In my notebook, I'm going to jot down a list of things that I find myself wondering as I read and write (Figure 6.4).

RECORD THINKING AND LEARNING

What do you wonder as you read and write? What topics are you passionate about? What questions do you investigate at home? Think about the questions you have and record some of them in your literacy notebook. How will these questions guide your work during literacy workshop? When you have the opportunity to explore one of these topics, which one would you start with? When you take something that you are wondering about and make it the focus of your reading and writing, it can shape your goals and work during literacy workshop and also guide your learning throughout your life.

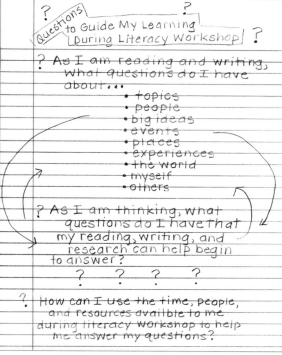

Figure 6.4
Karen's Literacy Notebook Entry: Asking Questions

(continues)

L E S S O N *CONTINUED*

WHAT'S NEXT?

While students are brainstorming their lists of questions, talk with them about their questions to learn more about their individual interests. You might want to record some of their questions and interests in your literacy notebook or electronic document to refer to in future demonstration lessons or to help guide students' book selections or writing topic choices. Your students' individual interests are a starting point for them as they read, write, and explore a wide range of personally meaningful topics.

BIG IDEA: PLAN

READING WORKSHOP	LITERACY WORKSHOP COMMON THREADS	WRITING WORKSHOP
	Plan	
How might I plan my reading based on my interests, needs, and goals?	What are the habits and behaviors of people who plan?	How might I plan my writing based on my interests, audience, and purpose?
How does my reading plan help me grow?	How might I plan my reading and writing based on what I already know?	How can I use writing to help create my plan and record my thinking?
Why does having a reading plan help me become an even better reader?	How can I plan an investigation based on my questions?	Why does having a writing plan improve my craft?
	Why does creating a plan for my learning time help me grow as a literate citizen?	

What Experts Say About Planning

Learners who are able to plan are better prepared for a variety of situations both in and out of school. Planning encourages students to think about not only what is occurring now but also what might happen in the future. It offers them time to prepare for situations that they may not have anticipated and create plans for them (Johnston 2004). When students are involved in developing their own procedures, you are helping them take ownership of their own learning. You are communicating to them that learning is an experiment (Harvey 2017), and, like any experiment, a proposed method is helpful in order to uncover results. You are also letting children figure out that there is more than one right way to go about learning something new, thus helping them to be flexible and adjust when things aren't going the way they predicted. By offering students different ways to design their learning path and then creating opportunities for your students to execute their plans, you are encouraging them to be more deliberate about how they are using their learning time. Here we offer two demonstration lessons to get your students started with planning. Use what you learned from your observations and interactions with children to revise or recast these learning experiences to fit your learners' needs.

L E S S O N PRIMARY

PLAN: MAKING A GENIUS PLAN

FOCUS PHRASES	MENTOR TEXT SUGGESTION

FOCUS PHRASES

- I plan an investigation to answer my question.

- I record the things I need to help me learn.

- I list the steps I will take to answer my question.

MENTOR TEXT SUGGESTION

Douglas, You're a Genius!
(Adamson 2018)

Why We Chose This Book: Nancy and her dog Douglas are playing outside when their ball goes through their backyard fence. When the ball mysteriously rolls back to their side of the fence, the pair propose plan after plan to find out who is on the other side of the fence. In the end, they discover a pair of Spanish-speaking friends, and the four work together to create "the most genius plan of all." The plans that Nancy and Douglas design include materials and steps in both pictures and words, providing helpful mentor texts for your young planners.

Additional Mentor Text Suggestions for Planning

- *Rulers of the Playground* (Kuefler 2017)

- *Shh! We Have a Plan* (Haughton 2014)

ANCHOR LEARNING IN LITERATURE/CONVERSE TO GROW THINKERS AND LEARNERS

BEFORE READING

- Set a Purpose: A genius is someone who works at being smarter every day and does smart things. I'm wondering what Douglas is going to do in this book to make someone call him a genius. As we read, we're going to notice the smart actions that Douglas and his friends do in this book.

- Discuss the Book Cover: Do you see the paper that the girl is pointing to underneath the title? Talk to your neighbor about what you think that might be. Notice the note on the ground next to the girl, it reads "¡HOLA," the Spanish word for Hello! I'm curious to see whether that note will be important to the story. Let's start reading to find out!

DURING READING

- "'What do you think?' Nancy asked." page: Look, it is a paper like the one on the cover of the book! Let's read it to see what Nancy included in her plan [the materials they would need and the steps they would have to follow to look over the fence].

- "'I'm not sure about this,' Douglas groaned." page: Why do you think Nancy made an "Even Better Plan"? I'm noticing that she doesn't give up. When one plan doesn't work, she creates another. Hmm! We might have to do this during literacy workshop.
- "'Fine, but I can already tell that this is a silly idea,' Nancy said." page: Turn and tell your friend what you think about Douglas's "Extremely Clever Plan."

AFTER READING

Why did Nancy think Douglas was a genius? [He made a simple plan that worked.] What did you notice about all of the plans in the book? [They had pictures and words]. We're going to use what we learned from *Douglas, You're a Genius!* to help us make our literacy workshop plans.

DEMONSTRATE HABITS AND STRATEGIES

- First, I'm going to look back at the questions on my question sheet and decide which question I'm the most interested in investigating. I think I'll begin with this question: "Where do the bees go in the winter?" Remember how the bees chased us when we were outside with our lunchboxes? I want to know where they all are right now!
- I'll write that question at the top of my Genius Plan Sheet (see Figure 6.5). That will help me stay focused during learning time.
- Now it's time to make a plan. Just like in the book we just read, I'm going to record the materials I think I will need to answer my question along with the steps I'm planning to take to find the answer so you can see how I do it.

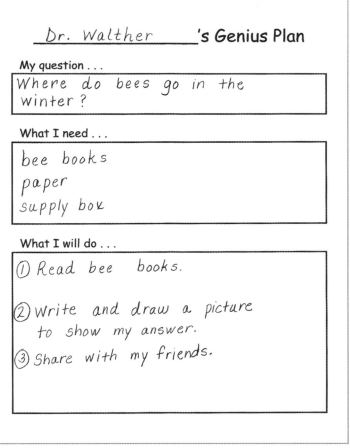

Figure 6.5   Literacy Notebook Entry: Maria's Genius Plan

(continues)

L E S S O N *CONTINUED*

RECORD THINKING AND LEARNING

- Today, during learning time, you are going to begin creating your plan. Just like I did on my Genius Plan Sheet, you are going to pick a question, write your materials, and then make your plan. I can't wait to read all of your genius plans! (See reproducible resource in Appendix 11 in the Online Resources.)

WHAT'S NEXT?

Guide students as they narrow their questions and create their plans. The completed planning sheets will assist you in gathering the materials and resources that students might need to execute their plans. If you are fortunate enough to have a teacher-librarian in your school, this would be an ideal time to enlist their help to locate both physical and online resources. Once students have a plan, they can use what they've learned from your previous demonstration lessons and literacy workshop experiences to read, write, and research in order to carry out their plan.

IDEAS TO PONDER

IDEAS TO TRY

L E S S O N   INTERMEDIATE

PLAN: CREATING A PLAN FOCUSES MY LEARNING

FOCUS PHRASES   MENTOR TEXT SUGGESTION

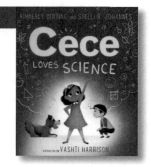

- I plan my learning
  to help me grow
  as a reader and a
  writer.

- I plan reading
  and writing
  that extends my
  experiences as a
  learner.

Cece Loves Science
(Derting 2018)
Why We Chose This Book: Cece loves
science and planning experiments with
her friend Isaac. Her latest investigation
involves her dog, Einstein, and wanting
him to eat vegetables (even though they
aren't Cece's favorite food). She creates a
plan, revises her plan, and re-revises her
plan based on how Einstein responds to
each of the trials that she plans to try to
get him to eat his veggies. Cece's experiences in this book show literacy workshop learners that plans are important,
yet flexible.

**Additional Mentor Text
Suggestions for Planning**

- *Cece Loves Science and
  Adventure* (Derting and
  Johannes 2019)

- *Two Problems for
  Sophia* (Averbeck 2018)

ANCHOR LEARNING IN LITERATURE/CONVERSE TO GROW THINKERS AND LEARNERS

BEFORE READING

- Set a Purpose: As we read *Cece Loves Science*, we're going to investigate how learners
  plan. Planning your learning helps you consider what you are doing now, what you
  need to do next, and the steps you will follow to reach your goals. Planning will help
  you be more prepared as you take on learning tasks, and it will also help you reflect
  on what you notice about yourself as a learner before, during, and after you do tasks.
- Discuss the Book Cover: What do you notice about the characters on the cover of the
  book? What do you think that they will be planning during the story? Why do you
  think that?

DURING READING

- Notice how Cece plans her experiment. How does she create her plan? How does she
  adjust her plan? What does she consider when she adjusts her plan? How did planning
  help her be successful?

AFTER READING

- What do you think about when the story ends? Was Cece a successful planner? How do you know? What might you have done differently if you were planning her experiment?
- Questions for Learners to Ponder:
  - » What does it mean to plan?
  - » How does planning my learning time help me grow as a reader and a writer?
  - » Why is planning important when setting and trying to reach my goals?

DEMONSTRATE HABITS AND STRATEGIES

As I read this book, I'm thinking about how important planning is to me as a literacy learner. Today, I'm going to create a plan for my work during literacy workshop. I'm going to use this planning sheet to record my goals and plan for the day. [Display Literacy Workshop Plan Sheet found in Appendix 12 in the Online Resources.] It's helpful for me to do this to stay focused during literacy workshop learning time. At the top of the planning sheet, I'm going to record my reading and writing goals. Then, I'll think about how I'm going to use my reading and writing to help work toward those goals. I'll jot down the books or writing pieces that I plan to read or work on today. I'm going to remember that, like Cece, I might have to revise my plan based on what I learn today. Let's think how writing our plans can help us in our work during workshop time.

RECORD THINKING AND LEARNING

Think about how you will plan your learning time during literacy workshop today and in the future. Begin with the goals that you have set for yourself as a reader and a writer. Then, decide how you will use your learning time to work toward those goals and challenge yourself to grow as a literacy learner. Fill out the top half of the sheet to plan your work for today. Toward the end of our learning time, we'll take a few minutes to reflect on how things went and jot down a celebration. After that, plan what you'll do as you begin your literacy work tomorrow. You'll be practicing the important habits and behaviors of readers and writers (Figure 6.6).

(continues)

Name: _____   Date: _____

Literacy Workshop Plan

My goal as a reader: _is to read 20 books by the end of the year_

My goal as a writer: _is to write diffrent Gunreas_

Today as a reader, I will: _read till the next 2 chapters_
_____

Today as a writer, I will: _work on my story_
_____

The book that I am reading is: _Tiny infinities_

In writing, I am working on: _I'm working on a story_
on the Coumputer.

A literacy celebration that I had today was: _I read past how_
far I wanted to.

During Literacy Workshop time tomorrow, I am planning to: _work on the_
new story.

Figure 6.6   Completed Literacy Workshop Plan Sheet

WHAT'S NEXT?

As students are working, check in with them to see whether they are focused on the goals that they set out for themselves on their planning sheet. Near the end of workshop time, remind them to reflect on their process and think about how that work will help them plan their work for tomorrow and beyond. Invite students to revise, add to, or change the planning sheet to work for them. Chances are they will come up with better ways to design the planning sheet and, in doing so, become even more invested in the process.

BIG IDEA: INVESTIGATE

READING WORKSHOP	LITERACY WORKSHOP COMMON THREADS	WRITING WORKSHOP
	Investigate	
How can I learn more about this topic by reading?	What are the habits and behaviors of people who investigate?	How can I figure out more about this topic by writing?
How can I investigate while I'm reading to better understand the meaning of texts?	How can I investigate big ideas through reading, writing, and research?	Where do I find information to support key points in my pieces?
How can reading help me investigate myself, others, and the world?	Why does investigating help me better understand my role as a literate citizen?	How can writing help me investigate myself, others, and the world?

What Experts Say About Investigating

Students who investigate the questions, wonderings, and topics that they are passionate about become more independent in their learning (Lehman 2012). However, creating these experiences can be messy as we shift the ownership to our learners and take on more of a *backseat* role. But in letting go, we give them permission to make mistakes and learn from those mistakes, making them more flexible thinkers ready to take on the next challenge that awaits them, whether it's in our classroom or out in the world (Keene 2018).

L E S S O N PRIMARY

INVESTIGATE: WE ARE INVESTIGATORS

FOCUS PHRASES   MENTOR TEXT SUGGESTION

- I investigate things in many different ways.

- I share the answers from my investigations with others.

Spring After Spring: How Rachel Carson Inspired the Environmental Movement (Sisson 2018)

Why We Chose This Book: Sisson's innovative and engaging illustrations help tell the story of Rachel Carson, who went to college to become a writer and ended up studying biology. Once out of college, she began researching and writing books about the ocean. Being a lifelong observer, she noticed that animals were dying, so she attempted to figure out why. Putting the pieces together, Rachel discovered the dangers of pesticides, which eventually prompted the formation of the Environmental Protection Agency. Throughout her life, Rachel practiced the habits and behaviors of an investigator, the same practices that we want to instill in our learners.

Additional Mentor Text Suggestions for Investigating

- *Otis and Will Discover the Deep: The Record-Setting Dive of the Bathysphere* (Rosenstock 2018)

- *Shark Lady: The True Story of How Eugenie Clark Became the Ocean's Most Fearless Scientist* (Keating 2017)

ANCHOR LEARNING IN LITERATURE/CONVERSE TO GROW THINKERS AND LEARNERS

BEFORE READING

- Set a Purpose: During literacy workshop, we've been learning about the habits of investigators. This biography is about an investigator like you! As we learn more about Rachel Carson, we'll find out different ways that you can investigate during literacy workshop.
- Discuss the Book Cover: What is Rachel doing on the cover? [Writing about something in her notebook.] Why do you think Stephanie Roth Sisson called this book *Spring After Spring*? What do you think that means? Think and share with a partner.

DURING READING

- "And wonders big . . . and small." page: Look at the illustrations. [It would be helpful to use the document camera to project the text so that students can get a close-up look.] What are some different ways that Rachel is investigating? [Looking, listening.] I'm going to jot down ideas in my literacy notebook so that we can remember them (Figure 6.7). [As you continue reading, jot down the various ways that Rachel investigates.]
- "Snuggled under a warm blanket," page: Look! I noticed some more ways that Rachel is investigating. What is she doing?
- "So Rachel did what she did best:" page: Now Rachel is grown up, and she is still investigating in different ways.

AFTER READING

- Once Rachel learned that the poisons were killing the animals, what did she do? [She spoke up about it.] Yes! She used what she learned in her investigations to convince people to stop using the chemicals. That's what literate citizens do!

DEMONSTRATE HABITS AND STRATEGIES

I'm going to use what I've learned from Rachel as I continue to investigate my questions during literacy workshop. I've been reading books about bees, but I haven't found the answer I'm looking for in just one book. So, I'm going to have to put together facts from different books to help me find the answer, just like Rachel did. Are any of you finding the same thing as you investigate? [It is most helpful if you can use a child's investigation as an example of how to put facts together. That way, you are not only helping that child move forward in his or her investigation but also showing the rest of your learners how to piece together

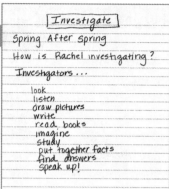

Figure 6.7   Maria's Literacy Notebook Entry: Ways to Investigate

information in a kid-friendly way. Putting together facts from various resources is a challenging task for young literacy learners. The best way we've found to do it is to show them how to write down the separate facts from each book in their own words (another challenge!), and then use the facts to draw a conclusion. See Figure 6.7.]

RECORD THINKING AND LEARNING

To help us remember the different ways we can investigate, let's take the ideas we jotted down while we were reading and make them into a chart (Figure 6.8). I'll post the chart where we all can see it to help us in our future literacy workshop investigations.

Figure 6.8   Anchor Chart: Literacy Workshop Investigators Anchor Chart

WHAT'S NEXT?

At this point in literacy workshop, try to keep in mind that you are teaching young learners the habits and behaviors for conducting their own investigations. Honor their approximations and focus more on the process than on the finished product (if they even get to that point!). Sometimes, after spending a great deal of time reading and writing, a student's interest in the topic might wane. That's okay. Let them abandon that investigation and begin anew until they find something that they want to spend their time and energy learning about through reading and/or writing.

L E S S O N   INTERMEDIATE

INVESTIGATE: I DEEPEN MY UNDERSTANDING THROUGH INVESTIGATION

FOCUS PHRASES

- I investigate to better understand my reading and writing.

- I use investigation to better understand the world around me.

MENTOR TEXT SUGGESTION

The Eye That Never Sleeps: How Detective Pinkerton Saved President Lincoln (Moss 2018)

Why We Chose This Book: Allan Pinkerton was a detective who worked for the Chicago Police Department solving crimes. He later established his own detective agency and solved more three hundred murders and recovered millions of dollars in stolen money. But his greatest accomplishment came when he saved President Lincoln by discovering a plot to assassinate him on the way to his 1861 inauguration. Pinkerton's investigative talents provide a window into the reasoning skills that people use when investigating a problem or question. The insights students gain from reading this book will help them as they prepare to investigate.

Additional Mentor Text Suggestions for Investigating

- *Georgia's Terrific, Colorific Experiment* (Persico 2019)

- *The Boo-Boos That Changed the World: A True Story About an Accidental Invention (Really!)* (Wittenstein 2018)

ANCHOR LEARNING IN LITERATURE/CONVERSE TO GROW THINKERS AND LEARNERS

BEFORE READING

- Set a Purpose: Have you ever thought about what the word *investigation* means from a learner's point of view? [It helps learners focus their learning and gives them purpose as they are doing their work.] Today, we are going to think about what it means to investigate a question, an idea, or anything else that you want to discover. When we investigate, it helps us learn about specific topics, but it can also help us learn about the world and about ourselves as learners, too. Let's take a look at a book about a famous detective and see what he did to make himself a great *investigator* as we think how we might apply that to our own learning.

- Discuss the Book Cover: What do you notice about the cover of this book? As we look at it, stop and think about what the illustrator is telling us about the characters in this book. What do you want to know more about each of them before we begin reading?

DURING READING

- Notice how Allan Pinkerton successfully conducts investigations throughout the book. What are Allan Pinkerton's habits and behaviors that made him a successful investigator? How could you apply those qualities when you are trying to find answers? How would they make you a successful literacy learner?

AFTER READING

- What does the author leave you thinking or wondering?
- Would Allan Pinkerton be a successful detective in today's world? Why or why not?
- Questions for Learners to Ponder:
  - » What does it mean to be an investigator?
  - » How does investigating help me in my reading and writing?
  - » How does investigating help me learn about the world?

DEMONSTRATE HABITS AND STRATEGIES

After reading and talking about this book, I'm reflecting on how investigation has helped me as a learner. When I want to find answers, I do a lot of different things. If I want a quick answer, I usually Google it even though I know that is not always the most reliable way to research a topic. Finding efficient ways to investigate is an important life skill for all of us, so I think it might be helpful to share some of the ways that I use reading and writing to learn more about books, topics, and the world. Here's a quick list of just a few of the ways that I investigate when I have questions about my reading and/or writing:

- Read texts about topics of interest
- Record ideas I've learned from my research
- Ask questions of an expert
- Visit places to learn more

After I investigate, I consider how I might apply what I've learned from my investigations beyond my own literacy to my world.

RECORD THINKING AND LEARNING

How do you investigate the questions you have related to your reading, writing, and the world? Create a list in your literacy notebook of ways to use your learning time to explore books, your own writing, and/or interesting topics (Figure 6.9). As you do this, you will be learning about not only yourself as a literacy learner but also the wider world. The choices you write in your notebook can become a part of your literacy workshop plan, providing you with opportunities to seek answers in your own way.

(continues)

L E S S O N CONTINUED

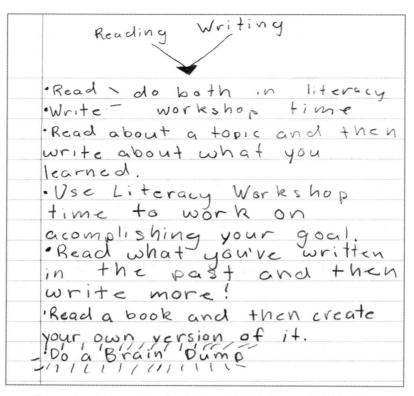

Reading   Writing

- Read ↘ do both in literacy
- Write ⌐ workshop time
- Read about a topic and then write about what you learned.
- Use Literacy Workshop time to work on acomplishing your goal.
- Read what you've written in the past and then write more!
- Read a book and then create your own version of it.
- Do a 'Brain' Dump

Figure 6.9   Literacy Notebook Entry: My Reading and Writing Investigations

WHAT'S NEXT?

As students are working on their lists, encourage them to collaborate with their classmates to brainstorm and discuss possible investigations that they might engage in as literacy learners. During sharing time, invite a few students to read aloud what they consider the most original idea from their list. As you confer with students to learn more about their investigations, you have an opportunity to reinforce the habits and behaviors of investigators as they pursue a variety of purposes for their learning.

BIG IDEA: INNOVATE

READING WORKSHOP	LITERACY WORKSHOP COMMON THREADS	WRITING WORKSHOP
	Innovate	
How can I learn about the innovation process through reading?	What are the habits and behaviors of innovative people?	How can I be innovative in my writing?
Where can I find texts to better understand the process of innovation?	How can I innovate by creating a new idea, an object, or a literacy product?	Where can I find texts to use as examples of innovative writing?
Where can I find texts about innovative people or characters?	How can being innovative help me grow as a literacy learner?	How can being innovative help me improve my craft?
How can being innovative help me grow as a reader?	How can being innovative help broaden my literacy horizons?	

What Experts Say About Innovation

Innovation is a skill that all of our learners need as they move toward their future. When innovating, individuals think about something differently and create something new based on their thinking (Wagner 2012). Many experts see overlap between innovation and creativity. This is why most educators often consider providing these types of learning opportunities mainly within students' STEM or STEAM time. However, we have realized that literacy workshop is a place where we can help learners begin to think about how they become innovators in their reading and writing lives. This allows us to broaden that definition of innovation to one that empowers learners to practice thinking outside of the box. Inviting students to be innovative in their reading and writing allows them to understand how innovation can help them create throughout their learning day.

L E S S O N PRIMARY

INNOVATE: WE ARE INNOVATORS

FOCUS PHRASES	MENTOR TEXT SUGGESTION

- I innovate by creating a new idea or object.

- I innovate by doing something in a new way.

Doll-E 1.0 (S. McCloskey 2018)
Why We Chose This Book: Charlotte is an innovator who loves everything related to technology, making her an ideal character to model innovation for literacy workshop learners. She and her dog Blutooth are happy "Tinkering. Toggling. Coding. Downloading." Worried their daughter is too techy, Charlotte's parents buy her a baby doll. Although she tries many things, the doll isn't very exciting until Charlotte realizes it has a battery pack. When Blutooth gets jealous and tears the doll apart, Charlotte innovates and designs Doll-E 1.0.

Additional Mentor Text Suggestions for Innovation

- *Ben Franklin's Big Splash* (Rosenstock 2014)

- *Going Places* (Reynolds and Reynolds 2014)

ANCHOR LEARNING IN LITERATURE/CONVERSE TO GROW THINKERS AND LEARNERS

BEFORE READING

- Set a Purpose: Today, we're going to be learning more about the word *innovate*. When you innovate, you figure out a new idea, or a new way, to do something. Innovators also can change the way things work. As we read *Doll-E 1.0*, let's think about the word *innovate*.
- Discuss the Book Cover: What do you notice on the cover of this book? [A girl is using tools and a computer to fix or do something to a doll.] Does anyone have any questions before we begin reading?

DURING READING

- "I know! I could run an update on you." page: Hmm! I notice something above Charlotte's head. [Light bulb.] Why do you think Shanda McCloskey put that there? [To show us that Charlotte has an idea.]
- "Charlotte couldn't let it end this way." page: What innovative things do you predict Charlotte is going to do to the doll?

AFTER READING

- How did Charlotte change the doll? [Added arms that could hold things. Made her say words other than *Ma-ma*.]
- After reading *Doll-E 1.0*, can you give other examples of ways to innovate?

DEMONSTRATE HABITS AND STRATEGIES

Now that I've answered my question about where bees go in the winter, I want to share it with you in an innovative or unique way. I'm thinking that I will use what I've learned from my investigation to pretend I'm a bee and write steps on how to survive winter for my bee friends:

Step 1: Find a lot of friends.

Step 2: Go to an underground hive.

Step 3: Snuggle together.

Step 4: Stay there until spring.

RECORD THINKING AND LEARNING

- Now that we know what it means to innovate, let's see if we can write some ideas on this chart (Figure 6.10). Let's ponder how we might use what we learned from Charlotte during literacy workshop. What are some of the ways that you might innovate as you are investigating or sharing what you've learned?
- Today, we used writing to help us better understand an idea that we read in a book. Then, I showed you one way that you might innovate while sharing your ideas. After that, we innovated and designed new ways that we could learn during literacy workshop. Are you ready to go out and innovate today?

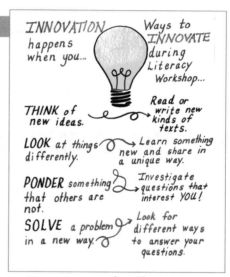

Figure 6.10 Anchor Chart: Innovation

WHAT'S NEXT?

As you are observing and conferring, select students who have done innovative things during learning time to share with the group. Add any new innovations to the anchor chart. Some students may choose to imitate your innovation; that's okay. They are standing on the shoulders of your work as they take steps toward independence. The more opportunities they have to see and hear about their classmates' innovations during sharing and celebrating time, the more ideas they will have to draw from as they expand their own repertoire of innovative ideas.

L E S S O N INTERMEDIATE

INNOVATE: I INNOVATE TO CREATE NEW IDEAS AND SOLUTIONS

FOCUS PHRASES

- I innovate by looking at a problem in a different way.

- I innovate by creating solutions that are unique ways to solve the problem.

MENTOR TEXT SUGGESTION

How to Build a Hug: Temple Grandin and Her Amazing Hug Machine (Guglielmo and Tourville 2018)
Why We Chose This Book: Temple Grandin was a girl who loved many things like folding paper airplanes, building things, and making obstacle courses. But there was one thing that she didn't like—hugs. She didn't like them because they felt like scratchy socks! Even though she didn't like them, she really wanted one. So, one day she decided to build one! Temple innovates to build a hug just as we want our students to be inventive during literacy workshop.

Additional Mentor Text Suggestions for Innovation

- *The Crayon Man: The True Story of the Invention of Crayola Crayons* (Biebow 2019)

- *Just Like Rube Goldberg: The Incredible True Story of the Man Behind the Machines* (Aronson 2019)

ANCHOR LEARNING IN LITERATURE/CONVERSE TO GROW THINKERS AND LEARNERS

BEFORE READING

- Set a Purpose: Today, we're going to be thinking about how everyday people innovate in their daily lives. What does *innovate* mean? Innovation is when you come up with a new way to do something. Oftentimes, it requires us to look at a problem or situation differently, especially if something about it isn't working. Let's meet Temple Grandin, a young girl with a unique situation that required innovation, creativity, and hard work to solve a problem.

- Discuss the Book Cover: What do you notice about the cover? How does the illustration on the cover help you think about what will happen in the book?

DURING READING

- Think about how Temple used innovation to help create a hug for herself. How did innovation help her throughout her life?

AFTER READING

- What do you think about who Temple was and who she became in her life? How did innovation help her be successful throughout her life?

- Questions for Learners to Ponder:
  » What does it mean to innovate?
  » When could I innovate outside of school?
  » Can I create innovative solutions to challenges when I'm reading and writing?
  » How might innovative thinking help me to meet my learning goals?

DEMONSTRATE HABITS AND STRATEGIES

As I read this book, I was thinking about what it means to innovate. Let's see if we can write some ideas on this chart (Figure 6.11). Now that we have a better understanding of the word *innovate* let's ponder how we might use what we learned from Temple during literacy workshop. What are some of the ways that readers and writers might use innovation during their work?

Innovation is...

- thinking outside the box
- being creative
- coming up with a new way of looking at an idea
- pushing yourself (and others) to try to stretch your perspective
- coming up with multiple ways to present your idea
- considering lots of choices
- being flexible and willing to try something new

Innovation in Literacy Workshop is...

- reading books that may be outside of your *comfort zone*
- getting or receiving book recommendations as you continue your literacy connections with others
- experimenting with a new form or style of writing
- receiving or giving feedback on writing as you learn to better understand your place in the literacy community
- researching topics that are important to you and then sharing your learning with others in your learning community and then beyond the four walls of your classroom
- taking risks as a reader and a writer to better understand yourself to grow as a literacy learner

Figure 6.11   Anchor Chart: Innovation

RECORD THINKING AND LEARNING

- Now it's your turn to think about innovation. We are going to create a chart that will begin with what happens when you innovate, and then we are going to think about some ways that you can innovate during your literacy workshop time. This chart will give you some ideas about how you can be innovative in your reading and writing work. Being innovative is one way that you can think about your literacy in new ways and approach your goals in new ways.
- Today, we used a chart to help us think about how we can use innovation not only to help solve problems but also to create new ideas. We extended that thinking into our literacy workshop work. How can we innovate in our reading and writing? How might that look in your work as readers and writers today?

WHAT'S NEXT?

As you are conferring with your learners, help them focus on what they are doing that is innovative in their reading and writing. Also, encourage students to share their literacy innovations in sharing time at the end of workshop.

CHAPTER 7

Demonstration Lessons—
Teaching Integrated Literacy Strategies

Congratulations! You've launched literacy workshop by teaching and modeling the behaviors used by literate citizens. After establishing expected student actions, you fostered independence by demonstrating how curious learners go about answering questions. At this point, your students are *feeling the flow* of the literacy workshop routines and are ready to deepen their understanding of a few literacy strategies that will support their comprehension and creation of texts. In our opinion, comprehension and creation go hand in hand. When learners are able to dig into texts with a firm foundation in their background knowledge and an eye toward connections they can make with the story or information, they become more skilled in writing with their audience in mind. Likewise, when they are able to discern the purpose of a text and imagine the world an author has created, they will begin to see the importance of a clear focus and sensory language when crafting their own engaging texts.

COMMON THREADS:
BIG IDEAS FOR TEACHING INTEGRATED LITERACY STRATEGIES

In this set of demonstration lessons, you will introduce and/or review strategies such as schema, relationships, focus, and imagination to help your students better grapple with and craft texts. Before using the literacy workshop structure, you might have taught similar minilessons in either reading *or* writing workshop. Here, we've blended them together to further solidify the relationship between the two. You will find that these lessons will build on and complement the demonstrations in Chapters 5 and 6 that were designed to develop the essential habits and behaviors of literacy learners. As you select the demonstration lessons that best meet your students' needs, you will continue to reinforce their prior learning by offering descriptive feedback that builds confidence and fosters independence.

As the seeds of literacy workshop grow in your classroom, watch for signs that your students' confidence is growing. It might be a moment when a craft technique they noticed while reading magically manifests itself in a piece of writing. Or when you overhear a conversation between learners who are sharing a strategy that they used as writers to help them better understand a book. Trust that your students are becoming confident, well-rounded learners as they read, write, converse, and listen to each other in order to better understand themselves and the reciprocity of reading and writing.

BIG IDEA: IDEAS (SCHEMA)

READING WORKSHOP	LITERACY WORKSHOP COMMON THREADS	WRITING WORKSHOP
	Ideas (Schema)	
How does activating and building my background knowledge help me better understand texts?	How do I build on what I already know to help me learn new things?	How does accessing my schema help spark ideas for writing?
How does connecting my schema to what is happening in the story help me better understand?	How do I share my ideas and new learning with others?	How does connecting to my readers' experiences help draw them into my writing?

What Experts Say About Activating Background Knowledge

Your learners have a helpful tool in their literacy toolbox—their schema: the innate ability to bring their unique knowledge base and life experiences to their reading and writing. Students' experiences come from daily occurrences, the books they read, the conversations that they have with others, and their curiosity about the world around them. Activating these *mental files* (Keene and Zimmerman 2007) enables learners to take the ideas that they have in those files and apply them to new scenarios. These novel situations include understanding a challenging text or brainstorming an idea for a piece that they are writing.

Learners who pause to activate their prior knowledge before tackling a reading or writing task are setting themselves up for success. Empowering students to be reflective and access their background knowledge prepares them for the challenging work they will be faced with in the future (Duckworth 2016).

L E S S O N PRIMARY

IDEAS: OUR SCHEMA GROWS ONE EXPERIENCE AT A TIME

FOCUS PHRASES   MENTOR TEXT SUGGESTION

- I am a learner who adds to my schema by reading.

- I am an author who uses what I've learned when I write.

Dreamers (Morales 2018)

Why We Chose This Text: Before reading this book to your students, take a moment to read Yuyi Morales's story in the back matter. Here you learn that *Dreamers* is based on her own experience of bringing her two-month-old son, Kelly, to America to meet his gravely ill grandfather. Then, after marrying Kelly's dad, she discovered that she was a "permanent resident" and had to stay in the United States. With a blend of Spanish and English, accompanied by Yuyi's signature illustrations, you discover the essential role that both books and libraries played in the young mother and son's lives. For Yuyi and Kelly, books were both teachers and inspirers, which is why we selected this book to highlight the role schema, or background knowledge, plays in our literacy lives. Books will teach your students many things and also inspire them to share their stories with the world through writing.

Additional Mentor Text Suggestions for Ideas

- *The Book Tree* (Czajak 2018)

- *Reading Beauty* (Underwood 2019b)

ANCHOR LEARNING IN LITERATURE/CONVERSE TO GROW THINKERS AND LEARNERS

BEFORE READING

- Set a Purpose: I'm so excited to read you this beautiful book. It is based on the life story of Yuyi and her son, Kelly. That's why I thought it would be the perfect book to talk about how thinking about your *schema* can help you during literacy workshop. Some people call schema *background knowledge*. Schema, or background knowledge, is all of the experiences you have in your brain. For instance, turn and tell you neighbor everything you know about school. [Pause to let students share their schema.] Wow! You have a lot of *school* schema. Now tell your friend something else you know a lot about. How did you learn so much about that topic?

- Discuss the Book Cover: [Open the book so that children can see the illustration on the front cover and back cover together. This is called a *wraparound cover*.] How does Yuyi Morales's cover illustration invite you into the story? What do you know after looking at this picture that you didn't know before? [Perhaps the main characters?] How does having this schema before reading help you as a reader? Do authors usually show the main characters on the cover? Why would they do that? Could you do that in the books you write?

DURING READING

- "There were so many things we didn't know." page. Why do you think they made mistakes? Do you think they were able to play in the fountains in their home country? When you make a mistake, you add to your schema. That's how we learn.
- "Unimaginable." page: Our schema can also help us figure out words. Have you heard of the word *imagine*? How can your schema help you figure out what the author means by *unimaginable* on this page?
- "Someday we will become something we haven't yet imagined." page: What do you dream of doing someday? How has what you've learned so far helped you to dream that dream?

AFTER READING

- What do you think this book is trying to tell us as learners?
- Does anyone want to work with a partner to study the pictures in this book and notice all of the book covers that are included in the illustrations? You can see how many of the books she pictured are part of your background knowledge. I'll put your names on a sticky note in the cover. When you're done, please pass it to the next partnership.

DEMONSTRATE HABITS AND STRATEGIES

Before we read the book, you shared some of your schema about your favorite topic with a friend. Because I'm much older than you are, I have more schema than you do! My schema helps me when I'm reading, writing, and even when I'm teaching. Since I have a lot of schema for the ways children might act, when I'm reading a book about kids, I can usually predict what they will do next. As a writer, I use what I know about how children learn to write emails to your families so they can help you at home. When I'm teaching, I think about what I've learned from my experiences to do things to help make learning fun for all of us.

RECORD THINKING AND LEARNING

In this story, Yuyi and her son learned how to read and to speak English and were inspired to write simply from reading all the books they found at the library. All of those books gave them schema. That's why we spend so much time during literacy workshop reading and writing! Their story shows the importance of books and experiences as part of our schema. Think about the books you've read or things you've done so far this year. Which books or activities have inspired you to write or draw something? [Share some examples.] As we continue to notice how schema helps us during literacy workshop, we'll write ideas on this chart (Figure 7.1).

(continues)

L E S S O N CONTINUED

WHAT'S NEXT?

Helping students access their background knowledge is an ongoing focus during literacy workshop. Being aware of your students' home lives, cultures, families, and interests will help you tap into their schema when supporting them in understanding and crafting texts. Before reading aloud or putting books into kids' hands, notice any vocabulary, text structures, illustrations, or story elements that might be unfamiliar (Ness 2019). Consider ways to frontload this information so that they can then transfer it to their written texts.

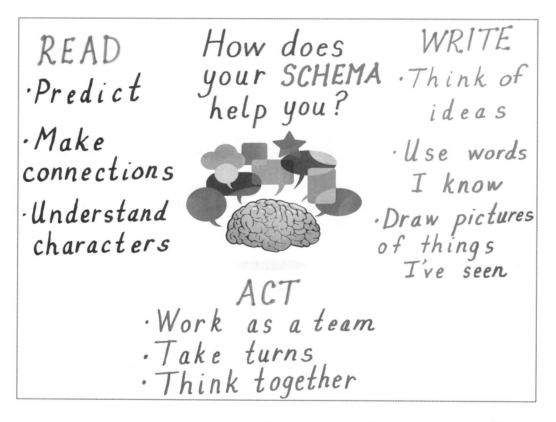

Figure 7.1 Anchor Chart: How Our Schema Helps Us

IDEAS TO PONDER

IDEAS TO TRY

L E S S O N   INTERMEDIATE

IDEAS: BUILDING ON WHAT I KNOW LEADS TO MORE THINKING

FOCUS PHRASE	MENTOR TEXT SUGGESTION

- I take what I know from my background and own ideas to enhance my learning.

The Day You Begin (Woodson 2018)
Why We Chose This Text: A young girl walks into a classroom and feels out of place because of all of the ways that she thinks she is different from everyone else in the room. Later, when she finds the courage to share her story, a classmate connects with her experiences. It is at this moment that she realizes that she can begin again in a new place. Through both words and illustrations, this book emphasizes that life experiences shape how children perceive themselves and the ways in which they engage with the world around them. For that reason, it is an ideal book to launch a discussion about how ideas, or *schema*, influence the choices students make during literacy workshop.

Additional Mentor Text Suggestions for Ideas

- *Little Red Reading Hood and the Misread Wolf* (Wilson 2019)
- *Mixed: A Colorful Story* (Chung 2018)

ANCHOR LEARNING IN LITERATURE/CONVERSE TO GROW THINKERS AND LEARNERS

BEFORE READING

- Set a Purpose: Today, we are going to think about how we use our background knowledge to help us become even better readers and writers. Learners take their life experiences and *mine* them to better understand what they read and to get ideas for writing. Let's consider how our everyday experiences will help deepen our comprehension and make the pieces that we write more relatable to our readers.
- Discuss the Book Cover: What do you notice about the cover of the book that we will be reading today? Notice that the door is made from a ruler. I wonder why Rafael López chose to do that. As we look at it, what can you tell about the girl who might be the main character in the story today? What might you infer about some of her experiences or her background based on what you see on the book's cover?

DURING READING

- Notice how Angelina begins her day at her new school. How was she feeling at the beginning of the book? How did those feelings change throughout the day? What happened that caused her feelings to change?
- What experiences did Angelina have that were different from those of her classmates? How did Angelina finally find the courage to share those experiences with her classmates?
- The experiences that she had were part of her schema or background knowledge. Where did her experiences come from? How did those experiences help her to connect with her classmates?

AFTER READING

- Let's think about how your ideas and experiences help you during your literacy workshop time. How might your background knowledge help to deepen your understanding of the books that you are reading?
- As a writer, your schema can help you develop pieces that are more interesting for your readers. When you draw upon your own unique experiences, you are better able to write pieces that engage readers or broaden their worlds. If you are an expert on a particular topic, you can take what you know about that topic to write a piece that informs your readers.
- Questions for Learners to Ponder:
  » How do I use what I already know to help me deepen my understanding of what I am reading?
  » How does my background knowledge help me write pieces that are more engaging for my reader?
  » How do my experiences help me learn new things?

DEMONSTRATE HABITS AND STRATEGIES

This book reminds me of how important it is, as people, to share our stories with each other. When I meet new people, I ask them questions to get to know more about their backgrounds and look for ways that our experiences connect. That's how friendships begin. It's the same for me when reading a book. I think about how my experiences compare to, or are different from, the character's life. When they are different, I might have questions. These questions often lead to research. I rely on my schema as a writer, too. I use what I've learned from studying the work of mentor authors and from my previous writing experiences to try to improve my written work.

(continues)

RECORD THINKING AND LEARNING

During literacy workshop time, reflect on or discuss how you are using your experiences and schema to support your literacy learning. When you stop to analyze how you use a literacy strategy, like accessing background knowledge, it helps you become more aware of how to use it effectively. If you pause now and then to think about your thinking, you can also figure out how to more effectively use the strategy in the future. At the end of workshop time today, take a moment to write a reflection about how you used your background knowledge to enhance the understanding of your reading or improve your writing.

WHAT'S NEXT?

As students are working, encourage them to share with each other how their schema helps enhance their reading and writing. As you listen in on these conversations, prompt students to reflect by asking

- How have you connected with this text that you have written or read through your own ideas?
- Have you created a text that is based on your experiences or background knowledge?
- How did using your schema help you better understand a text that you read or help you create a more interesting text for readers?

Students who understand the importance of using their background knowledge when interacting with texts will be better equipped to try new things that challenge them as literacy learners.

BIG IDEA: RELATIONSHIPS (CONNECTIONS)

READING WORKSHOP	LITERACY WORKSHOP COMMON THREADS	WRITING WORKSHOP
	Relationships (Connections)	
How does noticing characters' relationships help me better understand a story?	How does making connections between my reading and writing improve my craft?	How does developing a mentoring relationship with an author, an illustrator, or text improve my writing?
How does making connections among texts help me better understand my reading?	How does connecting with my classmates' thinking help make me smarter?	How does making connections among texts help me to see patterns in my writing and the writing of others?
	Why are relationships important in learning and in life?	

What Experts Say About Relationships

Meaningful relationships are an essential aspect of a healthy classroom culture. Without relationships, schools cannot be successful (Routman 2018). Students who build rapport with their teachers and their peers are more engaged with their learning (Goldberg 2018; Reeve 2002). As we previously shared, there is also a powerful connection between reading and writing (Graham and Hebert 2010). As your students bond with their peers and with the written word, you'll notice that their learning becomes personally relevant. Literacy workshop is designed to foster meaningful relationships between students' reading and writing and also within those literacy experiences to help them better understand themselves. During literacy workshop, your teacher actions will personally engage your readers and writers and foster trusting relationships as you make time for the following:

- Rich and diverse read-aloud experiences
- Collaborative conversations about reading and writing
- Self-selected, supported reading and writing
- Opportunities to reflect on and celebrate growth in their literacy lives

Just as the relationships we have with others grow and change, so do the interactions between and among characters in the stories your children will read and write. Drawing parallels between relationships in your classroom and those in books you read aloud or put in students' hands offers opportunities to discuss and apply lessons learned. Students can apply these insights while both crafting their own texts and caring for others.

It takes time to develop and maintain healthy relationships. That is why literacy workshop is essential in today's classrooms. The extended time your students will have during literacy workshop offers opportunities for students to expand their relationships with books, the written word, themselves, and each other. Creating consistent routines and practices that foster relationships is one of the most important investments that we can make for our learners.

L E S S O N PRIMARY

RELATIONSHIPS: BUILDING FRIENDSHIPS THROUGH STORIES

FOCUS PHRASES   MENTOR TEXT SUGGESTION

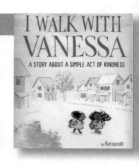

- I notice how an illustrator shows how characters feel about each other.

- I show how characters feel about each other when I draw.

- I show others I care by being kind.

I Walk with Vanessa: A Story About a Simple Act of Kindness (Kerascoët 2018)

Why We Chose This Book: While walking home, Vanessa, the new girl in school, is bullied. A girl in a yellow dress witnesses the bullying and Vanessa's ensuing tears. After sharing what she saw with her friends, they all go home feeling upset. That night, the witness has an idea. The next day she, her friends, and many others *walk with Vanessa,* showing the bully the power of friendship. Through illustrations, Kerascoët detail how the characters' choices impact their relationships. This wordless book is perfectly suited for literacy workshop because it promotes conversations about peer relationships and the author-illustrator-reader relationship. (Because the illustrations are small and detailed, we would suggest projecting this text. Plan to read, think, and talk about it for two days.)

Additional Mentor Text Suggestions for Relationships

- *Goodbye, Friend! Hell Friend!* (Doerrfeld 20

- *Maybe Tomorrow?* (Agell 2019)

ANCHOR LEARNING IN LITERATURE/CONVERSE TO GROW THINKERS AND LEARNERS

BEFORE READING

- Set a Purpose: When you are reading, you are listening to the words of the author and learning more from the pictures the illustrator created. When you are writing, you are sharing your ideas with a reader. The *relationship* between writer and reader is like a friendship. What are some ways you show your friends that you care about them? During literacy workshop, you show authors and illustrators you care by paying attention to their ideas, and you show readers you care by taking the time to do your very best writing and illustrating. As we carefully read the wordless book *I Walk with Vanessa,* we're going to think about how we can strengthen our relationships as readers, writers, and kind friends.

- Discuss the Book Cover: What can you infer about the two girls on the cover? What clues in the illustrations help you to know this? [Perhaps the two girls are friends. I know this because they are smiling and talking with each other. Maybe they are walking to school. I see they have backpacks on their backs. It's possible that one of the girls is Vanessa because her name is in the title.]

DURING READING

- [Vanessa's teacher introduces her to the class.] page: How do you infer Vanessa is feeling? What do you think the girl in the yellow dress is thinking? What words would you write in a thinking bubble above her head?

- [Bully confronts Vanessa.] page: Wow! A lot is happening on this page. How did the illustrators help you understand what the characters are doing, thinking, and feeling?
- [Girl in yellow dress has an idea.] page. How did the illustrators show us that the girl in the yellow dress has an idea? Could you use this same technique in your pictures?

AFTER READING

- What did you learn from *I Walk with Vanessa* that you could use an illustrator?
- What did you learn from reading and talking about this book that you can use as a friend?

DEMONSTRATE HABITS AND STRATEGIES

I noticed that the illustrators used a lot of different techniques or strategies to show us how the characters were feeling. I think I can learn something about drawing characters' feelings by studying some of the illustrations. Let me look back in the book at the characters' faces and see what I can learn.

RECORD THINKING AND LEARNING

I'm going to draw what I learn on this chart so that we can all use it later (Figure 7.2).

- On the first page, when the child with pigtails is raising her hand, her mouth is curved up. I'll draw a face like hers. How do you infer how she is feeling? We can write that word below her face.
- I notice when the bully is being mean to Vaness, her mouth is like an O. I'll draw a picture of a face that looks like that. How do you infer how she is feeling? We can write that word below her face.

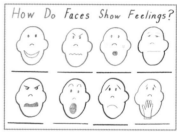

Figure 7.2   Anchor Chart: Faces Show Feelings

[Continue in the same fashion as you add additional faces to the chart. Another option is to invite children to come up and add their version of the different illustrated emotions to the chart.]

WHAT'S NEXT?

A child's ability to read, or infer, the feelings of others is an essential building block in fostering and maintaining friendships. Peter Johnston (2012) calls this capacity a child's *social imagination*. During literacy workshop, you can help children develop their social imaginations by offering opportunities for learners to read, study, and discuss books like *I Walk with Vanessa* where the illustrations clearly depict the characters' feelings. Asking questions like, "Can you infer how that character is feeling?" and noticing when a child adds voice to their illustrations by drawing expressive images of people will go a long way in helping children better identify and understand the role feelings play both in friendships and in books.

L E S S O N INTERMEDIATE

RELATIONSHIPS: RELATIONSHIPS HELP MY READING AND WRITING GROW

FOCUS PHRASE	MENTOR TEXT SUGGESTION

- I think about the relationship between my reading and writing to strengthen my learning.

Drawn Together (Lê 2018)

Why We Chose This Book: A young boy of Vietnamese American descent goes to visit his grandfather and feels frustrated because they are unable to communicate with each other. Feeling lonely, he pulls out some paper and begins to draw. When he does this, his grandfather sits down beside him with his sketchbook and ink. This surprises the young boy, and together they create a beautiful world. As they collaborate, they begin to understand that their communication happens through their images, rather than words, creating a special bond between them—the same bond that we want to develop among our students and with the written and illustrated word.

Additional Mentor Text Suggestions for Relationships

- *A Gift from Abuela* (Ruiz 2018)

- *Thank You, Omu!* (Mora 2018)

ANCHOR LEARNING IN LITERATURE/CONVERSE TO GROW THINKERS AND LEARNERS

BEFORE READING

- Set a Purpose: Relationships are an important part of life. We have many relationships both in school and out of school. Today, we are going to think about the important relationship that exists between readers and writers and how that makes us better literacy learners. That relationship allows us to understand ourselves, others, and the world around us. Our book, today, is about a boy and his grandfather who seem to not have anything in common, but much to their surprise, they do!

- Discuss the Book Cover: What do you notice about the title of this book, *Drawn Together*? What do you think it means? What do you notice about the illustration both on the dust jacket and on the cover of the book? How do you think that the title and the cover illustrations go together? How do they prepare us for what we are going to read in the story?

DURING READING

- At the beginning of the story, it appears that the boy and his grandfather have a communication problem. What are some clues that they aren't understanding each other? How do you know that based on what you notice in the illustrations?
- What is the turning point in the story? How does that impact the way they are interacting with one another?
- How does that change the way they view each other? How do you think they might spend their time together in the future?

AFTER READING

- Let's consider how relationships are important to literacy learners. We have been thinking about how reading and writing are connected to each other, but now, let's ponder how readers and writers are connected as well. As writers, we learn from authors and illustrators to help make our writing better. As readers, we learn from writers how text helps us understand ourselves and the world around us. Reading, writing, and talking about our literacy help us understand the craft of what we do and who we are as people. Our reading and writing relationships help us better understand our place in the world and our connections with others, just like the boy and his grandfather understood the special connection that they shared with each other.
- Questions for Learners to Ponder:
  - » Why are relationships important to me as a reader and writer? How do they help me improve?
  - » How do my reading and writing relationships make me a better person?
  - » What role do relationships play outside of school?

DEMONSTRATE HABITS AND STRATEGIES

As a learner, I notice how the relationships that I have with others, such as authors, illustrators, and my peers, help deepen my understanding. I know that my own reading and writing has improved because of the relationships that I have with others. I talk about what I'm reading and what I'm writing. They listen to me and make my thinking better when they give me feedback. I also learn from mentor authors and illustrators who can do things that I'd like to do in my own writing. Today, during literacy workshop time, think about how the relationships that you have with the authors of the books you are reading or the classmates with whom you share your writing and thinking help make you an even better reader and writer.

(continues)

LESSON *CONTINUED*

RECORD THINKING AND LEARNING

Before you get started on your work today, look back through your literacy notebook to notice any relationships that you might have formed with authors, illustrators, or your classmates. Reflect on how those relationships have helped you grow as a thinker and learner. As we continue our work together this year, you might want to create a symbol to mark those people who are influential in helping you develop your reading and writing identities.

WHAT'S NEXT?

During learning time, encourage students to think about and share with you who they have relationships with that help them grow as literacy learners. If they can't name authors, illustrators, or classmates who help them grow, help them explore their "Books I've Read" lists for favorite authors or think of friends with whom they share their reading to identify people with whom they have relationships, although they may not have realized it.

BIG IDEA: FOCUS (DETERMINING IMPORTANCE)

READING WORKSHOP	LITERACY WORKSHOP COMMON THREADS	WRITING WORKSHOP
	Focus	
How does determining importance in a text help me better understand it?	What are the habits and behaviors of focused people? How does being focused help me as a learner and a person? How does focus help me in setting and achieving my goals?	How does narrowing the focus for my writing help me create coherent pieces?

What Experts Say About Focus

Our learners are bombarded with information and images. In addition, their lives are often packed with activities and other events that pull their attention away from school and learning. Therefore, it is helpful if we intentionally guide students as they zero in on important ideas and their own learning goals. When you teach children how to direct their mental energy, they are better able to prioritize. Empowering students to determine importance in a text, to identify strengths and areas of improvement in written pieces, or to become a part of partners in the goal-setting process provides a path for success as they take ownership of their learning (Routman 2018; Thompson 2015; Yates and Nosek 2018).

During literacy workshop, you invite learners to set out their own goals. Goal setting is an effective way to encourage students to invest in the learning process. As we have worked with literacy workshop in our own classrooms, we've learned how important student goals are in the process of growing readers and writers. Goal-driven processing centered on integrated big ideas helps students apply literacy strategies in authentic ways.

L E S S O N PRIMARY

FOCUS: IMPORTANT IDEAS
PLANT SEEDS THAT HELP ME GROW

FOCUS PHRASES   MENTOR TEXT SUGGESTION

- I focus on important ideas when I read.

- I share important ideas when I talk or write.

- I learn important ideas from others.

Planting Stories: The Life of Librarian and Storyteller Pura Belpré (Denise 2019)

Why We Chose This Book: In the 1920s, Pura Belpré shared her abuela's stories from Puerto Rico with the children who gathered at her feet in the New York Public Library. As Pura told and published her stories, she planted seeds—seeds that changed many young readers' lives. When you read aloud *Planting Stories* during literacy workshop, you will be planting seeds for children who also have stories to tell.

Additional Mentor Text Suggestions for Focus

- *Malala's Magic Pencil* (Yousafzai 2017)

- *Ordinary, Extraordinary Jane Austen* (Hopkinson 2018)

ANCHOR LEARNING IN LITERATURE/CONVERSE TO GROW THINKERS AND LEARNERS

BEFORE READING

- Set a Purpose: Have you heard the word *focus* before? The word *focus* can mean different things, depending on the situation. Today, we are going to think about how, when we *focus* on something, we pay careful attention to it. As we read this biography about a librarian named Pura Belpré, we are going to *focus on*, or pay attention to, two things. First, I want you to think about what is important to remember *about* Pura after reading this book. Second, we are going to ponder what we can learn *from* Pura that we can use during literacy workshop.

- Discuss the Book Cover: What a beautiful cover! Let me open up the book so you can admire it for a moment. Did you notice that the woman holding the open book has a name tag on that reads *Pura* and she is sitting on the steps of the public library?

- What do you think the author means by the title *Planting Stories*? Is there anything in the illustration that has to do with planting? [Notice the flowers flowing out of the book Pura is reading to the children.]

DURING READING

- "Then—a golden opportunity!" page: A *golden opportunity* means that this is a perfect chance for Pura. Why do you think Pura would enjoy working in a library? Why do you suppose the same type of flowers we saw on the book cover are coming out of the library?
- "Now Pura has a wish, too: to plant her story seeds throughout the land." page: Pura really wants to share the stories she learned from her abuela in Puerto Rico with others. What steps might she take to go about sharing her stories? How do you share your stories?
- "Soon, *Pérez y Martina* is a book:" page: Think about Pura's wish. Do you think her wish came true? Did she meet her goal? I wonder what she will want to do next.

AFTER READING

- If you were going to tell someone about Pura Belpré, what's important for them to know?
- How did the author's words and the illustrator's images help you focus on the important parts of Pura's life?
- As fellow readers and storytellers, what can we learn from Pura?

DEMONSTRATE HABITS AND STRATEGIES

Did you know that the books we read during literacy workshop are all special to the authors who wrote them, just like Pura's book was special to her? How does it make you feel when you finish a book or project? Let's look back at the page where Pura's book was published. Look at how she's holding the book above her head, and there are stars coming out of it. Is that how you feel? Me too! Sometimes we have big wishes or goals, like Pura did. Other times our wishes or goals are smaller. As learners, we can think about our goals and then use what we learn from reading, writing, and talking with our friends to meet them. Sometimes it helps me to write down my goals and think about the steps I'm going to take to meet them. Let me show you what I mean.

RECORD THINKING AND LEARNING

After reading the biography about Pura Belpré, I'm interested in reading another biography. Then, I'm thinking I might make a little book to share what I've learned from the person in that biography. So, on my goal-setting sheet, I'll write those steps (Figure 7.3 and Appendix 14 in the Online Resources).

(continues)

L E S S O N *CONTINUED*

NAME _____

BIG IDEA

[   ]

I'm wondering . . . _____

_____

I'm going to . . .

I'm going to work . . .   by myself   with _____

Figure 7.3 Goal-Setting Sheet: Primary, Version II

WHAT'S NEXT?

Little learners will need support in setting attainable goals and following the steps to reach those goals. To support them in this work, consider continuing this demonstration for a few days as you follow the steps you set out to meet the goal. A demonstration sequence might sound something like this:

Day 2: [Show the biography you chose to read. Explain why you chose it, what you hoped to learn, and how you are going to go about reading it. During sharing time, share your progress and something you learned.] Before Learning Time: I decided to read *Malala's Magic Pencil* by Malala Yousafzai (2017) because I wanted to learn more about her magic pencil. Since there are some challenging words in this book, I decided to read it with a friend. During Share Time:

Today, we read up to the part where Malala was thinking about the kids who didn't have enough food and the girl who couldn't go to school. I learned that in some countries not everyone gets to go to school. I wrote that on a sticky note and stuck it on the page where I learned that so I will remember it tomorrow.

Day 3: [Share what you learned from reading the rest of the book. Explain what you learned *about* Malala and *from* Malala.] Before Learning Time: My plan today is to read the rest of this book. I'm hoping I learn more about her magic pencil today. I'm glad I decided to read it with my friend because we were able to work as a team to figure out some of the words. During Share Time: I finally learned more about her magic pencil! Malala decided to write about what was happening in her country. When she did that, she got famous and people all over the world wanted to hear her story. Some bad men tried to stop her, but she kept writing. I learned that something isn't right, you should speak up. I also learned that you have to be brave to do it! So, I wrote those ideas on sticky notes so I could use them when I make my Malala book.

Day 4: [Begin your little book by writing what we learned from the first biography.] I'm going to call my book *Keep Writing! What I Learned from Malala.* I'll write the title on the cover. I can draw my picture later. On page 1, I will write: *Lessons I learned from Malala.* On page 2: *Be brave!* On page 3: *Tell people when something isn't right.* On page 4: *Use your words to make the world better.* On page 5: *Keep writing!*

L E S S O N   INTERMEDIATE

FOCUS: GOALS HELP ME GROW IN MY READING AND WRITING

FOCUS PHRASE	MENTOR TEXT SUGGESTION

- I focus my learning to help achieve my reading and writing goals.

The One Day House
(Durango 2017)

Why We Chose This Book: Wilson has the best intentions to help fix Gigi's house, which isn't in the best condition, but something always seems to happen to keep him from achieving his goal of getting it done for her (and himself). Gigi has a positive attitude and keeps reassuring Wilson that he will someday get it done, but his hopes and dreams never seem to be enough to make it become a reality. One day Wilson realizes that he might need some assistance in order to get Gigi's house fixed, but will he be reaching out to others too late? Since one of the themes in this story is goal setting, we use this book to further our goal-setting conversation with students.

Additional Mentor Text Suggestions for Focus

- *Lubna and Pebble* (Meddour 2019)

- *my heart* (Luyken 2019)

ANCHOR LEARNING IN LITERATURE/CONVERSE TO GROW THINKERS AND LEARNERS

BEFORE READING

- Set a Purpose: Today, we are going to think about the goals that we have for ourselves and what we do to help make those goals become a reality. Wilson is a boy who has a goal to help his neighbor, Gigi. It is a big one, and it might be a bit bigger than he can manage by himself. Some goals that we have for ourselves we can manage on our own, and some goals may need support from others. How do we know the difference, and what do we do when we realize that we might need to reach out to others to make our goals a reality?

- Discuss the Book Cover: What do you notice about the book cover? Who do you see, and what are they doing? What can you infer about the characters in the story, and how might they be connected to one another? Also, why do you think the author may have named this book *The One Day House*? How do you think the title of this book and the illustrations on the cover connect to the story?

DURING READING

- At the beginning of the story, Wilson wants to help Gigi fix her house. He sets a goal to fix it, but we quickly realize that he might not be able to meet his goal. When do you—as the reader—realize that Wilson might need some help to meet his goal?
- When do you think Gigi realizes that Wilson has good intentions but might need some help to fix her house, or do you think that she even cares about having her house fixed up? How do you know?
- Why do you think that Wilson decides to ask others to help him with fixing up Gigi's house? How does he do this? Why do you think others decide to help him?
- Would you have asked others for help in the same way? What are some other ways that Wilson might have asked for help in helping Gigi with her house?

AFTER READING

- Questions for Learners to Ponder:
  - » What goals are important to me as a reader and writer?
  - » Why is goal setting helpful?
  - » When might goals focus my reading and writing work?
  - » How might others (teachers, parents, peers) support me in meeting my literacy goals?
  - » What kind of support is the most helpful?

DEMONSTRATE HABITS AND STRATEGIES

We are going to continue to think about how the goals we set as readers and writers help us focus during literacy workshop. Whether in school or outside of school, goals help move us forward. Throughout my life, I've set goals both as a reader and as a writer. Sometimes they are *small* goals: to write a few words in my notebook every day or to finish a chapter in a book that I've been reading. Other times, I've set *bigger* goals: to finish the book that I've been writing or to read an entire book series. Bigger goals like these require time, effort, and stamina.

Whether my goals are big or small, I have to focus on the individual tasks that are necessary to complete in order to move toward achieving these goals. Like Wilson, I've also had to recognize that I occasionally need the support of others to achieve these goals. So, I reach out to my book friends who recommend books to me and listen as I talk about my reading. They encourage me to think about and stick with the books that are important to me. When I am writing, I turn to my writing partners to cheer me on, give me feedback, and ultimately remind me that I *can* reach my goal even when I think that I can't.

(continues)

L E S S O N CONTINUED

RECORD THINKING AND LEARNING

Think of a reading and writing goal that will help you focus your work during learning time. To help you remember your goals, you will record each one on a speech bubble (Figure 7.4 and Appendix 15 in the Online Resources). These goals will help you grow as a literacy learner. Remember that goals can change over time based on your needs. You may meet a goal and change it, or you may decide that there is something else that you'd like to focus your attention on in your literacy life.

Figure 7.4   A Learner's Reading and Writing Goals

WHAT'S NEXT?

During literacy workshop, take time to confer with your students about their goals. Some students will have a clear plan about what they would like to work on in their reading and writing. Others might need a bit more guidance. Either way is okay. Think of it as another way to get to know them as readers and writers but, more importantly, for them to get to know themselves better. Empowering them and sharing the responsibility for their literacy lives and journey will add to their engagement as readers and writers.

BIG IDEA: IMAGINATION (VISUALIZATION)

READING WORKSHOP	LITERACY WORKSHOP COMMON THREADS	WRITING WORKSHOP
	Imagination (Visualization)	
How does visualizing while reading help me better understand a text?	How can I use my imagination to blend my reading and writing knowledge in fresh, new ways?	How does using my imagination help me create stories and illustrations?
What types of words and phrases help me visualize as I read?	Why is imagination important to readers, writers, and learners?	How does using figurative language when writing help make my piece more engaging?

What Experts Say About the Importance of Imagination

Think of a memorable book that you've read or a recent piece of writing. Close your eyes. What do you visualize? You probably see an image that connects you to that text in a meaningful way that is unique to you alone. Images are powerful and live in both our senses and emotions (Keene and Zimmerman 2007). Our imagination evolves with every experience. Each time we read or write a text, we strengthen our ability to create mental images. As literacy teachers, we know that "illustrations can provide the same information as written texts and can be independently decoded and comprehended" (Bryan 2019, 7). When you focus on imagination, you are guiding learners to understand the importance of images in books and consider how to enhance written texts by creating illustrations to engage or teach their readers.

During literacy workshop, we encourage you to take the concepts of imagination and creativity one step further. Future-ready learners are able to think creatively, work creatively with others, and implement innovation. Students who are able to continuously create and innovate will be prepared for the future challenges of society and the workplace (National Education Association 2011). Think back to the demonstration lessons found in Chapters 5 and 6 that were focused on habits and behaviors. As you guide your students in understanding the importance of imagination as a literacy strategy, think beyond texts and encourage students to consider the importance their imagination and creativity will play as literate citizens of the future.

L E S S O N PRIMARY

IMAGINATION: IMAGINATION MAKES WORDS COME TO LIFE

FOCUS PHRASES   MENTOR TEXT SUGGESTION

- I use my imagination to help me picture what I'm reading.

- I use my imagination when I write to help readers picture my ideas.

- I use my imagination to create.

My Heart Is a Compass
(Marcero 2018)

Why We Chose This Book: Compass Rose wants to discover something unique to bring to show-and-tell, so she creates her own maps and journeys to imaginary places. Her maps include a road map, a sky map, an ocean map, and an electonic map. The author, Deborah Marcero, is a former Chicago Public School literacy specialist, which is apparent when you see the illustration of the classroom on the front endpapers. This book could lead to students creating their own unique maps, as the kids are doing on the back endpapers. The way in which Deborah Marcero illustrates the differences between reality and fantasy will spark conversations about how our imaginations help us as readers, learners, and creators.

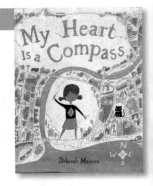

Additional Mentor Text Suggestions for Imagination

- *Flora's Tree House* (Alborozo 2019)

- *The Greatest Adventure* (Piedra 2018)

ANCHOR LEARNING IN LITERATURE/CONVERSE TO GROW THINKERS AND LEARNERS

BEFORE READING

- Set a Purpose: When do you use your imagination? Turn and tell a friend. We use our imagination in many different ways. Our imagination is at work when we play, create art, read, and write. Many of the stories you read came from someone's imagination, just like the one we are going to read today.

- Discuss the Book Cover: There is so much to look at in this cover illustration. I listened to an interview with Deborah Marcero, and she said that she used two different illustration styles in this book: one style that shows the main character's real world and another that reveals her imagination. As we read *My Heart Is a Compass*, let's see if we can figure out the difference between the two styles.

DURING READING

- "Rose longed to be an explorer, a pioneer, a trailblazer." page: What do you notice about the pictures on the two sides of this page? Which do you think is Rose's real world and which is her imagination? [On the left-hand side, Deborah Marcero chose to use the color palette of old printed maps for Rose's real world and on the right-hand side, she used a single color, blue. The blue line that runs from Rose's pencil through the book ties the two together.]

- "It could have been anything." page: These pages show Rose's imagination at work. How can you tell she's imagining? [She sees a giant butterfly, a dragon, and a mermaid.]
- "She found herself in the same place she began." page: Wait! Why is that? Where are all of her maps?

AFTER READING

In this book, Rose creates places that no one has ever seen before. Her maps are so detailed that we can imagine what we would see and experience if we visited each place. As authors and illustrators, we add details that help our readers imagine the ideas or places we create. It's important as readers to pay attention to the author's and illustrator's details. The details in books help us to imagine or make mental images of the characters, setting, and other important events in a story. Wow! It seems like imagination is a pretty important tool for learners, doesn't it?

DEMONSTRATE HABITS AND STRATEGIES

On the back endpapers, the author invites us to make our own imaginary maps. Sometimes books like this one give us ideas about how to use our imagination in unique ways. Since I'm interested in the idea of creating my own map, I think I'll take her challenge. Some of you might want to join me (Figure 7.5). This book also got me thinking more about maps. I have a basket of books about maps here if you're interested in doing some research.

Figure 7.5   Literacy Workshop Entry: Imaginary Map

RECORD THINKING AND LEARNING

Rose's maps have so many details to notice. Who would like to work with a partner to study a map and share what you've noticed? [List the four types of maps—road map, sky map, ocean map, and electronic map—on a sticky note. Jot down the names of each interested partnership next to the type of map. Give each partnership some time to notice and share.]

WHAT'S NEXT?

We want our classroom to be places where children are encouraged to imagine, create, and think outside of the box. Continue to foster these behaviors as you invite students to read, write, research, converse, and create products during literacy workshop.

L E S S O N INTERMEDIATE

IMAGINATION: IMAGINATION HELPS ME READ, WRITE, AND CREATE

FOCUS PHRASE

- I use my imagination to extend the worlds in which my reading and writing exist.

MENTOR TEXT SUGGESTION

Imagine! (Colón 2018)
Why We Chose This Book: In this beautiful wordless picture book, Colón shares how he became interested in art. It tells the story of a young boy who passes a museum every day until one day when he decides to go in to explore the art housed there. As he does, he becomes fascinated by the beautiful artwork, so much so that the artwork comes to life. As he enters the *living world* of the pictures, he begins to understand the beauty of art, and it changes his life forever.

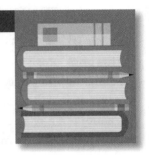

Additional Mentor Text Suggestions for Imagination

- *Another* (Robinson 2019)
- *Inside My Imagination* (Arteaga 2012)

ANCHOR LEARNING IN LITERATURE/CONVERSE TO GROW THINKERS AND LEARNERS

BEFORE READING

- Set a Purpose: During our time today, we are going to consider how our imagination helps us as readers and writers. When we can visualize what is happening in a book, we better understand the text. Imagination also helps make our writing more creative. The book that we are reading today is about a young man who not only discovers the magic of art through his imagination but also learns that art is something that he wants to do for his life's work.
- Discuss the Book Cover: As you look at the cover of the book what do you see? How are the illustrations on the cover and the title connected to each other?

DURING READING

- What do you know about the boy in this book? What might he be interested in at the beginning of the book?
- What clues is the author giving us that the boy has a vivid imagination?
- Where is he going, and how does he use his imagination once he gets there?
- How do we know that his experiences using his imagination throughout the book will follow him throughout his life?

AFTER READING

- Questions for Learners to Ponder:
  » How does my imagination help me as a reader and a writer?
  » How does my reading and writing help develop my imagination?
  » How can I use my imagination to combine my reading and writing to create something new?

DEMONSTRATE HABITS AND STRATEGIES

Imagination is an amazing tool for readers and writers. I know that I use it almost every time that I read and write. When I'm reading, I use my imagination to think about the stories that I am reading. I also love to use my imagination to create stories. I will often think about pieces of a book that I have read and think about how I might use a character or a setting in a story that I'm writing. Imagination is one of my favorite literacy tools!

RECORD THINKING AND LEARNING

Think about how imagination is important to you as a literacy learner. How do you use it in your reading and writing? Do you use it to *picture* the characters and settings in the books that you are reading? How about the experiences that you have when you're not in school? How might you capture those so that you can use them in your writing? Let's create a mind map of words and pictures that will show some of the things that are in your imagination that will help enhance your literacy life! (See Figure 7.6.)

Figure 7.6
Literacy Workshop Entry: Imagination Mind Map

WHAT'S NEXT?

Take time to chat with your students during literacy workshop about how they are using their imaginations when they read and write. Encourage them to reflect on how visualization supports them as readers. Discuss which types of books demand more visualization on their part. Guide them as they transfer this knowledge to their written pieces. Prompt them to consider how much visual support their audience may need to understand their ideas. You might notice it is easier for learners to make mental images in fiction and narrative texts, so you may have to demonstrate the importance of visualization in informational texts. Capitalize on the power of your conversations with learners and their discussions with each other to help them better understand and apply literacy strategies.

CHAPTER 8

Demonstration Lessons—
Teaching the Elements of Fiction

Stories bind us together. They connect us to the past, to each other, and to worlds that exist only in an author's imagination. The power of story is evident as you observe your literacy learners in action. The narratives they choose to read, discuss, write, and tell each other are one of the many delicate threads that weave together to create a classroom community. Immersing learners in a wide range of stories during literacy workshop will strengthen their understanding of the elements of a well-written narrative. As your students engage with fictional tales, your deliberate teacher actions can nudge them toward deeper understanding of texts, of themselves, and of the world in which they live. There is nothing like gathering your class around you to share a memorable story. Cherish these moments with your learners. The conversation that surrounds an engaging read-aloud builds relationships and, at the same time, deepens students' understanding of the inner workings of a narrative text.

COMMON THREADS:
BIG IDEAS FOR TEACHING THE ELEMENTS OF FICTION

The demonstration lessons in this chapter draw attention to the big ideas related to the elements of fiction that are essential for comprehending and composing narrative texts. We present the demonstrations in the order that you might choose to teach them, keeping in mind that the needs of your students may take you in a different direction. Embrace the flexibility of literacy workshop. With your students as your guides, introduce or review these concepts as your learners show you they're ready. Over time, we've learned that the big ideas explored in the demonstration lessons that follow are most effective when they are spiraled throughout your literacy workshop lessons. So, you may want to introduce an element of fiction and then circle back to it with increasingly complex texts to fine-tune your students' understanding.

BIG IDEA: CHARACTER/PERSON

READING WORKSHOP	LITERACY WORKSHOP COMMON THREADS	WRITING WORKSHOP
How do I get to know a character?	Character/Person What can I learn from book characters and biographies of interesting people to help make me a better person? What can I learn from the character's journey to help me in my own life?	How do I create memorable characters?

What Experts Say About Understanding Characters

In the past, most children's books were predominantly peopled with characters who didn't reflect the variety of cultures, histories, and opinions that our students possess. Fortunately, the world of children's literature is evolving, and we are beginning to see readers reaching for books with characters, settings, and experiences as diverse as the children who learn with us in our classrooms (Kids and Family Reading Report 2019). As readers widen their reading repertoires, they may meet characters who offer new perspectives. Readers who are open to this possibility and read with what Kylene Beers and Robert Probst (2017) dub *compassion,* considering the thoughts and feelings of fictional characters, have a chance to refine and improve their thinking. In addition, by promoting compassionate reading, you are supporting their growth into empathetic adults who carefully consider the ideas and perspectives of others. As readers live vicariously through the characters' experiences, they are learning to navigate an ever-changing world.

Introducing students to a variety of multidimensional characters will not only provide them with the opportunity to experience the world through the pages of a book but also build their skills when writing stories with well-developed characters. Noticing the ways in which authors portray the experiences, emotions, and inner thoughts of characters gives writers an inside look into the craft of making characters come alive on the page. Although your learners may be used to writing about their own thinking and life experiences, during literacy workshop, you can expand their viewpoint by inviting them to incorporate what they've learned from influential characters that have helped them better understand a book, a particular situation, or their worldview.

L E S S O N PRIMARY

CHARACTER/PERSON: LEARNING ABOUT AND FROM CHARACTERS

FOCUS PHRASES	MENTOR TEXT SUGGESTION

- I learn *about* characters by paying attention to the pictures and words.

- I create characters by showing their personality with my pictures and words.

- I learn important lessons *from* the characters in the books I read.

Natsumi! (Lendroth 2018a)

Why We Chose This Book: Natsumi did everything in a big way. From her parents and grandmother, she heard, "Not so fast. Not so hard. Not so loud." One evening, her wise grandfather assures her she will find an activity that fits her personality if she keeps looking and listening. On the day of the traditional Japanese festival, Natsumi surprises her family by being one of the taiko drummers. Lendroth's story is an exemplar text for this demonstration because Natsumi is a distinctive character possessing traits students can relate to and discuss. In addition, the author and illustrator paint a clear picture of her personality through dialogue and illustrations showing her actions.

Additional Mentor Text Suggestions for Character

- *I Will Be Fierce!* (Birdsong 2019)

- *Unstoppable Me* (Verde 2019)

ANCHOR LEARNING IN LITERATURE/CONVERSE TO GROW THINKERS AND LEARNERS

BEFORE READING

- Set a Purpose: Each of you has your own personality. Some of you prefer quiet activities while others love to yell and run around. Book characters are the same way. Because characters live inside the pages of a book, authors and illustrators make them come to life through words and actions. As a reader, we use those clues to help us get to know a character. While writing, we give our readers clues to help them get to know our characters. It's also smart to ponder the lessons we might learn *from* the characters in the books we read. We're going to read about a character named Natsumi. Let's see what we can learn from her.

- Discuss the Book Cover: Why do you suppose Natsumi's name has an exclamation mark after it? What can you tell about Natsumi's personality simply by looking at the illustration on the cover?

DURING READING

- "For a small girl, Natsumi did everything in a big way." page: What do you think the author means when she says, "Natsumi did everything in a big way"? Do you know anyone like Natsumi? Do you think doing things in a big way might cause some problems?

- "She jumped high, played hard, and slurped noodles like a sumo wrestler." page: Why do you suppose Grandfather didn't say anything? I wonder if that will be important as we continue to learn more about Natsumi.

- "That evening, Grandfather found her slumped outside." page: What are some of the activities that are a right fit for your personality? Turn and talk about them with a friend. I notice that it is Natsumi's grandfather who is giving her advice. What do you remember about him from earlier in the story?
- "BOOM!" page: What do you predict is going on in the village hall? Does it sound like an activity that is a good fit for Natsumi? Why or why not?

AFTER READING

- What did you notice about Natsumi as a character? What are some of the clues in the words and pictures that helped you to get to know Natsumi?
- If you wrote a sequel this book, what do you suppose Natsumi might do next?

DEMONSTRATE HABITS AND STRATEGIES

As a writer, I like to study how other authors and illustrators create memorable characters. To do this, I go back into the book to notice three things:

1. What the character says (their words or dialogue)
2. What the character does (their actions)
3. How the character is feeling throughout the story

Let me show you how I would do that in the book *Natsumi!*

RECORD THINKING AND LEARNING

I'm going to use this chart to write down what I discover (Figure 8.1). [As you flip through the pages of the book, invite students to notice Natsumi's words, actions, and feelings. Then, in the days that follow, revisit the book to add ideas to the last two columns of the chart. When finished, this chart can serve as a model if children want to try the same type of character study with another book. If children need a guide to do this, they can use A Character Study reproducible resource found in Appendix 16 in the Online Resources.]

	Readers Learn About Characters	People Learn From Characters	Writers Create Characters
Main Characters Words	Natsumi says. "No matter what I do, something always goes wrong."	It helps to tell others how you are feeling.	Write words that help readers get to know your characters.
Main Character's Feelings	Beginning-sad End-excited	Characters feelings change-so do ours!	Draw characters' faces so that readers see how they're feeling.
Main Character's Actions	Natsumi does everything with a lot of energy. She does things her own way.	Be yourself!	Show characters doing things they ♡.
Other Characters Words/Actions	Grandmother: "Not so fast." Mother: "Not so loud." Grandfather smiled. ☺	Find people who understand you.	Use other characters' words or actions to help readers know main character.

Figure 8.1 Anchor Chart: A Character Study—*Natsumi!*

WHAT'S NEXT?

As you continue to read aloud and confer with your students about understanding and creating books with memorable characters, notice and discuss the following questions:

- How do words and pictures help bring characters to life?
- Why do you think there are so many different kinds of characters?
- How do the main character's words and actions give you clues to their personality?
- How can you use what you learned from this author and illustrator to create your own memorable characters?

L E S S O N : INTERMEDIATE

CHARACTER/PERSON: WHO MAKES ME A BETTER READER AND WRITER?

FOCUS PHRASE

- I identify how others influence and help me grow as a learner.

MENTOR TEXT SUGGESTIONS

Carmela Full of Wishes (de la Peña 2018)

Why We Chose This Book: Carmela wakes up on her birthday ready to take on new responsibilities, which include joining her brother on the family errands. When she finds a dandelion growing in the pavement, her brother tells her that she can make a wish. For the rest of the day, she imagines what she will wish for with her special find. Before she makes her wish, the dandelion is crushed on the sidewalk, and she is heartbroken. As the day ends, her brother helps her discover that there is more than one way to make a wish and that sometimes what you wish for may be in front of you all along. The relationship between Carmela and her brother highlights the ways in which characters interact and support each other, which can lead to a conversation about influential people in your students' lives.

Additional Mentor Text Suggestions for Character

- *Rocket Says Look Up!* (Bryon 2019)
- *The Rough Patch* (Lies 2018)

ANCHOR LEARNING IN LITERATURE/CONVERSE TO GROW THINKERS AND LEARNERS

BEFORE READING

- Set a Purpose: Today, we are going to think about how other people influence us and help us grow. One characteristic of successful literacy learners is that they are able to take input from others and use it to strengthen their reading and writing. They also observe and learn from others who have more experience to improve their skills. Let's take a look at a character who was able to change throughout a story because of the actions and influence of someone who is older and wiser.
- Discuss the Book Cover: What do you notice about the cover of the book? As you look at it, what do you think that the girl on the cover might be thinking or feeling at that particular moment? What might you infer about her as you look at the setting in which the cover illustration takes place? How might the cover illustration connect to the title of the book?

DURING READING

- Notice how Carmela begins her day. Can you infer how she is feeling? Why do you suppose she is feeling that way? How did her emotions change throughout the day? Who or what influenced Carmela's feelings as they changed during her day?
- What kind of relationship did Carmela have with her brother? How do you know that he was someone who was important to her and would have an impact on what she did and how she felt throughout the day? How did his actions show that Carmela was important to him and that he wanted to have a positive influence on her?
- What lessons did Carmela learn throughout the day? How did her brother help influence how she felt about herself and the experiences that she had?

AFTER READING

- Questions for Learners to Ponder:
  - » How do I use what I learn from others to help me grow as a reader and a writer?
  - » Who is someone who influences my literacy life? How do they do that?
  - » Do I influence others' reading and writing? How?

DEMONSTRATE HABITS AND BEHAVIORS

- The relationship between Carmela and her brother reminds me that I'm not alone in my literacy life, that I've had lots of people around to guide me as I've become even better at what I do. Some of the people who have supported me are my students (Yes, you!), my teachers, my family, other caring adults, and even my peers. Because I've surrounded myself with caring people who have the same interests, I find that they are better able to offer help when I need it. Some of the ways these people have helped me are giving me book recommendations to share with you in class, brainstorming ideas for writing with me, and helping me edit something before I get ready to publish it. These are the people who have helped me become a better literacy learner. Who are the people who support you in your literacy learning?
- I also try to be a positive influence on the literacy lives of others. I do this by sharing the books that I am reading with others who I think might enjoy them. After they've read the book, I ask them their opinion. Sometimes their opinion of the book is the same as mine, other times it is different. I think that differing opinions lead to the most interesting book discussions. When my doctoral students are working on their dissertations, I support them as writers by giving them descriptive feedback. That means I don't fix their work for them; instead, I notice things they are doing well and tell them. I also ask them questions about parts of their writing that I don't understand. Can you share an example of when you've been a positive influence on someone else's literacy life? How did that make you feel? Let's work together to be positive influences on each other's literacy lives as, together, we become even better readers and writers.

(continues)

L E S S O N CONTINUED

RECORD THINKING AND LEARNING

As you are reading and writing, think of one way that someone has helped you become an even better reader or writer. It may be something as simple as giving you feedback on a piece that you have written or talking to you about parts of a book you're struggling to understand. These small actions make a big difference because the relationships we have with others positively impact the way we grow as literacy learners (Figure 8.2).

• After you have identified one way people have influenced you, take a moment and think about something that you have done (or could do) for someone else to help them grow. What do you do well that you could share with someone else to move their reading or writing forward? Maybe you are good at adding details to a piece of writing to make it more interesting or you have thought of a unique way to create a book review. These are just two examples of ways that you might help someone else with their literacy. I'm sure you can think

of many more areas of expertise. We're going to put these together so that when you need help, you know who you can ask.

Carmela Full of Wishes	
Person	Wish
The Person that I have helped and has helped me is Abby. I think this because She has rec-mended many books to me and I have recomended, many books to her. We also have done partner writing in a google doc. I also introduced her to a Author named Kwame Alexander	I wish I could be better at writing for longer amounts of time, and making sure that I dont get distracted while im reading. I also wish that I could be able to pick really good books without anyones help at School.

Figure 8.2   Literacy Notebook Entry: Thinking About Relationships

WHAT'S NEXT?

After students are done generating their areas of expertise, gather them on a chart, note cards, or an electronic document to create a registry for students to access when they need support during learning time. Teach and model the difference between helping others and doing for others. During sharing time, celebrate learners who successfully support each other to strengthen their reading and writing, letting them demonstrate their process. Reinforce that thinking and learning together is how we improve. Developing a cohesive classroom culture where you've given children time to build and sustain relationships will support them both as literacy learners and as citizens of tomorrow.

BIG IDEA: STRUCTURE

READING WORKSHOP	LITERACY WORKSHOP COMMON THREADS	WRITING WORKSHOP
	Structure	
What is happening in the story?

How does figuring out the plot structure help me better understand the story? | How do the plots in stories help me to better understand my life and the lives of others?

How can I apply what I've learned from reading texts with various structures to my own writing? | What is the best structure to help move the action of my story forward?

How can I create plots that will keep a reader on the edge of their seat? |

What Experts Say About Understanding Text Structures

Structures come in all shapes and sizes. Just like constructing a building, the inner workings of a text are often designed long before they are built. Without a framework, sturdy buildings and well-written texts probably wouldn't have turned out the way that we see or experience them in their final form. Readers enjoy texts that are written with innovative structures. When your learners can see the *bones* of a narrative text, they are able to use this structure to connect new ideas. Moreover, they will be able to understand and remember more of what they've read (Taberski 2011).

As your students read widely, they encounter various ways that mentor authors use structures in the texts that they create (Ray 1999). Introducing writers to inventive text structures expands their writing repertoire, so they can match their organization to their audience and purpose. Use your deliberate teacher actions to work alongside your learners as they study the structures authors use in the books that they are reading. Scaffold (no pun intended!) their understanding of how a particular structure can both engage readers and support their understanding of the text. Your goal is for your writers to become thoughtful decision makers when they select the best structures to help communicate their message. Isn't this what you want for your learners? The cyclical nature of literacy workshop supports students as they continue to make reading-understanding-thinking-noticing-deciding-applying-sharing connections (Figure 8.3).

CYCLICAL NATURE OF LITERACY WORKSHOP

I read to learn more.
I understand what I read.
I think about the author and illustrator's craft choices.
I decide whether the techniques are helpful to me as a writer.
I apply what I've learned from my reading to my writing.
I share with others to see their reaction.

Figure 8.3 The Cyclical Nature of Literacy Workshop

L E S S O N PRIMARY

STRUCTURE: UNCOVERING INVENTIVE TEXT STRUCTURES

FOCUS PHRASES	MENTOR TEXT SUGGESTION

- I notice how authors organize stories in different ways.

- I think about how I can organize my stories.

Ten Rules of the Birthday Wish
(Ferry 2019)

Why We Chose This Book: In this inventive book, readers learn the ten rules of a birthday wish with some exceptions that come from the animal world. Using a numerical structure, Beth Ferry's text offers literacy workshop learners a fresh way to write about a familiar topic like blowing out birthday candles. Tom Lichtenheld's bright illustrations sprinkled with visual humor will also inspire your budding artists.

Additional Mentor Text Suggestions for Structure

- *How to Give Your Cat a Bath in Five Easy Steps* (Winstanley 2019)

- *How to Walk an Ant* (Derby 2019)

ANCHOR LEARNING IN LITERATURE/CONVERSE TO GROW THINKERS AND LEARNERS

BEFORE READING

- Set a Purpose: How many of you have made a birthday wish? What are your rules? Turn and share with your friends. I wonder what the ten rules are in this book. In the title, Beth Ferry gives us a clue as to how this story is going to be organized, or how it is *structured*. The *structure* of a story is kind of like the bones that make up your skeleton. Without them, you wouldn't be able to sit up and listen to this book or run and play at recess. Just like your bones are the framework for your body, the structure holds the story together. What do you predict the structure might be in this book? As we read, we'll see whether our prediction is correct. We can notice how this structure helps us as readers and think about how we might use a structure like Beth's in our own writing.
- Discuss the Book Cover: What do you notice on the cover that you've seen or had at your own birthday parties? Do you suppose any of those items have to do with the rules of a birthday wish?

DURING READING

- "Rule no. 1 It must be your birthday." page: I notice that at the end of this rule it reads, "Unless you are a beetle, bug, or insect . . ." The word *unless* signals that there is an exception to the rule. That means that there is some reason that or situation when people won't have to follow the rule. I wonder if there will be exceptions to all of the rules.

- "Rule no. 4 You must have a light (or lights) to blow out." page: How is the structure of counting the rules from one to ten helping you as a reader? What have you noticed about the exceptions?
- "Rule no. 8 You must make a wish." page: What are some of the things kids are wishing for on this page? How did Tom Lichtenheld show you that in his illustrations?

AFTER READING
- Are those the rules you follow when making a birthday wish?
- Which rules were the same, and which were different?

DEMONSTRATE HABITS AND BEHAVIORS

I notice that Beth Ferry used a counting structure to list the rules from one to ten. That helped me as a reader because I could predict the way the story was going to go. As a writer, sometimes I might choose to borrow a structure. That means I can use the ideas of rules or tips but write them about something else. To help me remember my ideas, I'm going to write a list of other things I might write rules or tips about:
- Three Tips for Being a Friend
- Five Rules for Catching a Bug
- Four Rules for Riding a Bike
- Six Tips for Eating an Ice Cream Cone

I'm sure you can think of a lot more! [Invite learners to share their own ideas and record them along with yours.]

RECORD THINKING AND LEARNING

As you're reading and writing over the next few days, if you notice any interesting text structures mark them with a sticky note. If you like, you can give them a name. We'll learn more about what you've discovered during sharing time. I can't wait to see what you find out.

WHAT'S NEXT?

To broaden your students' expertise in understanding and using text structures as scaffolds for their writing, introduce and study the following innovative structures:
- Seesaw Structure—Mentor Text Examples: *Tough Boris* (Fox 1994); *Lost. Found.* (Arnold 2015)
- Circular Structure—Mentor Text Examples: *If You Give a Mouse a Cookie* (Numeroff [1985] 2010); *A Hippy-Hoppy Toad* (Archer 2018)
- Cumulative Structure—Mentor Text Examples: *The Napping House* (Wood 1984); *One Day in the Eucalyptus, Eucalyptus Tree* (Bernstrom 2016)

L E S S O N INTERMEDIATE

STRUCTURE: CRAFTING INVENTIVE TEXTS TO ENGAGE READERS

FOCUS PHRASES   MENTOR TEXT SUGGESTIONS

- I recognize how authors use structure to help readers understand texts.

- I create texts that have unique structures to engage readers.

The Epic Adventures of Huggie and Stick
(Daywalt 2018)
Why We Chose This Book: Stick is cheerful and Huggie, a stuffed bunny, is quite grumpy. One day while traveling on a bike with their boy, they get thrown from the bike and an adventure begins! Because their adventure is told through diary entries, it provides a jumping-off point for literacy workshop conversations about unique narrative structures. From pirates to stampeding rhinos, from Africa to Europe, it may not be surprising that the two characters' perceptions of these experiences are a bit different. However, when they finally find their way home, the story appears to be over . . . but is it?

Additional Mentor Text Suggestions for Structure

- *I'm Trying to Love Math* (Barton 2019)

- *When Grandma Gives You a Lemon Tree* (Deenihan 2019)

ANCHOR LEARNING IN LITERATURE/CONVERSE TO GROW THINKERS AND LEARNERS

BEFORE READING

- Set a Purpose: We are going to read a book about a stuffed rabbit and a stick that go on an adventure and share their stories through diary entries. We often see diary entries used in nonfiction texts, but today we will see an author use this structure in a fiction text. Their entries give us insights into what they are thinking and feeling about where they are and what is happening to them. Let's think about why the author chose to use diary entries to share what is happening to the characters during the story.

- Discuss the Book Cover: What do you notice about the cover of the book? What can you tell about the characters in the book? How do you think they feel about their adventures? How do you know? What do you think the phrase *epic adventures* might mean? How does the cover show some of the adventures that Huggie and Stick might go on in the book?

DURING READING

- Notice how Huggie and Stick begin their journey. What do you know about each of them? How are they the same and/or different? How might that affect their perception of their journey?

- How does the author help you know that time is passing?

- Who seems to be enjoying his adventures the most? How do you know? Who seems to have a less than positive attitude toward their travels? How do you know?
- How do Huggie and Stick finally return home? What do you think life has in store for them after their homecoming?

AFTER READING

- Questions for Learners to Ponder:
  » How do authors use various text structures (like diary entries) to support readers' understanding of the plot while at the same time engaging them in the story?
  » What can I learn from studying texts with unique text structures to help me when we're writing fiction?

DEMONSTRATE HABITS AND BEHAVIORS

I was thinking to myself, what if Drew Daywalt chose to write this story using a traditional story structure, telling it only from Huggie's perspective? Would I have enjoyed it as much? Would it have been as funny? Would I know the characters as well as I do from reading their diary entries? Some of my favorite books are written using different or unique structures. I think that they are my favorite because the author's choice of structure made the story more interesting or engaging. While Drew Daywalt chose diary entries to tell his story, other authors choose structures like timelines, alternating voices, verse novels, and graphic novel format, among just a few. I find that unique structures help me follow along with the story, constructing meaning along the way. Recognizing the story structure is one more way to increase our ability to comprehend the books we're reading and one more choice we have as writers.

RECORD THINKING AND LEARNING

If you're interested in exploring how Drew Daywalt's choice of diary entries gave you insights into the characters' perspectives, you might choose to make a T-chart. Label the left side *Huggie* and the right side *Stick*. Write down your observations about Huggie and Stick. Focus on who they are, how they feel, and how they evolve throughout the story. Pay close attention to how the author's use of diary entries helped you learn about their personalities and opinions (Figure 8.4).

Huggie and Stick	
Huggie	Stick
• Huggie is moodie and not a huggie type of person	• Stick is like Happy adventsrous and kind of positive.
• Huggie does not like the boat or the trip	• Stick Loves the new adventure awaiting them
• Huggie is the oposite of Stick hates the trip	• Tells the story opisite of Huggie always happy.
• Huggie hates his life and hes very negitive	• Thinks the sand is kissing him when its eating him.
• He really hated his trip so much, am grry	• I think he had a good time on his trip

Figure 8.4   Literacy Notebook Entry: Characters' Perspectives

(continues)

If you want to try your hand at writing a diary entry from a character's point of view:

- Choose a character from a book you're reading or have recently read.
- Write a diary entry from that character's point of view. Consider these things:
  - » What is your character thinking during that time during the story?
  - » How is your character feeling? How can you share that with the reader of your diary entry?
  - » What does your character think about other characters in the story? How do they show that through their words and actions? (See Figure 8.5.)

As you're reading or writing, you could continue to document your new learning about text structures in a few different ways:

- Look back at the books you've read so far this year. Do you notice any patterns in the types of text structures you prefer? Jot down what you notice.
- Think of a narrative story that you have written in your notebook or that you are working on in your writing. How might you use a different structure (or structures) to tell that story to your reader? Decide what structure you might try and how it might be incorporated into your story.

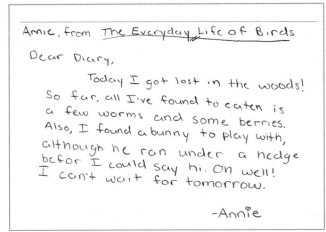

Figure 8.5   Literacy Notebook Entry: Diary Response

WHAT'S NEXT?

If noticing and using unique structures in their narrative writing is a new experience for your students, you'll find it helpful to collect a stack of mentor texts that they can read and discuss as they consider how to weave different text structures into their stories. In your conferences with students, guide them by questioning how they are experimenting with a structure (or two) in their writing. Encourage writers to explain how their chosen structure is helping to tell the story, to support the reader's understanding of what is happening to the characters, and to move the plot forward. Also, don't forget to give students time to share with one another. Their collaborative conversations together will further support them as they process their thinking about the use of structures they're reading in books and using in their narrative writing.

BIG IDEA: THEME

READING WORKSHOP	LITERACY WORKSHOP COMMON THREADS	WRITING WORKSHOP
	Theme	
How does inferring the theme help me better understand the deeper meaning of the story?	How does thinking about theme help me as a reader, a writer, and a person? What life lessons can I learn and apply?	How do authors reveal the theme? How can I develop themes in my own writing?

What Experts Say About Inferring Themes and Applying Life Lessons

How do children learn the life lessons that help them better understand themselves and the world around them? Some are taught within their families, and others are learned through experiences.

Many of our students learn valuable lessons from the characters in the books that they read. Through the pages of a book, children encounter situations that they may or may not have experienced yet. To uncover themes, learners have to dig into the deeper meanings that lie beneath the surface of the story. When contemplating the theme of a story, it is also helpful for readers to consider the author's purpose. As Katherine Paterson, author of *Bridge to Terabithia* states, "We are trying to communicate that which lies in our deepest heart, which has no words, which can only be hinted at through the means of a story" (1990, 153).

As literacy learners become more experienced at catching the author's hints, you can encourage the deeper thinking that comes from the "change, friction, or discomfort that leans against what we already know or believe" as they apply new insights about themselves or the world (Angelillo 2003, 19). As they read more complex texts, it allows them to examine how authors create stories that not only engage readers but also get them to think deeply about the world that they live in and their responsibility to themselves and others.

L E S S O N PRIMARY

THEMES: THINKING ABOUT THEMES

| FOCUS PHRASES | MENTOR TEXT SUGGESTION |

- I read, think, and talk to better understand big ideas.

- I write to figure things out.

- I use what I've learned from books in my own life.

What Is Given from the Heart (McKissack 2019)

Why We Chose This Text: In this heartwarming story, James Otis and his mother have their health and strength but not much else. After losing both his dad and their family farm, James and Mama are barely making ends meet. In early February, Reverend Dennis announces that is time to make *love boxes* for needy families. After much debating, James decides to make a special book for the girl in the family they're supporting. In the end, James and his mom receive their own *love box*. When a book touches your heart, it has a lasting impact. We're hopeful the themes in James Otis's story will stay with literacy workshop learners and guide their future decisions.

Additional Mentor Text Suggestions for Themes

- *Forever or a Day* (Jacoby 2018)

- *The Sloth Who Slowed Us Down* (Wild 2017)

ANCHOR LEARNING IN LITERATURE/CONVERSE TO GROW THINKERS AND LEARNERS

BEFORE READING

- Set a Purpose: Some books help us to learn lessons we might use in our own lives. *What Is Given from the Heart* is one of these books. When we are trying to figure out the lesson, theme, or big idea of a book we think about what happens in the book. Then, it is helpful if we can talk it over with a friend.

- Discuss the Book Cover: When you look at the illustration on the cover, how does it make you feel? Do you predict this is going to be a funny book or a more serious book? What makes you think that? What do you notice about the illustrations? [April Harrison used a lot of different art techniques. Some parts of the picture are even created using collage with various items.]

DURING READING

- "We got an early snowfall in November and Christmas was skimpy, but we made it through to the new year." page: What have we learned so far about James Otis and his mama? I wonder if knowing they are poor will be important as we think about the big ideas in this book.

- "'James Otis, we need to help out,' Mama said on the cold walk home." page: What do you suppose it means to give something from the heart? What is something you have that would be really hard to give away?

- "That made me study harder on what I could contribute." page: What happened to cause James Otis to spend so much time thinking about his contribution to the love box? What do you think he is going to give?

- "Seeing li'l Sarah happy made me happy, too." page: Hmm! Let's stop and think and talk together. Why do you think giving something to someone else made James Otis feel happy?

AFTER READING
- What do you think Patricia McKissack is trying to teach us in this book?
- What are the big ideas?

DEMONSTRATE HABITS AND STRATEGIES

This book gave me a lot to think about. Sometimes when I'm done reading books like *What Is Given from the Heart,* it helps me to write and draw in my literacy notebook (Figure 8.6). When I write and draw, I choose a few important parts from the book because I can't write or draw about everything.
- I'll start with a big heart in the middle of the page because this book touched my heart.
- Sometimes I write a quote from the book that helps me understand the big idea or theme. That means I write down important words from the book. When I write the exact words from the book, I put quotation marks around the words to show that they are not my words. I'm going to write the quote in the middle of the heart.
- Next, I'll draw what James Otis and Mama put in the love box because their gifts were important to the big ideas of the story.
- Finally, I'll write down some of the big ideas or themes that I noticed while we were reading.

RECORD THINKING AND LEARNING

Writing and drawing helps me think and remember. If you would like to try writing and drawing about this book or another book you're reading during literacy workshop, let me know, and I'll be happy to help you get started.

Figure 8.6 Maria's Literacy Notebook Entry: Sketchnotes

WHAT'S NEXT?

In *Ink and Ideas* (2019, 13), Tanny McGregor offers the following research-based reasons to introduce sketchnoting to your students:
- Makes intentional, designed thinking visible through words and images
- Celebrates students' thinking and offers choice
- Increases memory and focus
- Promotes deceleration and relaxation

Because it blends reading, writing, drawing, and thinking, sketchnoting is one way literacy workshop learners may choose to record their thinking. Like the sample in this demonstration lesson, we keep it very simple for our youngest learners.

L E S S O N INTERMEDIATE

LANGUAGE THEME: BIG IDEAS HELP ME LEARN LIFE LESSONS

FOCUS PHRASES   MENTOR TEXT SUGGESTIONS

- I look for the big ideas (themes) in the books that I read.

- I create texts that teach big ideas (themes) to readers.

the remember balloons (Oliveros 2018)

Why We Chose This Book: James's grandpa has balloons that represent the memories that they both share. The silver balloon is filled with their favorite memory of a fishing trip that they took together. James becomes concerned when he notices that Grandpa's memories begin to float away as he begins to forget about the things that he has known for what seems like always to James. He even lets go of the silver balloon with the memory of their fishing trip together. James becomes so upset and even angry, until his mother explains that now it is his turn to be the keeper of the balloons and the memories. He will keep and tell Grandpa of the special memories that he has shared, especially the one of the fishing trip that they have shared.

Additional Mentor Text Suggestions for Theme

- *The Last Tree* (Silva 2019)
- *A Plan for Pops* (Smith 2019)

ANCHOR LEARNING IN LITERATURE/CONVERSE TO GROW THINKERS AND LEARNERS

BEFORE READING

- Set a Purpose: Books give us opportunities to learn from the experiences of others without having to go through those experiences ourselves. With each book we read, we broaden our perspectives, our understanding of others, and our place in the world. The lessons that we learn from these books also seep into our writing. We learn ways to help our readers better understand themselves and their world by writing from the heart, just like the author of this book did. As you're listening to *the remember balloons*, think about the special lessons that we learn from the books that we read and how we can take that wisdom and apply it to our relationships with others.
- Discuss the Book Cover: Take a look at the illustration on the cover. What do you notice? Why do you think the characters all have balloons? How do you think that the illustration on the cover and the title (*the remember balloons*) connect to each other?

DURING READING

- Think about the balloons that each of the characters have. Why do some characters have more balloons and some have fewer?

- What seems to be happening with the balloons of James's grandfather? Why do you think that may be happening?
- How is James feeling because his grandfather is losing his balloons? Why do you think he might be feeling that way? What do you think he might do because his grandfather is losing his balloons? How might he help with that situation?

AFTER READING

- Questions for Learners to Ponder:
  - » Why do I think the author and illustrator choose to use balloons as a symbol for the memories? How does this symbolism help me understand the theme?
  - » How does that choice cause me to pause and think about not only memories but also the life that I share with those I love?
  - » When and why might I use symbolism in my writing?

DEMONSTRATE HABITS AND BEHAVIORS

When I'm thinking about the themes in a book, I try to think beyond the plot action. I know that themes are revealed in different ways. So, I ask myself these questions:
- Did the main character change over the course of the story?
- How did the main character respond to the conflict in the story?
- Has the main character come to understand something about themselves?
- Has the main character come to understand something about themselves, others, or the world around them?
- What big idea (or ideas) does the author leave me thinking about after I have finished reading the book?

Authors give us an opportunity to think about big ideas when we read. These themes are important lessons that help students learn about themselves and the world that they live in with others. I know that, as we think about these big ideas in the books that we read, it helps us better understand ourselves and the world that we live in, but it also prepares us to be citizens of the world.

RECORD THINKING AND LEARNING

After reading *the remember balloons*, you may want to reflect on how the author has led you to understand the theme. Here's how:
- Create a T-chart with *What I Notice* on the left side and *What It Means* on the right. Record how the author revealed the big ideas of what *the remember balloons* means and how the characters in the story evolved based on what was happening in their lives (Figure 8.7).
- After you've finished your reflection, take a look at what you have written and ponder the big question: What have you learned about yourself, your life, or the world from reading this book?

(continues)

L E S S O N CONTINUED

- If this book touched your heart, you might want to illustrate your own memories in *remember balloons*. What memories do you carry around with you that are special? They may be happy, sad, or just significant to you. Write one in each of your balloons. You may also color each balloon if you'd like. How might the colors enhance the memory contained in each balloon? Think about how each of your memories might be pieces of writing or stories you might tell. *The remember balloons* has taught us that our memories are treasures to keep for ourselves or to share with others. What will you do with your *remember balloons*? (See Figure 8.8.)

- As you are reading, think about how the author who has written the text you are reading has helped you think about a big idea. How do they hint at the theme through the character's development, the conflict or problems that they might be facing, and how they attempt to solve or overcome them? Also, what does the author leave you thinking about after you finish reading the text?

- Think about how you might do this for your readers in the texts that you write. What big ideas or themes are important to you? How might you share those with your readers through the texts that you create? Think about what you want to leave your readers thinking about after they finish reading a piece of your writing and how you do that. How might you do that more effectively based on what you learn from the authors you read?

Figure 8.7 Literacy Notebook Entry: Response to *the remember balloons*

Figure 8.8 Literacy Notebook Entry: Remember Balloons

WHAT'S NEXT?

Encourage conversations between your readers as they explore how these texts are crafted and then help them become authors of texts that will engage their readers to think about big ideas. Talking about the books they read and hear becomes the rehearsal for writing about reading as well as the preparation for writing their own pieces with messages for their readers. The more our students read, write, and think, the more they'll realize they have valuable messages to share with the world. Help them find their voice and then a way to share those big ideas with their readers through thoughtful, well-crafted texts.

BIG IDEA: STYLE

READING WORKSHOP	LITERACY WORKSHOP COMMON THREADS	WRITING WORKSHOP
	Style	
How does recognizing the different styles authors use to create and tell stories help me as a reader?	Which styles do I prefer?	What can I learn from an author's/ illustrator's style that I can use in my own writing?
How does noticing the style help me to better understand the plot, characters, and mood?	How do I develop my own unique style?	
	How does developing my own style help me as a reader, a writer, and a person?	How do the decisions I make about the selection and arrangement of my words or pictures impact the meaning?

What Experts Say About Understanding an Author's Writing Style

If each individual has their own personal style, then doesn't it make sense that so do the books students read and the pieces they write? Taking time during your workshop to reflect on the importance of style and what draws readers and writers to texts is important as your students are developing their own *literacy identities*. Your learners have already developed a collection of favorite books and authors. They can probably even show you pieces that they have written that are favorites of theirs. But now is the time to begin the conversation about what it is about those books and pieces that makes them favorites. What is it about a book or a piece of writing that sticks with us after we close the cover? What are the qualities of good writing that make an author's work something that we want to mimic in our own? These are often the elements of style—an important tool to add to our ever-growing literacy toolbox.

Style is often as important as the story itself, because it is what helps us *reflect* on a particular *aspect* of the story (Tunnell and Jacobs 2008). As our students reflect on the style of the books they read and even the texts they create, they think about how the words are crafted into the story on the page; they also think about how the illustrations complement the text or how they might move the story along on their own. The language, pictures, and development of the text often reflect the unique personality of the writer and are developed over time. This reminds our literacy learners that writing takes time, so be patient.

L E S S O N PRIMARY

STYLE: SENSING THE STYLE OF A STORY

FOCUS PHRASES	MENTOR TEXT SUGGESTION

- I read books by my favorite authors and illustrators.

- I think about what authors and illustrators do to make them my favorite.

- I use what I've learned from authors and illustrators when I write.

Blue (Seeger 2018)

Why We Chose This Book: From the cover illustration to the very last page, Laura Vaccaro Seeger's unique style helps create the changing moods of this story. The book begins with a dog and a baby boy sleeping on a blue blanket. We watch as the boy and dog grow up, the dog ages, and then, sadly, the dog passes away. On the next page, the young man meets a girl with the dog, and we're left to imagine what happens next. Readers have to look carefully at illustrations to infer what is happening in the story. Also, watch as the blue blanket becomes the dog's neckerchief.

Additional Mentor Text Suggestions for Style

- *Green* (Seeger 2012)
- *My Forest Is Green* (Lebeuf 2019)

ANCHOR LEARNING IN LITERATURE/CONVERSE TO GROW THINKERS AND LEARNERS

BEFORE READING

- Set a Purpose: I've noticed that some of you prefer to wear clothes from your favorite sports teams. Others have shirts with characters from movies or video games. A few of your outfits are decorated with butterflies, hearts, and rainbows. When we choose what we want to wear, that is one way we show our style. We all have unique styles that will grow and change as we do. Like us, authors and illustrators tell their stories in unique ways—in their own *style*. When we notice how a book makes us feel or the mood the author and illustrator created, we are noticing one part of their style. As we read *Blue*, we are going to focus on noticing the choices that Laura Vaccaro Seeger made and how they make us feel.
- Discuss the Book Cover: Look very carefully at the cover. What color is it? What else do you see? [Notice the dog paw print.] Why do you suppose Laura Vaccaro Seeger painted a paw print on the cover?

DURING READING

- "baby blue" page: How does this page make you feel? [Peaceful, sleepy.] What about the style of this page makes you feel this way? [As you continue reading, pause now and then to notice the feeling or mood the pages evoke.] Watch when I turn to the next page. I see that there is a hole cut in the page. This is called a *die-cut*. Let's notice if there are any more die-cut pages. Perhaps that is part of the author's style.

- "ocean blue" page: What do you notice about both the boy and the dog? [They are growing older.] Have we seen the blue scarf that is around the boy's neck somewhere else in the story? Let's go back and look.
- "my blue" page: The dog is tugging at the boy's scarf. I wonder who is going to get it.
- "silly blue" page: Now the blue blanket, scarf, is the dog's neckerchief.
- "true blue" page: How does this page make you feel? Do you have any predictions about what might happen next? Share them with your friend.

AFTER READING
- I wonder why Laura Vaccaro Seeger chose the word *Blue* for the title of this book and the color blue for the pages. Do you know any other meanings for the word *blue*?

DEMONSTRATE HABITS AND BEHAVIORS

As a reader, there are certain authors whose books I love to read again and again. I'm excited when they have a new book coming out because I know I'll probably like that book, too. Laura Vaccaro Seeger is one of those authors. I think she has a unique style. Let me go back through the book to show you two of the elements of style I notice in this book:
- Word Choice: Every page had only two words and one of them was blue. When you read through the pages without stopping, you also hear that they rhyme. So, she chose each word very carefully.
- Images: Every illustration was a two-page spread so I could see all the details of what was happening. On each spread, she changed the shade of blue so that each page turn had a different feeling, or mood. She also used die-cut pages, I don't see that very often in books. I loved how it made one illustration blend into the next one.

RECORD THINKING AND LEARNING

- In this book, the word *blue* had more than one meaning. Since word choice is an important part of style, I'm thinking it might be helpful to us as readers and writers if we wrote down other words that mean the same as *sad* or *blue* (Figure 8.9).
- I've gathered all of Laura Vaccaro Seeger's books in a basket. If you're interested, you can study the rest of her books to see if they have a similar style.

Figure 8.9 Anchor Chart: Other Words for *Sad*

WHAT'S NEXT?

As you continue to explore the elements of style with your literacy workshop learners, introduce students to authors and illustrators with unique styles. Your goal is to broaden their knowledge of authors and illustrators so that they are better able to self-select books that appeal to their personal tastes and begin to develop their own writing style. In addition to Laura Vaccaro Seeger, some authors that we've used to discuss the elements of style include Todd Parr, Micha Archer, and, of course, Mo Willems. Don't forget to include your own students' writing in your stack of exemplars. As you read aloud and confer with students, highlight and discuss the following:

- Words that create vivid mental images through sensory details
- Pages or passages that have a rhythm or flow
- Voiceful writing that brings the characters to life

IDEAS TO PONDER   ## IDEAS TO TRY

L E S S O N · INTERMEDIATE

STYLE: I LOVE THIS BOOK AND NOW I THINK I KNOW WHY

FOCUS PHRASES	MENTOR TEXT SUGGESTIONS

- I identify stylistic aspects of favorite books through their writing and illustrations.

- I develop my own writing style by using what I've learned from reading.

Poetree (Reynolds 2019)

Why We Chose This Book: Sylvia is so excited that spring is here that she decides to write a poem and tie it to the branch of her favorite tree. When she returns the next day, her poem is gone, and a new poem is in its place. Could it be that the tree is actually a magical Poetree? She decides to test the tree by leaving another poem to see what happens next. She is surprised to find out who the secret poet really is and a new friendship blossoms with poetry as its roots. Reynolds's stylistic choice to intersperse the children's poetry with the prose of the story offers a unique approach to study during literacy workshop.

Additional Mentor Text Suggestions for Style

- *How to Read a Book* (Alexander 2019)

- *The Panda Problem* (Underwood 2019c)

ANCHOR LEARNING IN LITERATURE/CONVERSE TO GROW THINKERS AND LEARNERS

BEFORE READING

- Set a Purpose: Have you ever thought about why some books are your favorites? Why you can't wait to read another book by your favorite author or illustrator? What is it about those books that you love? What is it that stays with you long after you close the cover or makes you want to reread it over and over again? We refer to this special quality as an author's or illustrator's *style*. Style is the way an author or illustrator creates a story that draws the reader into the experience in their own unique way. It is that uniqueness that makes you remember or want to read or reread the same book or similar books. *Style* is also what we, as writers, develop over time as we use the books that we love as mentor texts for our own writing.

- Discuss the Book Cover: As you look at the book cover, think about what choices both the author and the illustrator made to engage the reader and draw them into the story. Why do you think the author chose the title *Poetree* for the book? Why do you think the illustrator chose the colors that she used for the art on the cover? Based on these choices, what are you thinking about before we begin reading the story?

DURING READING

- As we read *Poetree*, we are going to think about how authors and illustrators help engage us in the books that we read. Sylvia is excited that winter is changing into spring and decides to share her poetry with her favorite tree. Let's notice how the story is shared with us as the readers through both the text and the illustrations.
- Why do you think Sylvia decided to hang her poem on the tree? How do the illustrations help you see what is happening to the characters, including how their feelings change?
- What happens when Sylvia thinks that the tree is writing poetry back to her? How does she feel?
- What happens when she learns that her tree is not a Poetree? How do the author and illustrator help us understand the characters' emotions at the end of the story?

AFTER READING

- Questions for Learners to Ponder:
  - » How did the author help the reader understand how the characters were thinking and feeling throughout the story?
  - » How did the illustrator create images to engage the reader and help them understand what was happening throughout the story?
  - » How did the style of both the author and the illustrator add to the understanding of the text?
  - » How did the style of both the author and the illustrator add to the enjoyment of the text?

DEMONSTRATE HABITS AND BEHAVIORS

- I've been pondering why I have favorite books, authors, and illustrators. What is it about their work that makes it so special to me and makes it something that I want to try in my own writing pieces? We've been discussing a variety of favorite books in our literacy workshop, and I'm wondering whether there is something that makes those texts and people stand out from all the others. I think that it might be the style of the work. Style is what makes authors or illustrators work unique or different from someone else's work. It is that quality that makes it stand out and makes it *identifiable*. As I'm reading, I'm going to make a list of what qualities I see in the books that I read that draw me in. As I recognize those qualities, then I'm going to think about how I might integrate those qualities from my reading into the texts that I write.

RECORD THINKING AND LEARNING

- After reading *Poetree* today, you might want to think about what qualities this text has that makes it engaging for you, as the reader. Record as many of them as you noticed in this text (Figure 8.10).

(continues)

L E S S O N CONTINUED

- Over the next several days, notice the different styles of the texts you're reading or writing. What is it that makes the text unique? Consider how the author's and illustrator's choices related to character development, language, structure, and theme make their work memorable. Capture some of your thinking in your notebook so you can share it with your classmates in case they, too, might want to read a book with that particular style. Studying the styles of others is also helpful as you develop your own unique style of writing. Don't you want to create texts that your readers will remember, unique only to you? Who will you be as a writer? What stylistic qualities will help your readers love your texts and want to reread them over and over again?

Figure 8.10   Literacy Notebook Entry: Noticing Author's Style

WHAT'S NEXT?

Continue to converse with your literacy learners about the texts that they are reading independently and encourage them to think about the styles the authors they are reading have developed over their writing careers. Help them understand that writing styles evolve over time and invite them to think about who they are as writers and their own individual *writing identities*. These conversations can also grow beyond teacher-student to student-student as learners begin to confer with one another about their writing and appreciate the unique perspectives they bring to their own texts. Sit back, enjoy, and appreciate who your literacy learners are becoming because of the reading, writing, and conversing they are doing!

IDEAS TO PONDER

IDEAS TO TRY

CHAPTER 9

Demonstration Lessons— Teaching the Elements of Nonfiction

Huddled in the corner of the classroom with pencils in hand, Moriah and Jordan are drawing diagrams of a giant squid. They've read and reread Candace Fleming's *Giant Squid* (2016) so many times, they almost have it memorized. For many readers, informational texts are as surprising and intriguing as stories. More and more nonfiction texts are available in unconventional formats such as narrative nonfiction, which seamlessly blends fiction and nonfiction to tell true stories of people or events with many of the same elements of fiction, including characters, setting, plot, and dialogue. Many nonfiction texts include visual images, such as photographs, captions, charts, and graphs, to focus readers' attention to help them process factual information (Stone 2019). As you and your students are exploring informational books, be confident that you are helping them develop critical thinking and reading skills. Take advantage of your interactions as learners explore their preferred topics to deepen their understanding of the natural world, the people who have helped shape history, and those who can inspire them today. For your writers, literacy workshop offers time to approach topics of interest with a "passionate curiosity" (Portalupi and Fletcher 2001, 7) and then to craft texts or create products to share their discoveries with others.

COMMON THREADS: BIG IDEAS FOR TEACHING THE ELEMENTS OF NONFICTION

To prepare children to be literate global citizens, we need to be intentional in teaching students to read and write informational texts (Duke and Bennett-Armistead 2003). The demonstration lessons in this chapter will help you do just that. By modeling the habits and behaviors of an inquisitive learner, you will encourage your students to follow their curiosities and stretch their minds through the parallel processes of reading and writing.

BIG IDEA: TOPIC

READING WORKSHOP	LITERACY WORKSHOP COMMON THREADS	WRITING WORKSHOP
	Topic	
How does reading a well-written nonfiction book spark my curiosity?	How do reading, writing, and talking about nonfiction texts help me better understand the topic?	How do I narrow my focus so that readers better understand the main idea?
How does using the nonfiction text features help me better understand the topic?	How does researching help me better determine a topic for my informational text or product?	How does adding nonfiction features help focus the reader's attention?

What the Experts Say About Investigating Intriguing Topics

Children are naturally inquisitive. They enter our classrooms brimming with questions every day. As their teachers, it is one of our responsibilities to surround them with a wealth of quality nonfiction literature and guide them as they find answers to topics of interest. Reading to find answers has an added benefit: it prompts more questions—questions that lead children to inquire, investigate, share, and ideally, act. For inquiry like this to be authentic, there must be *discovery* on the part of the learner and a transformation of that learning into something new—creating new knowledge or learning from their research (Fraser 2019). Literacy workshop is the place for curiosity and knowledge to flourish. A time for students to become like scientists and poets who "search the world and find knowledge and wonder in equal parts" (Salas 2019, n.p.).

When guiding learners to seek out topics that spark wonder, encourage them to pursue ideas that not only interest them but also drive them to read, write, and research (Harvey 1998). Connecting topics to life experiences is one way to make research meaningful to students. During learning time, confer with readers as they find nonfiction books on topics that meet their specific interests. Encourage them to spend some time doing what William Zinsser (1988) calls "exploratory writing" in their literacy notebook—freewriting about the topic to explore new learning and generate questions. Once they've become experts on the topic, it's up to them to decide how they might share their new learning with others. It's important to note that their discoveries about a topic, particularly those that prompt "passionate curiosity," may lead your students to take action. We've seen many literacy learners extend their newfound expertise of a topic far beyond the classroom to social action (Ahmed 2018). Organizing food drives, fund-raisers, or letter-writing campaigns are just a few ways that our students enter the world of literate citizenship.

L E S S O N PRIMARY

TOPIC: ZOOMING IN ON INTERESTING TOPICS

FOCUS PHRASES

- I figure out the main topic in books.

- I learn more about interesting topics.

- I focus my writing on a main topic.

MENTOR TEXT SUGGESTION

Apex Predators
(Jenkins 2017a)

Why We Chose This Book: When we are looking for enticing nonfiction texts to share with our learners, Steve Jenkins is one of our go-to authors. Like all of his books, *Apex Predators* draws readers in with his detailed torn- and cut-paper collage illustrations and fascinating facts. As a mentor text for literacy workshop, this book offers readers enough facts about a variety of deadly animals to pique their interest and provides a model for writers who want to home in on the most significant facts about their topics.

Additional Mentor Text Suggestions for Topic

- *Cute as an Axolotl: Discovering the World's Most Adorable Animals* (Keating 2018)

- *Look Again: Secrets of Animal Camouflage* (Jenkins 2019)

ANCHOR LEARNING IN LITERATURE/CONVERSE TO GROW THINKERS AND LEARNERS

BEFORE READING

- Set a Purpose: As we read nonfiction texts, it is smart to think about the main topic of the book or section. Luckily, writers give us clues to help us do this. Noticing the clues will help you remember the important facts and, when you're writing nonfiction, give the same clues to your readers. Jenkins starts giving us hints to the main topic right on the cover of *Apex Predators*.

- Discuss the Book Cover: Notice where he put the title of the book! [In the mouth of the animal.] Why would he do that? Do you see the words at the top of the page? They are called the *subtitle*. The subtitle of a nonfiction book often tells us more about the main topic of the book. This subtitle reads, "The World's Deadliest Hunters, Past and Present." Hmm! I'm inferring that apex predators are hunting animals. Would you agree? Let's continue reading to see if we're right.

DURING READING

[With a book like *Apex Predators*, where each page is about a different topic, we typically read just the first few pages for our demonstration lesson, enough to make our point. Then, if students' interest remains high, we continue reading the rest of the book a bit at a time during future read-aloud experiences or put it into students' hands to explore on their own.]

- "Predators are animals that kill and eat other animals" page: Did you notice that Steve Jenkins did two things to prepare readers? First, he explains the definition of an apex predator. Second, he tells us exactly what we will be learning about in this book. This is called an *introduction*. Many nonfiction books have an *introduction* to help readers get their brain ready to learn new information. That's something nonfiction writers, like you, do.
- "The **Komodo dragon** is the world's deadliest lizard." page: Wow! There is a lot to notice and learn on this page. Let's look at one part at a time:
- What did you learn about Komodo dragons after reading the text? What would you say is the most important thing to remember about Komodo dragons? [They are the world's largest lizards.] Notice that Steve Jenkins wrote that sentence first. It is called the *topic sentence*. The *topic sentence* is another cue nonfiction authors often give to help us figure out the main idea.
- See the green band at the top of the page? It reads, "MODERN-DAY PREDATOR." Remember the introduction? Share with your neighbor an example of a modern-day predator. I'm guessing that the band at the top of the pages with predators from the past might be a different color. Let's look to see. How does the color code help us as a reader? Could you do this as writers?
- Why does he show a silhouette of a man and a Komodo dragon? I see that a Komodo dragon is ten feet long. It is taller than an average man. How does this comparison help you as a reader? How might you use this idea as writers?

[Each page in *Apex Predators* follows the same format. The number of pages you need to read and study together will depend on how experienced your readers are with reading and writing nonfiction text. We would suggest studying no more than two or three pages during each demonstration lesson.]

AFTER READING
- What are some of the clues we noticed to help us figure out the main idea?

DEMONSTRATE HABITS AND STRATEGIES

As a reader of nonfiction, I use clues like we did today to focus on the main topic and remember the most important details. I know I will not be able to remember everything. So, I think about what I learned that I would like to share with others. When I go home tonight, I might tell my family something like this: "Today, I read a book about apex predators. They are at the top of the food chain. The one that was the most fascinating to me was the Komodo dragon because they are giant lizards. I'm glad I don't live where they live!" Now I'm really curious about Komodo dragons. Does that ever happen to you after you read a nonfiction book? When I'm curious about a topic that I've read, I try to find some other books or information about the topic, do some research, and share with others what I've learned. That's one of the many things you can do during literacy workshop learning time.

(continues)

L E S S O N CONTINUED

RECORD THINKING AND LEARNING

I learned a lot about apex predators from reading a few pages of Jenkins's book. Sometimes drawing or writing in my notebook helps me remember what I've read (Figure 9.1). So, I'm going to write what I learned in the introduction and make a place to write down the animals that I might want to read or write about during learning time. If this book was interesting to you, you might want to study it a bit more. Maybe you can form a research group and report back to us about apex predators.

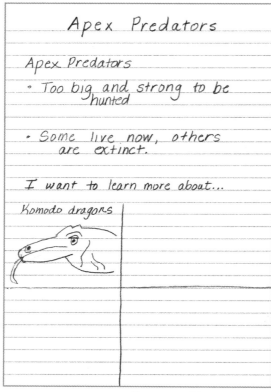

Figure 9.1 Maria's Literacy Notebook Entry: *Apex Predators*

Figure 9.2 First Graders Comparing Sizes of Apex Predators

WHAT'S NEXT?

When you read aloud books like *Apex Predators,* you may have students who can't get enough and want to dig deeper. For instance, when Maria read this to her first graders, she had a group of children who wanted to compare the size of each predator. During learning time, they collaborated to create a chart of all the animals and their sizes to share with their classmates and other interested kids in the school (Figures 9.2 and 9.3). Capitalizing on opportunities such as these will expand your students' background knowledge and prepare them to tackle a broader range of topics in their reading and writing.

Figure 9.3   First Graders' Apex Predator Chart

L E S S O N INTERMEDIATE

TOPIC: RESEARCHING AND SHARING INTERESTING FACTS TO CHANGE MY WORLD

FOCUS PHRASES	MENTOR TEXT SUGGESTION

- I read about interesting topics.

- I identify topics I'm curious about to research.

- I share my discoveries with others.

- I integrate information from others with my discoveries to create new knowledge.

Don't Let Them Disappear: 12 Endangered Species Across the Globe (Clinton 2019)

Why We Chose This Book: Through the course of one day, readers learn about twelve animals from around the world, including their endangered status, and the reasons these animals are facing extinction. After the perils of the animals are discussed, solutions are presented to help reduce endangerment before it is too late! The call-to-action at the end of the book prompts students to do something with the facts they've learned.

Text Suggestions for Topic

- *Little Dreamers: Visionary Women Around the World* (Harrison 2018)

- *Enough! 20 Protesters Who Changed America* (Easton 2018)

ANCHOR LEARNING IN LITERATURE/CONVERSE TO GROW THINKERS AND LEARNERS

BEFORE READING

- Set a Purpose: Today, we are going to think about how learners choose topics to research, how they might further explore those topics through their writing, and then how they share their discoveries with others. Chelsea Clinton wrote this book to teach us about an important topic and how it impacts our world. As you listen to *Don't Let Them Disappear,* you may get ideas for your own research, writing, or both.
- Discuss the Book Cover: Take a look at the cover of this book. What do you notice about the illustration? What animals do you see? What do you think they might have in common? How do you think the animals on the cover connect to the title of the book?

DURING READING

- Notice how the author begins the book. How do you think the key on the first page of the book will help you understand the information presented throughout the text? How might you use a feature like this in your own nonfiction writing?

- What topics are discussed throughout the text? Why do you think Chelsea Clinton chose these twelve animals? What kinds of information did she share about each animal? Why do you suppose she repeated the phrase "don't let them disappear" on each page?
- What did you learn about these animals? At the end of the book, she ends with the following statement: "Let's make a pledge as fellow inhabitants of Planet Earth, that we won't let any of these species disappear." Why do you think she chose to end the book with that pledge? What does it mean to you? As a citizen of the world, what could you do to honor this pledge?

AFTER READING

- Questions for Learners to Ponder:
  » How do I use nonfiction texts to help spark ideas for my own informational research and writing?
  » How does writing or talking about a topic help me better understand it and narrow my focus prior to creating a product?
  » Why is nonfiction reading important in helping me understand the world and my responsibility to it?

DEMONSTRATE HABITS AND BEHAVIORS

Reading nonfiction books like *Don't Let Them Disappear* helps me gather topic ideas for my writing. I enjoy learning about animals. This book gave me information about a variety of endangered animals and made me think about how I can help them. Other places that I get topics for my writing are

- thinking about what I am learning about in science or social studies,
- talking to others about their interests or expertise, and
- keeping my senses open and noticing what is happening around me.

There are so many ideas there that I am either learning about now or might be interested in learning more about in the future. All I have to do is *notice* them and then take a moment to *jot* down those topics in my notebook. Then, when I have some time to write or research, I have a collection of ideas to choose from during literacy workshop time.

RECORD THINKING AND LEARNING

During literacy workshop time, think about a topic that you might be interested in doing some research and writing about during the next few days. You may want to create a product to share with others or you may just want to gather some information to save for your own learning (Figure 9.4). Your topic may be based on a book that we have shared together, or it may be an idea that you have been thinking about learning on your own.

(continues)

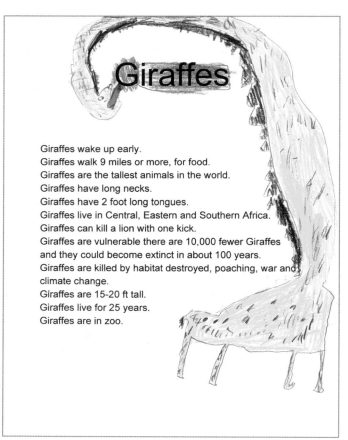

Giraffes

Giraffes wake up early.
Giraffes walk 9 miles or more, for food.
Giraffes are the tallest animals in the world.
Giraffes have long necks.
Giraffes have 2 foot long tongues.
Giraffes live in Central, Eastern and Southern Africa.
Giraffes can kill a lion with one kick.
Giraffes are vulnerable there are 10,000 fewer Giraffes
and they could become extinct in about 100 years.
Giraffes are killed by habitat destroyed, poaching, war and
climate change.
Giraffes are 15-20 ft tall.
Giraffes live for 25 years.
Giraffes are in zoo.

Figure 9.4
Literacy Notebook Entry: Independent Research Writing

WHAT'S NEXT?

As students are generating topic idea lists, encourage them to share their ideas with you and with each other, adding to their lists as they are conversing with others. Helping learners understand that their informational topic lists will continue to grow—just like their lists of narrative story ideas—will help them always have ideas for their informational writing. Developing a classroom community where curiosity and collaboration are celebrated will help prepare your learners to research their world!

BIG IDEA: STRUCTURE

READING WORKSHOP	LITERACY WORKSHOP COMMON THREADS	WRITING WORKSHOP
	Structure	
What is this text teaching me? How does figuring out the nonfiction text structure help me better understand the topic?	How do noticing, reading, writing, and discussing a variety of nonfiction text structures help improve my ability to learn new things?	How can I apply what I've learned about various text structures to my own writing? How does selecting a text structure to best match my purpose and audience help me create a meaningful informational text or product?

What Experts Say About Understanding Nonfiction Text Structures

Structure is the inner workings of a text. In nonfiction texts, the clear arrangement of information helps readers stay engaged with the topic. Selecting the best organizational structure to communicate information is one of the challenges of writing nonfiction. To support your young nonfiction writers, immerse them in well-organized informational texts to use as exemplars as they choose ways to shape their facts. It is well worth your instructional time to stop and notice the structures of texts and then envision what writers can learn from the same texts to use in their own works (Dorfman and Cappelli 2009) (Figure 9.5). When you capitalize on these opportunities, you inspire learners to approach informational writing in creative ways. Studying texts also encourages readers to reach for nonfiction texts that have innovative structures.

When you study various ways that nonfiction authors arrange their texts, it prompts learners to consider how best to present their own information. This not only prepares students to write texts but also presents options for sharing their learning in other creative ways such as sketchnotes, posters, slide presentations, and videos. As they begin to take their learning public, they become *literary scholars* (Graves 1983) and assume the responsibilities that go along with that published work. Empowering students to make decisions about research topics, which big ideas they will share, their audience, and in what format they will present that information increases their passion and enthusiasm for their topic and their desire to take their learning public.

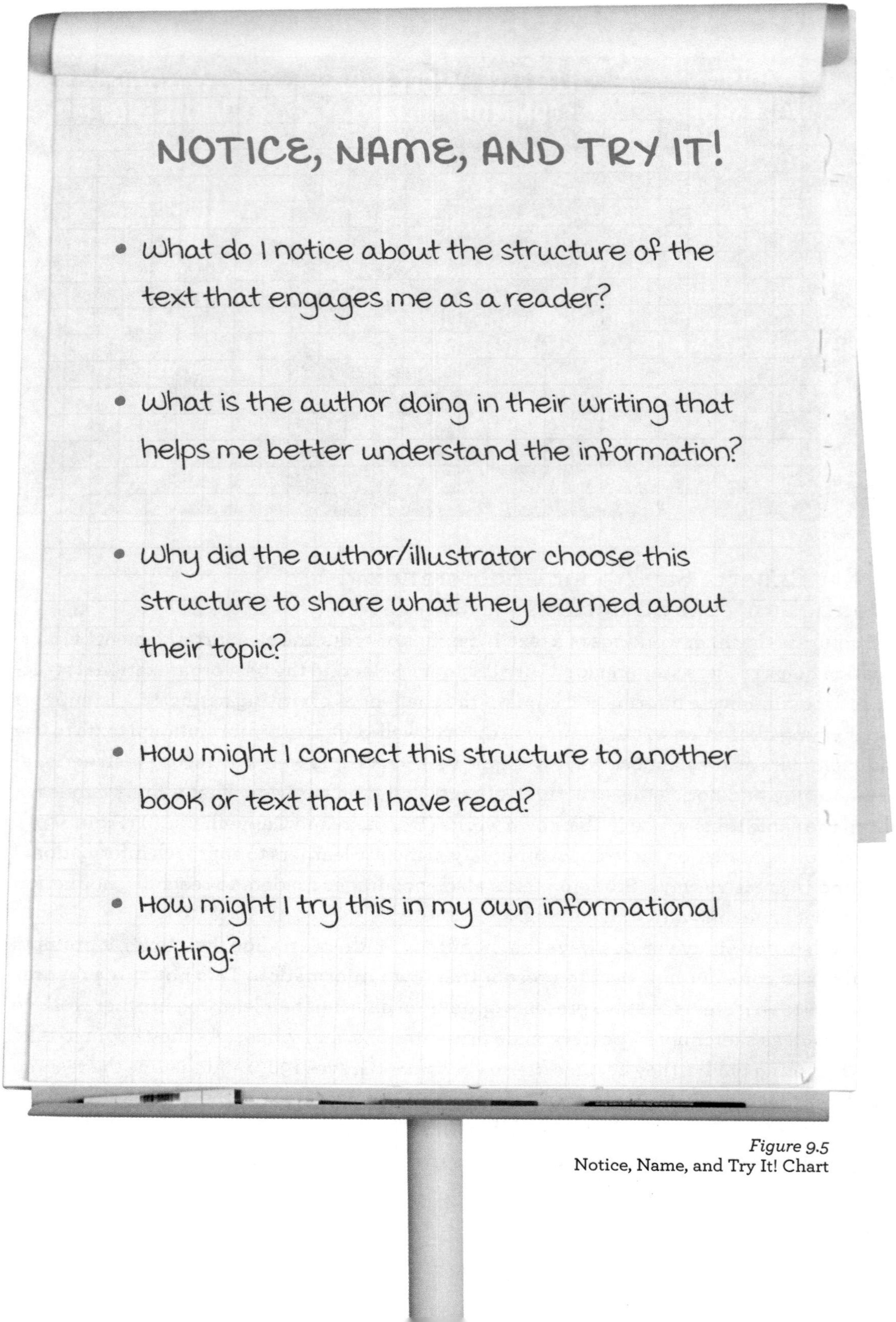

NOTICE, NAME, AND TRY IT!

- What do I notice about the structure of the text that engages me as a reader?

- What is the author doing in their writing that helps me better understand the information?

- Why did the author/illustrator choose this structure to share what they learned about their topic?

- How might I connect this structure to another book or text that I have read?

- How might I try this in my own informational writing?

Figure 9.5
Notice, Name, and Try It! Chart

IDEAS TO PONDER

IDEAS TO TRY

L E S S O N PRIMARY

STRUCTURE: TUNING IN TO NONFICTION TEXT STRUCTURES

FOCUS PHRASES   MENTOR TEXT SUGGESTION

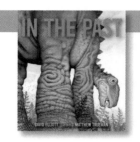

- I figure out how nonfiction texts are organized.

- I organize my information in different ways.

In the Past (Elliott 2018)
Why We Chose This Book: Kids who dig dinosaurs will pore over the pictures and poems in this book. The poems are organized in chronological order by geologic era from the Cambrian to the Quaternary period. Back matter gives pronunciations and additional information about each creature. The chronological structure of this nonfiction text is accessible and replicable for early readers and writers. Also, the author's choice of poetry as a vehicle to share information broadens learners' awareness of innovative ways to deliver information.

Additional Mentor Text Suggestions for Structure

- *Hey Ho, to Mars We'll Go! A Space-Age Version of "The Farmer in the Dell"* (Lendroth 2018a)

- *Snails Are Just My Speed* (K. McCloskey 2018)

ANCHOR LEARNING IN LITERATURE/CONVERSE TO GROW THINKERS AND LEARNERS

BEFORE READING

- Set a Purpose: Writers organize nonfiction texts in different ways. They put their ideas together in a way that best matches their topics. Sometimes information is organized in time order, or *chronologically.* Can you think of any topics that it would make sense to organize in time order? Have you already read any books organized chronologically?

- Discuss the Book Cover: Can you infer from the cover what this book might be about? Why do you think the author chose the title *In the Past*? If you were going to write a book about dinosaurs how might you organize your information? As we're learning, let's think about how David Elliott chose to organize the information in this book.

DURING READING

[With a book like *In the Past*, where each page is about a different topic, we typically read just the first few pages for our demonstration lesson, enough to make our point. Then, if students' interest remains high, we continue reading the rest of the book a bit at a time during future read-aloud experiences or put it in students' hands to explore on their own.]

- "Trilobite" page: What do you notice about this text? [It's a poem.] Interesting! David Elliott chose to share facts about prehistoric animals through poetry. Sometimes in nonfiction books, the authors give us more information at the end of the book. It makes sense that the information on the pages in the back of the book is called *back matter.* Let's check to see whether there is back matter that tells us more about the trilobite. [David Elliott's additional information is helpful to read because he explains why he chose certain facts to create each poem.]

- "Astraspis" page: Hmm! Another poem. Was it helpful to read the back matter to understand the first poem? Perhaps we should try that again. I also notice this rectangle at the bottom of the page that read, "Ordovician Period." It's different from the one on the first page. Let's flip through the book to see what happens with these rectangles. [Notice that the pages are organized in chronological order by time periods.]

AFTER READING

- Do you think chronological order was a helpful structure for you as a reader? Why or why not?
- What other ways might David Elliott have organized this text?

DEMONSTRATE HABITS AND BEHAVIORS

[For this demonstration, we suggest gathering a few nonfiction texts as exemplars of other text structures. A few are listed in Figure 9.6.] When I'm reading a nonfiction text to help me remember what I've read, I think about how the text is organized. Because *In the Past* was organized in time order, it helps me to remember which creatures lived long, long, long ago and which were around more recently. Did you know that nonfiction authors organize their texts in other ways? I found some of my other favorite nonfiction texts to show you what I mean. [In the days that follow, do a quick book talk of the other titles in your stack, and highlight their organizational structures.]

RECORD THINKING AND LEARNING

Think about a structure that might be helpful as you write down your facts. Feel free to take one of these texts to study as you decide how you might want to organize your information.

WHAT'S NEXT?

Nell Duke (2014) reminds us that it is more important to teach students to figure out how a particular informational text is structured than to have them memorize the most commonly used informational text structures (description, sequence, problem/solution, cause and effect, and compare/contrast). To that end, as you continue to read aloud informational texts and your students independently read and write their own, focus your teaching points on uncovering the structure of the text.

Figure 9.6   Exemplar Texts for Nonfiction Text Structures

ALPHABET AND COUNTING BOOK STRUCTURE
100 Bugs! A Counting Book (Narita 2018)

The Icky Bug Alphabet Book (Pallotta 1986) [Jerry Pallotta has a few other engaging nonfiction alphabet books.]

COMPARE AND CONTRAST
Cats vs. Dogs (Carney 2011)

Whale vs. Giant Squid (Who Would Win?) (Pallotta 2012) [There are many other books in this series.]

QUESTION-ANSWER
What Will Grow? (Ward 2017)

Who Am I? An Animal Guessing Game (Jenkins 2017b)

SEQUENCE
From Caterpillar to Butterfly (Heiligman 1996)

From Tadpole to Frog (Pfeffer 1994)

L E S S O N INTERMEDIATE

STRUCTURE: BUILDING NONFICTION TEXTS TO INFORM AND ENGAGE READERS

FOCUS PHRASES   MENTOR TEXT SUGGESTION

- I identify text structures in nonfiction books.

- I notice how structures help me better understand nonfiction texts.

- I create nonfiction texts that integrate different text structures.

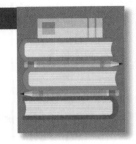

When Angels Sing: The Story of Rock Legend Carlos Santana (Mahin 2018)

Why We Chose This Book: Carlos Santana grew up listening to his father play the violin in a small town in Mexico. He fell in love with the music his father played; it was as if he were hearing angels sing. At an early age, he decided he wanted to play music that would also make the angels sing. He tried the violin and the clarinet, and finally began to play the guitar. He and his family moved to the United States, and although life was difficult for him, it was there that he discovered jazz. Throughout tumultuous times, he developed his own style of Afro-Cuban music and finally was able to hear the angels sing. Mahin's use of chronological structure with milestone dates blending into the vibrant illustrations and his choice of second-person voice provide a jumping-off point for literacy workshop learners' exploration of nonfiction text structures.

Additional Mentor Text Suggestions for Structure

- *Go for the Moon: A Rocket, a Boy, and the First Moon Landing* (Gall 2019)

- *How to Be an Elephant: Growing Up in the African Wild* (Roy 2017)

ANCHOR LEARNING IN LITERATURE/CONVERSE TO GROW THINKERS AND LEARNERS

BEFORE READING

- Set a Purpose: We are going to study *When Angels Sing* through both our readers' eyes and our writers' eyes to help us understand the choices that Michael Mahin made to select the structures for this book. Noticing the structure of a nonfiction text is important for a few reasons. The structure is designed to engage the reader and help them better understand the information. Structure is also important for us as writers, because it gives us an organizational framework for sharing information. Let's look into how one author created a biography of an immigrant musician in a unique and memorable way. The structure he uses may be one that you want to try out in your own writing.

- Discuss the Book Cover: Take a look at the cover. What do you notice about the illustration? Why do you think that the illustrator chose to use the colors that he did? Now read the title of the book. What do you suppose the title means? Remember the title. It will be important to both the subject of this book, Carlos Santana, and his life story.

DURING READING

- As we read *When Angels Sing: The Story of Rock Legend Carlos Santana*, we are going to think about how the author tells Carlos's story. What do you notice about how the author tells his story? Who is the story about? How do you know? Why does the author choose to tell the story this way?
- When does Carlos's love of music begin? What is he looking for as he plays?
- How does Carlos's music evolve as he grows? Who and/or what influences his music?
- When Carlos and his family move to America, what is his experience like? How does he feel about being an immigrant in a new country?
- Did Carlos ever hear *the angels sing*? When and why did that happen? What do you think we can learn from his life experiences?

AFTER READING

- Questions for Learners to Ponder:
  - » How did the author's choice of nonfiction text structure help me better understand the information?
  - » How do authors use nonfiction text structures to help them organize their information?
  - » What are some of the different nonfiction text structures I might use?

DEMONSTRATE HABITS AND BEHAVIORS

As a nonfiction reader, I'm always on the lookout for books that tell true stories or factual information using unique text structures. I notice I'm more engaged when learning about people, places, and things if the author uses a structure that does not read like a textbook. As a writer, when I notice text structure I haven't seen before, it challenges me to think about new ways to creatively structure my information. When I do this, I'm crafting texts that are more interesting for my readers, and it is also stretching my abilities as a writer.

RECORD THINKING AND LEARNING

- To record my thinking about what I've learned from this book or other books like it, I usually make a T-chart in my literacy notebook. For this book, I will write *Notice/Why Important* on the left side and *Facts About Him* on the right. Then, I reread or skim the book to add ideas to my chart. If you're interested in exploring the book in this way, it will be right here (Figure 9.7).
- If not, you could think about someone that you'd like to research, and then tell their life story using a unique text structure. Think back to the example we looked at today in *When Angels Sing*, where author Michael Mahin used both a timeline structure and second-person narrative to tell Carlos Santana's story. You might want to use what you've learned to experiment with chronological structure (Figure 9.8).

(continues)

L E S S O N CONTINUED

- Perhaps you've noticed other structures in the nonfiction books that you've read. You could go back to those books as mentor texts for your writing. Literacy learners are constantly going back and forth between reading and writing to think about what structures they might want to try as they research and share their information.

When Angels Sing	
Notice / Why Important	Facts About Him
Someone else is telling the story it is not in first person. The book is kind of like a Timeline, because theres a date on each page. It Tells us how old he is. Pictures show us he is getting older. He would not give up, he ran all the way home to improve.	His father was someone who plays the violen. Carlos was born in 1947. He did not like the sound of Jazz at all he didnt like the sound of violen. He finally got a guitar, really liked it, played songs to the radio. He couldn't read the english tests that they were giving him.

Figure 9.7   Literacy Notebook Entry: *When Angels Sing* Response

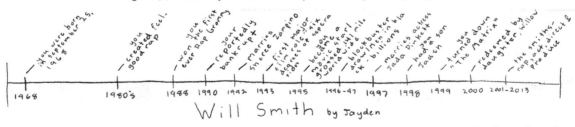

Figure 9.8   Literacy Notebook Entry: Timeline of Will Smith's Life

WHAT'S NEXT?

Gather and continue to share nonfiction texts with unique organizational frameworks to further enrich your students' knowledge of text structures. When you increase the amount of informational texts in your classroom, students are more likely to match their interests and answer their own questions. Create and share the anchor chart found in Figure 9.9 to remind your students to intentionally view the structures of nonfiction texts with their readers', writers', and literacy learners' eyes.

EYES CHART

READER'S EYES

How is this text structured to help me better understand the facts?

How do the key words help me identify the text structure?

How do the images support the text so that I can better understand the facts?

How do the words and images work together to support the understanding of the information?

LITERACY LEARNERS' EYES

How can thinking about texts help me appreciate how they are both structured by authors and consumed by readers?

What can I learn from these texts that extends my experiences as a learner to prepare myself for research?

What can I learn from these texts that extends my thinking about others and the world around me?

WRITERS' EYES

How might I re-create this text structure in my own nonfiction writing?

How can I use key words when creating my own nonfiction texts?

How might I use images in my own writing to enhance its meaning?

What can I learn from this author that I can add to my own style of nonfiction writing?

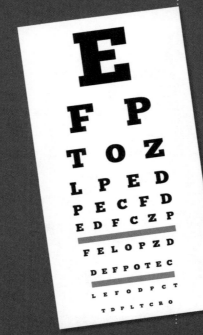

Figure 9.9
Viewing Nonfiction Text Structures Through Literacy Learners' Eyes Chart

IDEAS TO PONDER	IDEAS TO TRY

BIG IDEA: AUTHOR'S PURPOSE

READING WORKSHOP	LITERACY WORKSHOP COMMON THREADS	WRITING WORKSHOP
	Author's Purpose	
What clues does the author give me to their purpose for writing the text? How does figuring out the author's purpose help me better understand the topic?	How does figuring out the author's purpose help me understand how others might influence my thinking? How does considering the author's purpose influence my actions or reactions?	What clues can I give my readers to indicate my purpose for writing the text? How does having a clear purpose and audience help me create meaningful and engaging nonfiction texts?

What Experts Say About Determining the Author's Purpose

Why would an author choose to write a nonfiction book rather than a fiction one? What motivates them to write a biographical account of a person's life instead of historical fiction? Authors who write nonfiction books are curious individuals. They investigate topics about which they are *passionate*. As they write, they aim to leave their readers thinking about *big ideas* and, perhaps, acting based on what they've learned. Determining the author's purpose is an important skill for readers to understand and writers to consider as they delve into nonfiction during literacy workshop.

As nonfiction texts have evolved, so have the purposes that writers choose for sharing information with others. Compelling nonfiction texts have themes related to real-life information that help learners *make meaning* from and *mediate* their world (Ahmed 2015). When students are reading a biography about Rachel Carson and understand that the author wants them to think about their impact on the environment, they are comprehending the message and may be prompted to mediate their world by making more earth-friendly decisions. To determine the purpose of the text, readers engage in reflective inquiry—viewing the text through a critical lens by asking, "What do I think this author wants me to know, consider, or do?" On the flip side, writers ask a similar question: "What do I want my readers to know, consider, or do?" When learners have the opportunity to view an author's purpose from both the readers' and the writers' perspectives, they clearly see how it impacts the way in which we process and produce texts.

L E S S O N PRIMARY

AUTHOR'S PURPOSE: FIGURING OUT THE AUTHOR'S PURPOSE

FOCUS PHRASES

- I wonder about why the author wrote the book.

- I think about what the author wants me to learn, ponder, or do.

- I keep my reasons in mind when I'm writing nonfiction books.

MENTOR TEXT SUGGESTION

Snowman – Cold = Puddle: Spring Equations (Salas 2019)

Why We Chose This Book: In this unique, brainteasing book, readers discover the science and poetry behind the processes of nature that occur as winter turns to spring. Each page features a word equation and a brief, poetic scientific description that explains the equation. Laura Purdie Salas shares her purpose for writing this book in the author's note: "I hope you notice how our world changes every day all around us."

Additional Mentor Text Suggestions for Author's Purpose

- *Lovely Beasts: The Surprising Truth* (Gardner 2018)

- *Sea Bear: A Journey for Survival* (Moore 2019)

ANCHOR LEARNING IN LITERATURE/CONVERSE TO GROW THINKERS AND LEARNERS

BEFORE READING

- Set a Purpose: Did you know that authors write nonfiction books for different purposes? Thinking about the author's purpose for writing a nonfiction book is like figuring out the big idea, or theme, in a fiction book. After reading a nonfiction book, we can ask ourselves, "What did the author want us to learn, ponder, make, or do after reading the book?"
- Discuss the Book Cover: Look at the unique title of this book. It's an equation! We usually see equations during math, not on the cover of a book. Look at the illustration and tell a friend what you think the equation means. Did you notice that the illustrator, Micha Archer, made her pictures in a unique way? She used collage, which means she cut and tore pieces of paper and put them together very carefully to make this beautiful scene. Isn't that amazing?

DURING READING

- [With a book like *Snowman – Cold = Puddle*, where each page is about a different topic, we typically read just the first few pages for our demonstration lesson, enough to make our point. Then, if students' interest remains high, we continue reading the rest of the book a bit at a time during future read-aloud experiences or put it into students' hands to explore on their own.]

- "science + poetry = surprise" page: Here Laura Purdie Salas gives us a hint about one of her purposes for writing this book. I think that she wants us to look at our world like both scientists and poets. What do scientists do when they look at nature? How about poets?
- "EARLY SPRING" *page*: I'm going to read the equation. Then, I want you to look at the picture to see whether you can figure out what the equation means. Talk with a friend. Now read the author's explanation to see whether her reasons match your thinking or were a bit different.

[Continue in the same fashion as time and student interest dictate.]

AFTER READING
- What are you learning about in this book?
- As a reader, what were you having to do to understand Laura Purdie Salas's equations? [Think. Look at the illustrations. Read the explanation. Talk to a friend.]
- Why do you think she wrote this book? What was her purpose? Do you think she wanted us to learn, ponder, make, or do something? Did she want us to do more than one thing?

DEMONSTRATE HABITS AND BEHAVIORS

As a reader, I like to try to figure out the author's purpose. It is like being a detective. I can use clues from the book and from other places to help me. Here are some of the places that I can look for clues:

- Back matter. In *Snowman - Cold = Puddle* Laura Purdie Salas writes us an author's note and, at the end, gives us a hint when she says, "I hope you notice how our world changes every day all around us." Sometimes authors will include more information in the back of the book to give clues about why they wrote about a topic.
- Author's backflap biography. Her biography (or *bio* for short) says that she loves spring and poetry. It makes sense that she would write a book that combines the two.
- Author website. Sometimes, when you learn more about the author, you can get clues to their purpose for writing a book.
- After reading thoughts or actions. When I'm done reading a book, I consider what it left me thinking about or wanting to do, which is often a clue to the author's purpose.

RECORD THINKING AND LEARNING

Some of you had so much fun figuring out the equations in this book that I thought you might like to try some of your own. I made a paper to help organize your thinking or you can write them in your literacy notebook (see Figure 9.10 and Appendix 17 in the Online Resources).

L E S S O N CONTINUED

WHAT'S NEXT?

While reading aloud or conferring with readers about nonfiction books, help them to access the different parts of the book and electronic resources that Maria outlined as she was demonstrating her habits and behaviors. The more adept children become at considering the author's purpose, the better able they will be at critically reading nonfiction texts both in print and online.

Name: Shreya   Class: IJW

My Summer Equation
Inspired by
Snowman—Cold = Puddle ~ Spring Equations
By: Laura Purdie Salas

bug x bug x bug = army

I went to Florida. They're a lot of bugs so thats why I did army of bugs.

Figure 9.10
Literacy Notebook Entry: An Equation

IDEAS TO PONDER

IDEAS TO TRY

L E S S O N   INTERMEDIATE

AUTHOR'S PURPOSE: CONSIDERING THE AUTHOR'S PURPOSE

FOCUS PHRASES   MENTOR TEXT SUGGESTION

- I consider why authors create texts.

- I have a purpose for creating texts.

- I consider how authors' purposes impact my life and my world.

What Can a Citizen Do? (Eggers 2018)
Why We Chose This Book: Citizenship begins in your own backyard. It begins by helping those around you and thinking about others. We often think that citizenship happens in big moments when you step into the voting booth or you volunteer to make your community better when you grow up. This book reminds readers that social responsibility happens even for the youngest citizens in small, but powerful, ways.

Additional Mentor Text Suggestions for Author's Purpose

- *Peaceful Fights for Equal Rights* (Sanders 2018)

- *Raise Your Hand* (Tapper 2019)

ANCHOR LEARNING IN LITERATURE/CONVERSE TO GROW THINKERS AND LEARNERS

BEFORE READING

- Set a Purpose: Why do authors write books? Is it just to entertain you, to teach you information, or is it something more? One of the decisions that writers make when creating a text is what they want people to think about during and after they finish reading. We often refer to this as *author's purpose*, but you will see that illustrators also influence what readers think about during their time with a text. Today, we are going to interact with a text called *What Can a Citizen Do?* As we are reading, ponder what the author and the illustrator may have been hoping you'd think about when they were creating it and what meaning you would take away from their text after finishing it.
- Discuss the Book Cover: Let's begin by thinking about why the author chose a question as the title of the book: *What Can a Citizen Do?* What do you think that question means? Now take a look at the illustration. What do you notice about what the characters have in their hands? How do you think it might relate to the title?

DURING READING

- What do you notice about what the characters are doing throughout the book? What are some of the activities that they are participating in both individually and with each other? What do you think is motivating them to do these things?

- How do the characters throughout the book make their community a better place?
- What is a citizen? How do all of the behaviors demonstrated throughout this text demonstrate citizenship?

AFTER READING

- Questions for Learners to Ponder:
  - » What different purposes do authors have when creating nonfiction texts?
  - » How do authors influence me through the texts that they create?
  - » How can I create texts that help readers think about others and the world?

DEMONSTRATE HABITS AND BEHAVIORS

I notice that Dave Eggers crafted a text to make me think about how citizenship is a responsibility that all of us have, not just grown-ups. Before reading this book, I mainly thought of citizenship as something related to adults—for example, when we make a *choice* about voting for our political leaders, such as president, senators, mayors, and even school board members. After reading this book, I'm rethinking my original idea of citizenship. His book made me realize that citizenship is about our daily choices and actions. When we help others in our community,

like our friends and our neighbors, we are being responsible citizens. So, I'm inferring that this is what Dave Eggers set out to do when writing this book. I'm reminded that through their books authors can reinforce, change, or even offer us new thinking about big ideas and our place in the world.

RECORD THINKING AND LEARNING

I did quite a bit of reflecting while reading *What Can a Citizen Do?* Maybe you also have some thoughts swirling around in your head that you want to record in your literacy notebook (Figure 9.11). Now that you have some ideas about what being a citizen means to you, choose one of your ideas and share with a partner how you might be an active citizen in your community by doing this. What would you do? Why is your idea important to you? How would it make a difference in your community?

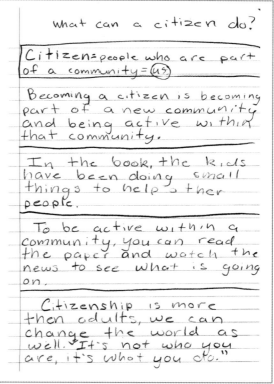

Figure 9.11 Literacy Notebook Entry: The Meaning of Citizenship

(continues)

L E S S O N CONTINUED

WHAT'S NEXT?

As your learners immerse themselves in nonfiction texts and read information via print and electronic sources, it is essential for them to realize that authors write that content with a particular purpose in mind. Providing students with questions to ask themselves, like those found in Figure 9.12, will help them consider an author's purpose as a way to refine their ability to read information with a critical eye. Critical reading is imperative as students become informed citizens in their ever-changing world. The knowledge they gain from reading critically empowers them to write in a way that will inform and nudge their readers to make choices and take action that will make a difference in society.

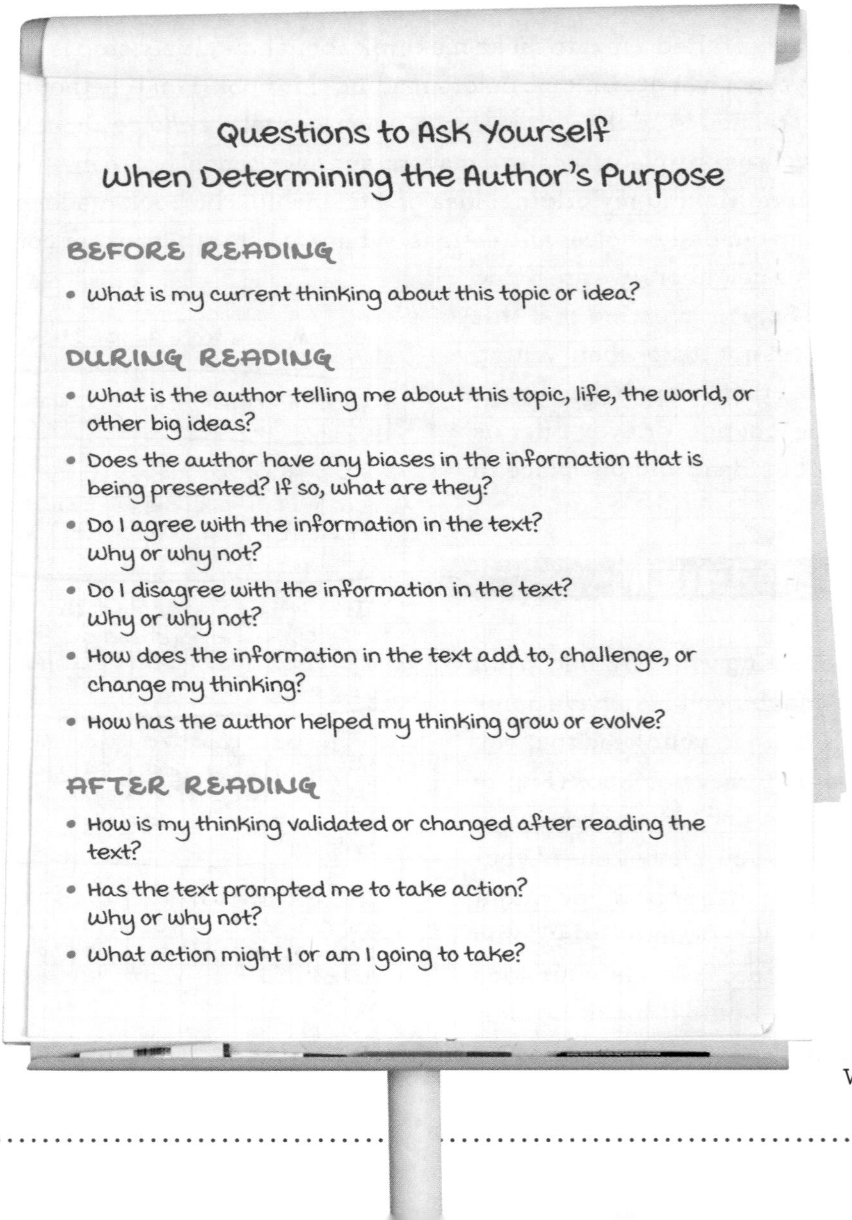

Questions to Ask Yourself
When Determining the Author's Purpose

BEFORE READING

- What is my current thinking about this topic or idea?

DURING READING

- What is the author telling me about this topic, life, the world, or other big ideas?
- Does the author have any biases in the information that is being presented? If so, what are they?
- Do I agree with the information in the text? Why or why not?
- Do I disagree with the information in the text? Why or why not?
- How does the information in the text add to, challenge, or change my thinking?
- How has the author helped my thinking grow or evolve?

AFTER READING

- How is my thinking validated or changed after reading the text?
- Has the text prompted me to take action? Why or why not?
- What action might I or am I going to take?

Figure 9.12
Questions to Ask Yourself
When Determining Author's
Purpose Chart

BIG IDEA: STYLE

READING WORKSHOP	LITERACY WORKSHOP COMMON THREADS	WRITING WORKSHOP
	Style	
How does recognizing the different styles authors use to share facts help me as a reader? How does noticing an author's style help me better understand the information and their purpose?	Which nonfiction styles do I prefer? How do I develop my own unique nonfiction style? How does developing my own style help me as a reader, a writer, and a person?	What can I learn from an author's/illustrator's style that I can use in my own writing? How do the decisions I make about the selection and arrangement of my words or pictures impact the information?

What Experts Say About Noticing an Author's Writing Style

Over the course of our careers, the selection and quality of nonfiction books have greatly improved. The most significant change that we have seen is in the diversity of writing styles they offer our learners. Many informational texts now have stylistic qualities similar to those in fiction texts, and sometimes even more of them. Studying well-crafted mentor texts during literacy workshop will help you share *writers' secrets* (Anderson 2005) that students can sprinkle into their own writing. When we invite students into the world of nonfiction where the players look, sound, and act like the ones in the fiction books, they are more likely to write texts about the real-life people they are learning about in their content-area studies. Also, when they see that writing about an informational topic can be done with engaging styles—like writing from the perspective of a germ or sharing what they have learned through a chart or infographic—writing nonfiction becomes fun!

Incorporating these experiences into your workshop routines communicates to your learners that the words and images on the page have power, that they are important to both the reader and the writer. Isn't this one of the most important lessons that we want our readers and writers to walk away with during literacy workshop time? As authors engage audiences in their own unique way, we are drawn into their texts. Students can take those lessons and think about what their own individual style might be and create texts that don't look like anyone else's. What an amazing gift—to have been a part of a young reader and writer's journey to discover their own unique writing style during literacy workshop time!

L E S S O N PRIMARY

STYLE: NOTICING NONFICTION STYLE

FOCUS PHRASES	MENTOR TEXT SUGGESTION

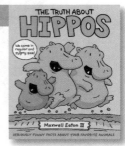

- I read nonfiction books about interesting topics.

- I think about what authors and illustrators do to make the facts interesting.

- I use what I've learned from authors and illustrators when I write.

The Truth About Hippos (Eaton 2018a)
Why We Chose This Book: The books in Eaton's The Truth About series are written in such an engaging and kid-friendly way, they make learning information fun. His books are sure to inspire your literacy workshop learners to try out speech bubbles—and more—in their own nonfiction writing. In this book, readers learn the differences between regular- and pygmy-sized hippos.

Additional Mentor Text Suggestions for Style

- *Hippos Are Huge* (London 2015)

- *The Truth About Bears* (Eaton 2018b)

ANCHOR LEARNING IN LITERATURE/CONVERSE TO GROW THINKERS AND LEARNERS

BEFORE READING
- Set a Purpose: Are you ready to learn about hippos? I chose the book *The Truth About Hippos* because the author Maxwell Eaton III has a unique writing and illustrating style. We can learn a lot from him about hippos and about writing our own nonfiction books.
- Discuss the Book Cover: When you look at the illustration on the cover, is it the kind of picture you would usually see on a fiction or a nonfiction book? I know from reading this book that it's a nonfiction book, but the author chose to draw the images rather than use photographs. What do you think about that? Also, see the speech bubble: the hippos are talking. Does that usually happen in nonfiction books? We're already noticing some unique choices that the author made. What else will we discover as we read?

DURING READING
- "A common hippo can weigh as much as four cows." page: Let's zoom in on this page for a minute to notice what the author did to help us learn facts and make the book interesting.
  - » I'm noticing that we can learn facts from the text [words on the page] and from the signs the author has drawn on the pages. They have extra or fun facts.
  - » What do you see that makes the book interesting or funny? [Speech bubbles. A baby pygmy hippo calf looking for his mom.]

  [Continue highlighting these stylistic features as you read aloud from the rest of the book.]

- "Hippo File" page: Maxwell Eaton also designed this back matter in an interesting way. What do you notice on these pages? [It looks like a real file folder with notes, maps, photos, and more.] I'm thinking you could create a page like this in the back of your nonfiction books. If you were writing a book about your favorite animal, what might you include on a page like this?

AFTER READING
- What did Maxwell Eaton do to make this book interesting to you?
- Were the extra things he added helpful or distracting?

DEMONSTRATE HABITS AND BEHAVIORS

As I read *The Truth About Hippos,* I thought to myself, *Why do I like this book so much?* I think it was Maxwell Eaton's style. I've read a lot of other nonfiction books about animals, but very few of them have the animals saying funny things in speech bubbles. I'm wondering how I can use what I've learned from him when I'm writing about my favorite topics.

RECORD THINKING AND LEARNING

If you're writing today, look back through the nonfiction pieces you've written. Can you find a place where you can add a detail or two to give your book a bit of style? If you want to learn more about animals and further explore Maxwell Eaton's writing style, I've checked out a few more of his books that you can read on your own or with a friend.

WHAT'S NEXT?

While reading aloud or conferring with students about informational texts, guide learners to continue noticing engaging style elements, including when authors
- directly address the reader,
- ask the reader questions,
- choose humorous or little-known facts,
- tell facts from a unique point of view,
- include an effective ending,
- present information in a unique way, and
- invite the reader to do something with the information.

Then, as students experiment with these elements in their writing, invite them to share with their classmates. That way, students can see and learn from the emerging styles of writers their own age.

L E S S O N INTERMEDIATE

STYLE: INCORPORATING EFFECTIVE NONFICTION AUTHOR'S STYLES

FOCUS PHRASES

- I consider nonfiction styles of nonfiction authors and illustrators.

- I develop my own style of informational writing based on what I'm learning from my reading.

MENTOR TEXT SUGGESTIONS

Sylvia's Bookshop (Burleigh 2018)
Why We Chose This Book: Shakespeare and Company is a legendary bookshop opened in Paris by Sylvia Beach. Told from the perspective of the bookstore itself, we hear of how Sylvia's love for books helped her establish a place not only for fellow booklovers but also for authors who need a place to congregate, share their stories, and find their unique voices.

Additional Mentor Text Suggestions for Style

- *Moon! Earth's Best Friend* (McAnulty 2019)

- *Martin and Anne: The Kindred Spirits of Dr. Martin Luther King, Jr. and Anne Frank* (Churnin 2019)

ANCHOR LEARNING IN LITERATURE/CONVERSE TO GROW THINKERS AND LEARNERS

BEFORE READING

- Set a Purpose: Today, we are going to think about how some nonfiction books pull us in as readers and make us want to go to our notebooks and mimic their style. What are those stylistic qualities that help us create meaning and learn about topics in engaging ways?
- Discuss the Book Cover: What do you notice about the cover of the book? Let's begin with the title of the book. How do you think the title of the book connects with the illustration on the cover? Who do you think the people shown on the cover might be and how might they be connected to Sylvia's bookshop? What do you think we might learn about Sylvia's bookshop as we read this text today?

DURING READING

- As we are reading today, let's pay attention to how the author chooses to teach us about this very special bookshop, Shakespeare and Company. Who is the narrator of the story? How do you know? Why do you suppose the author chose this narrator?
- How does the choice of the narrator help you engage with Sylvia's story? Do you think hearing the story from the bookshop's point of view gives you a unique insight into Sylvia's and her bookshop?
- How does the choice of narrator help you understand Sylvia and her friends' love of books? Do you think you would have this understanding if the author had used a different style to share the story? Why or why not?

AFTER READING

- Questions for Learners to Ponder:
  - » What techniques did the author use to share the information?
  - » How did the illustrator's images focus your attention, clarify the content, or enhance the textual information?
  - » How did the style of this book help you engage with, understand, and enjoy learning about this topic?

DEMONSTRATE HABITS AND BEHAVIORS

What is it about some nonfiction books that make them more interesting and engaging than others? I notice that some nonfiction books simply state the facts in a straightforward manner like a social studies textbook would, but others pull me in as a reader and make me want to read the book again and again. When I think about the qualities that differentiate those two types of books, I refer to that as *style*. Style in nonfiction books refers to the craft choices authors make to engage readers and make their work unique. I can identify and mirror these qualities to improve my own informational writing. Sound familiar? It's what literacy learners do when they learn from their reading to make their writing better.

RECORD THINKING AND LEARNING

Now let's think about how we can incorporate stylistic elements into your own informational writing. Maybe you want to try using a unique perspective to help share information about a person or a place like Robert Burleigh did in *Sylvia's Bookshop* or some other element that you have seen in a nonfiction text that you've been looking at recently (Figure 9.13). Considering how stylistic elements in nonfiction incorporate topic, structure, purpose, and even some story elements (character, setting, theme, perspective) will help you as you develop your personal writing style.

WHAT'S NEXT?

As your learners are developing their *literacy identities*, continue to support them as they grow as readers and writers. Immersing them in texts that offer a variety of stylistic choices will give them tools that they might eventually use in their own writing. Don't forget to encourage them to lean on one another as mentors as well. Sit back and watch your students as they discuss the stylistic content within their own texts. What a celebration as you see your literacy community grow as your learners make those connections between the books that they have been reading and their own writing! Isn't this the ultimate goal of your literacy workshop?

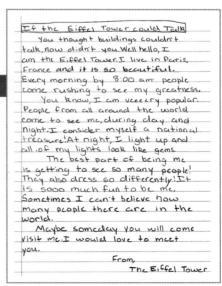

Figure 9.13   Literacy Notebook Entry: If the Eiffel Tower Could Talk

PROFESSIONAL BIBLIOGRAPHY

Ahmed, Sara. 2015. *Being the Change: Lessons and Strategies to Teach Social Comprehension.* Portsmouth, NH: Heinemann.

Allington, Richard L. 2002. "What I've Learned About Effective Reading Instruction from a Decade of Studying Exemplary Elementary Classroom Teachers." *The Phi Delta Kappan* 83 (10): 740–747.

Allington, Richard L., and Rachel E. Gabriel. 2012. "Every Child, Every Day." *Educational Leadership* 69 (6): 10–15.

Allyn, Pam, and Ernest Morrell. 2016. *Every Child a Super Reader: 7 Strengths to Open a World of Possible.* New York: Scholastic.

Anderson, Jeff. 2005. *Mechanically Inclined: Building Grammar, Usage, and Style in Writing Workshop.* Portland, ME: Stenhouse.

Angelillo, Janet. 2003. *Writing About Reading: From Book Talk to Literary Essays, Grades 3–8.* Portsmouth, NH: Heinemann.

Atwell, Nancie. 2015. *In the Middle: A Lifetime of Learning About Writing, Reading, and Adolescents.* 3rd ed. Portsmouth, NH: Heinemann.

Beers, Kylene, and Robert E. Probst. 2017. *Disrupting Thinking: Why How We Read Matters.* New York: Scholastic.

Biggs-Tucker, Karen, and Brian Tucker. 2015. *Transforming Literacy Instruction in the Era of Higher Standards 3–5.* New York: Scholastic.

Bryan, Trevor. 2019. *The Art of Comprehension: Exploring Visual Texts to Foster Comprehension, Conversation, and Confidence.* Portland, ME: Stenhouse.

Calkins, Lucy. 1983. *Lessons from a Child: On the Teaching and Learning of Writing.* Portsmouth, NH: Heinemann.

———. 1994. *The Art of Teaching Writing.* 2nd ed. Portsmouth, NH: Heinemann.

Carreker, Suzanne. 2011. "Teaching Spelling." In *Multisensory Teaching of Basic Language Skills,* ed. Judith R. Birsh, 251–291. Baltimore: Paul H. Brookes.

Coppola, Shawna. 2017. *Renew! Become a Better—and More Authentic—Writing Teacher.* Portland, ME: Stenhouse.

Couros, George. 2015. *The Innovator's Mindset: Empower Learning, Unleash Talent, and Lead a Culture of Creativity.* San Diego, CA: Dave Burgess Consulting.

Cruz, M. Colleen. 2018. *Writers Read Better: Nonfiction.* Thousand Oaks, CA: Corwin.

———. 2019. *Writers Read Better: Narrative.* Thousand Oaks, CA: Corwin.

Culham, R. 2018. *Teach Writing Well: How to Assess Writing, Invigorate Instruction, and Rethink Revision.* Portland, ME: Stenhouse.

Cunningham, Anne E., and Jamie Zibulsky. 2014. *Book Smart: How to Develop and Support Successful, Motivated Readers.* New York: Oxford University Press.

Cunningham, Patricia M. 2009. *What Really Matters in Vocabulary: Research-Based Practices Across the Curriculum.* New York: Pearson.

Daniels, Harvey. 1994. *Literature Circles: Voice and Choice in the Student-Centered Classroom.* York, ME: Stenhouse.

Dillenbourg, Pierre. 1999. "What Do You Mean by Collaborative Learning?" In *Collaborative-Learning: Cognitive and Computational Approaches,* ed. Pierre Dillenbourg. Oxford, England: Emerald Publishing.

Dorfman, Lynne R., and Rose Cappelli. 2007. *Mentor Texts: Teaching Writing Through Children's Literature, K–6.* Portland, ME: Stenhouse.

———. 2009. *Nonfiction Mentor Texts: Teaching Informational Writing Through Children's Literature, K–8.* Portland, ME: Stenhouse.

———. 2017. *Mentor Texts: Teaching Writing Through Children's Literature.* 2nd ed. Portland, ME: Stenhouse.

Duckworth, Angela. 2016. *Grit: The Power of Passion and Perseverance.* New York: Simon and Schuster.

Duke, Nell K. 2004. "The Case for Informational Text." *Educational Leadership* (61) 6: 40–44.

———. 2014. *Inside Information: Developing Powerful Readers and Writers of Informational Text Through Project-Based Instruction.* New York: Scholastic.

Duke, Nell K. and V. Susan Bennett-Armistead. 2003. *Reading & Writing Informational Text in the Primary Grades: Research-Based Practices.* New York: Scholastic.

Duke, Nell K., Gina N. Cervetti, and Crystal N. Wise. 2018. "Learning from Exemplary Teachers of Literacy." *The Reading Teacher* 71 (4): 395–400.

Farris, Pamela J. 2005. *Language Arts: Process, Product, and Assessment.* 4th ed. Long Grove, IL: Waveland.

Fessler, Leah. 2018. "'You're No Genius': Her Father's Shutdowns Made Angela Duckworth a World Expert on Grit." *Quartz at Work.* March 26. https://work.qz.com/1233940.

Fisher, Douglas, and Nancy Frey. 2018. "Raise Reading Volume Through Choice, Discussion, and Book Talks." *The Reading Teacher* 72 (1): 89–97.

Fletcher, Ralph. 1993. *What a Writer Needs.* Portsmouth, NH: Heinemann.

———. 2010. *Pyrotechnics on the Page: Playful Craft That Sparks Writing.* Portland, ME: Stenhouse.

———. 2017. *The Writing Teacher's Companion: Embracing Choice, Voice, Purpose, and Play.* New York: Scholastic.

Fletcher, Ralph, and JoAnn Portalupi. 2001. *Writing Workshop: The Essential Guide.* Portsmouth, NH: Heinemann.

Flitterman-King, Sharon. 1988. "The Role of the Response Journal in Active Reading." *The Quarterly* 10 (3): 4–11.

Foorman, Barbara R., and David J. Francis. 1994. "Exploring Connections Among Reading, Spelling, and Phonemic Segmentation During First Grade. *Reading and Writing* 6:65–91.

Fountas, Irene C., and Gay Su Pinnell. 2018. "Every Child, Every Classroom, Every Day: From Vision to Action in Literacy Learning." *The Reading Teacher* 72 (1): 7–19.

Fraser, Cathy. 2019. *Love the Questions: Reclaiming Research with Curiosity and Passion.* Portland, ME: Stenhouse.

Goldberg, Gravity. 2016. *Mindsets and Moves: Strategies That Help Readers Take Charge.* Thousand Oaks, CA: Corwin.

———. 2018. *Teach Like Yourself: How Authentic Teaching Transforms Our Students and Ourselves.* Thousand Oaks, CA: Corwin.

Graham, Steve, and Michael Hebert. 2010. *Writing to Read: Evidence for How Writing Can Improve Reading.* A Carnegie Corporation Time to Act Report. Washington, DC: Alliance for Excellent Education.

Graves, Donald H. 1983. *Writing: Teachers and Children at Work.* Portsmouth, NH: Heinemann.

Hancock, Marjorie R. 1993. "Exploring and Extending Personal Response Through Literature Journals." *The Reading Teacher* 46 (6): 466–474.

Hansen, Jane. 2001. *When Writers Read.* Portsmouth, NH: Heinemann.

Harvey, Stephanie. 1998. *Nonfiction Matters: Reading, Writing, and Research in Grades 3–8.* Portland, ME: Stenhouse.

———. 2017. "From Striving to Thriving: The Best Intervention Is a Good Book." Keynote address at the Literacy for All Conference, Providence, RI, October 24.

Harvey, Stephanie, and Anne Goudvis. 2000. *Strategies That Work: Teaching Comprehension to Enhance Understanding.* Portland, ME: Stenhouse.

Harvey, Stephanie, and Annie Ward. 2017. *From Striving to Thriving: How to Grow Confident, Capable Readers.* New York: Scholastic.

Heard, Georgia. 2016. *Heart Maps: Helping Students Create and Craft Authentic Writing.* Portsmouth, NH: Heinemann.

Hoyt, Linda. 2002. *Make It Real: Strategies for Success with Informational Texts.* Portsmouth, NH: Heinemann.

Johnston, Peter H. 2004. *Choice Words: How Our Language Affects Children's Learning.* Portland, ME: Stenhouse.

———. 2012. *Opening Minds: Using Language to Change Lives.* Portland, ME: Stenhouse.

Keene, Ellin. 2018. *Engaging Children: Igniting a Drive for Deeper Learning K–8.* Portsmouth, NH: Heinemann.

Keene, Ellin, and Susan Zimmerman. 2007. *Mosaic of Thought: The Power of Comprehension Strategy Instruction*. 2nd ed. Portsmouth, NH: Heinemann.

———. 2011. *Comprehension Going Forward: Where We Are/What's Next*. Portsmouth, NH: Heinemann.

Kids and Family Reading Report. 2019. 7th ed. Scholastic. www.scholastic.com/readingreport/home.html.

Kittle, Penny. 2012. *Book Love: Developing Depth, Stamina, and Passion in Adolescent Readers*. Portsmouth, NH: Heinemann.

Knight, Jim. 2016. *Better Conversations: Coaching Ourselves and Each Other to Be More Credible, Caring, and Connected*. Thousand Oaks, CA: Corwin.

Laminack, Lester L., and Reba M. Wadsworth. 2015. *Writers ARE Readers: Flipping Reading Instruction into Writing Opportunities*. Portsmouth, NH: Heinemann.

Lehman, Chris. 2012. *Energize Research Reading and Writing: Fresh Strategies to Spark Interest, Develop Independence, and Meet Key Common Core Standards, Grades 4–8*. Portsmouth, NH: Heinemann.

McGregor, Tanny. 2019. *Ink and Ideas: Sketchnotes for Engagement, Comprehension, and Thinking*. Portsmouth, NH: Heinemann.

Meek, Margaret. 1988. *How Texts Teach What Readers Learn*. Stroud, Gloucestershire, UK: Thimble.

Miller, Debbie. 2013. *Reading with Meaning: Teaching Comprehension in the Primary Grades*. Portland, ME: Stenhouse.

———. 2018. *What's the Best That Could Happen? New Possibilities for Teachers and Readers*. Portsmouth, NH: Heinemann.

Miller, Debbie, and Barbara Moss. 2013. *No More Independent Reading Without Support*. Portsmouth, NH: Heinemann.

Miller, Donalyn. 2009. *The Book Whisperer: Awakening the Reader in Every Child*. Hoboken, NJ: Jossey-Bass.

National Education Association. 2011. "Creativity and Innovation." In *Partnership for 21st Century Students for a Global Society: An Educator's Guide to the "Four Cs."* P21.org, May 16. http:// p21.org/index.php?option=com_content&task=vie w&id=262&Itemid=120.

———. 2012. *Preparing 21st Century Students for a Global Society: An Educator's Guide to the "Four Cs."* Washington, DC: National Education Association.

National Governors Association Center for Best Practices (NGA Center) and Council of Chief State School Officers (CCSSO). 2010. *Common Core State Standards Initiative*. Washington, DC: NGA Center and CCSSO.

Ness, Molly. 2019. "Leveling the Playing Field: Considerations to Make When Building Background Knowledge." *Literacy Today* 36 (4): 36–37.

Nichols, Maria. 2009. *Expanding Comprehension with Multigenre Text Sets.* New York: Scholastic.

———. 2019. *Building Bigger Ideas: A Process for Teaching Purposeful Talk.* Portsmouth, NH: Heinemann.

Pantaleo, Sylvia. 1995. "What Do Response Journals Reveal About Children's Understandings of the Working of Literary Texts?" *Reading Horizons* 36 (1): 77–93.

Paterson, Katherine. 1990. "Hearts in Hiding." In *Worlds of Childhood: The Art and Craft of Writing for Children,* ed. William Zinsser. Boston: Houghton Mifflin.

Paul, Annie. 2013. "The Science of Interest: Cognitive Research to Engage Students and Foster Real Learning." *School Library Journal* 59 (11): 11–13.

Pearson, P. David. 2002. "Thinking About the Reading/Writing Connection with P. David Pearson." *The Voice,* March–April, 6 and 9.

Pearson, P. David., and Margaret D. Gallagher. 1983. "The Instruction of Reading Comprehension." *Contemporary Educational Psychology* 63 (5): 317–344.

Perkins, David. 1995. *Outsmarting IQ: The Emerging Science of Learnable Intelligence.* New York: Free Press.

Portalupi, JoAnn, and Ralph Fletcher. 2001. *Nonfiction Craft Lessons: Teaching Informational Writing K-8.* Portland, ME: Stenhouse.

Ray, Katie Wood. 1999. *Wondrous Words.* Portsmouth, NH: Heinemann.

———. 2002. *What You Know by Heart: How to Develop Curriculum for Your Writing Workshop.* Portsmouth, NH: Heinemann.

Ray, Katie Wood, and Lisa B. Cleaveland. 2004. *About the Authors: Writing Workshop with Our Youngest Writers.* Portsmouth, NH: Heinemann.

Reeve, Johnmarshall. 2002. "Self-Determination Theory Applied to Educational Settings." In *Handbook of Self-Determination Research,* ed. Edward L. Deci and Richard M. Ryan, 183–203. Rochester, NY: University of Rochester Press.

Robb, Laura. 2017. *Read, Talk, Write: 35 Lessons That Teach Students to Analyze Fiction and Nonfiction.* Thousand Oaks, CA: Corwin.

Rosenblatt, Louise. 1978. *The Reader, the Text, the Poem: The Transactional Theory of Literary Work.* Carbondale: Southern Illinois University.

Routman, Regie. 2003. *Reading Essentials: The Specifics You Need to Teach Reading Well.* Portsmouth, NH: Heinemann.

———. 2018. *Literacy Essentials: Engagement, Excellence, and Equity for All Learners.* Portland, ME: Stenhouse.

Shanahan, Timothy. 2008. "Teaching Disciplinary Literacy to Adolescents: Rethinking Content Area Literacy." *Harvard Educational Review* 78 (1): 40–59.

Sims Bishop, Rudine. 1990. "Mirrors, Windows, and Sliding Glass Doors." *Perspectives: Choosing and Using Books for the Classroom* 1 (3): ix–xi.

Stead, Tony. 2002. *Is That a Fact? Teaching Nonfiction Writing K–3*. Portland, ME: Stenhouse.

Stone, Tanya Lee. 2019. "Nonfiction Authors Dig Deeper." *Celebrate Science* (blog). June 10. http://celebratescience.blogspot.com/2019/06/nonfiction-authors-dig-deep-by -tanya.html.

Taberski, Sharon. 2011. *Comprehension from the Ground Up: Simplified, Sensible Instruction for the K–3 Reading Workshop*. Portsmouth, NH: Heinemann.

Thompson, Terry. 2015. *The Construction Zone: Building Scaffolds for Readers and Writers*. Portland, ME: Stenhouse.

Tunnell, Michael O., and James S. Jacobs. 2008. *Children's Literature, Briefly*. 4th edition. Columbus, OH: Pearson.

Wagner, Tony. 2008. *The Global Achievement Gap: Why Even Our Best Schools Don't Teach the New Survival Skills Our Children Need—And What We Can Do About It*. New York: Basic Books.

———. 2012. *Creating Innovators: The Making of Young People Who Will Change the World*. New York: Scribner.

Walther, Maria. 2016. *Transforming Literacy Instruction in the Era of Higher Standards K–2*. New York: Scholastic.

Yates, Kari, and Christina Nosek. 2018. *To Know and Nurture a Reader: Conferring with Confidence and Joy*. Portland, ME: Stenhouse.

Zhang, Shenlan, Nell K. Duke, and Laura M. Jiménez. 2011. "The WWWDOT Approach to Improving Students' Critical Evaluation of Websites." *The Reading Teacher* 65 (2): 150–158.

Zinsser, William. 1988. *Writing to Learn*. New York: Harper and Row.

Zwiers, Jeff, and Marie Crawford. 2011. *Academic Conversations: Classroom Talk That Fosters Critical Thinking and Content Understandings*. Portland, ME: Stenhouse.

CHILDREN'S LITERATURE BIBLIOGRAPHY

Adamson, Ged. 2018. *Douglas, You're a Genius!* New York: Schwartz and Wade Books.

Agell, Charlotte. 2019. *Maybe Tomorrow?* New York: Scholastic.

Agee, Jon. 2018. *The Wall in the Middle of the Book.* New York: Dial Books for Young Readers.

Ahmed, Roda. 2018. *Mae Among the Stars.* New York: HarperCollins.

Alborozo, Gabriel. 2019. *Flora's Tree House.* New York: Henry Holt.

Alemagna, Beatrice. 2016. *On a Magical Do-Nothing Day.* New York: HarperCollins.

Alexander, Kwame. 2014. *The Crossover.* New York: Houghton Mifflin.

———. 2019. *How to Read a Book.* New York: HarperCollins.

Andros, Camille. 2019. *Charlotte the Scientist Finds a Cure.* New York: Houghton Mifflin Harcourt.

Antony, Steve. 2017. *Unplugged.* New York: Scholastic.

Archer, Micha. 2019. *Daniel's Good Day.* New York: Nancy Paulsen Books.

Archer, Peggy. 2018. *A Hippy-Hoppy Toad.* New York: Schwartz and Wade Books.

Arnold, Marsha Diane. 2015. *Lost. Found.* New York: Roaring Brook Press.

Aronson, Sarah. 2019. *Just Like Rube Goldberg: The Incredible True Story of the Man Behind the Machines.* New York: Beach Lane Books.

Arsenault, Isabelle. 2019. *Albert's Quiet Quest.* New York: Random House.

Arteaga, Marta. 2012. *Inside My Imagination.* Madrid, Spain: Cuento de Luz.

Atkinson, Cale. 2018. *Off & Away.* New York: Disney-Hyperion.

Averbeck, Jim. 2018. *Two Problems for Sophia.* New York: Simon and Schuster.

Baines, Becky. 2016. *Dolphins.* New York: Scholastic.

Bang, Molly. 2018. *When Sophie Thinks She Can't . . .* New York: Scholastic.

Barnes, Derrick. 2017. *Crown: An Ode to the Fresh Cut.* Chicago: Bolden.

Barnett, Mac. 2017. *The Wolf, the Duck, and the Mouse.* Somerville, MA: Candlewick.

———. 2019. *Just Because.* Somerville, MA: Candlewick.

Barrows, Annie. 2019. *What John Marco Saw.* San Francisco: Chronicle Books.

Barton, Bethany. 2019. *I'm Trying to Love Math.* New York: Viking.

Beaty, Andrea. 2013. *Rosie Revere, Engineer.* New York: Abrams.

———. 2016. *Ada Twist, Scientist.* New York: Abrams.

Beckmeyer, Drew. 2018. *The Long Island.* San Francisco: Chronicle Books.

Berger, Samantha. 2018a. *What If . . .* New York: Little, Brown.

———. 2018b. *Rock What Ya Got.* New York: Little, Brown.

Bernstrom, Daniel. 2016. *One Day in the Eucalyptus, Eucalyptus Tree.* New York: HarperCollins.

Biebow, Natascha. 2019. *The Crayon Man: The True Story of the Invention of Crayola Crayons*. New York: Houghton Mifflin Harcourt.

Birdsong, Bea. 2019. *I Will Be Fierce!* New York: Roaring Brook Press.

Boynton-Hughes, Brooke. 2019. *Brave Molly*. San Francisco: Chronicle Books.

Britt, Paige. 2017. *why am I me?* New York: Scholastic.

Bryon, Nathan. 2019. *Rocket Says Look Up!* New York: Random House.

Burleigh, Robert. 2019. *Sylvia's Bookshop*. New York: Simon and Schuster.

Byrne, Richard. 2018. *The Case of the Missing Chalk Drawings*. New York: Henry Holt.

Campbell, Marcy. 2018. *Adrian Simcox Does Not Have a Horse*. New York: Dial Books for Young Readers.

Carney, Elizabeth. 2011. *Cats vs. Dogs*. Washington, DC: National Geographic Children's Books.

Cena, John. 2018. *Elbow Grease*. New York: Random House.

Chung, Arree. 2017. *OUT!* New York: Henry Holt.

———. 2018. *Mixed: A Colorful Story*. New York: Henry Holt.

Churnin, Nancy. 2019. *Martin and Anne: The Kindred Spirits of Martin Luther King, Jr. and Anne Frank*. Berkeley, CA: Creston Books.

Clinton, Chelsea. 2018. *She Persisted Around the World: 13 Women Who Changed History*. New York: Philomel Books.

———. 2019. *Don't Let Them Disappear: 12 Endangered Species Across the Globe*. New York: Philomel Books.

Colón, Raúl. 2018. *Imagine!* New York: Simon and Schuster.

Coppo, Marianna. 2018. *Petra*. New York: Tundra Books.

Cordell, Matthew. 2017. *Wolf in the Snow*. New York: Feiwel and Friends.

Cornwall, Gaia. 2017. *Jabari Jumps*. Somerville, MA: Candlewick.

Cummings, Troy. 2018. *Can I Be Your Dog?* New York: Random House.

Czajak, Paul. 2018. *The Book Tree*. Cambridge, MA: Barefoot Books.

Daywalt, Drew 2018. *The Epic Adventures of Huggie and Stick*. New York: Penguin Random House.

Deenihan, Jamie L. B. 2019. *When Grandma Gives You a Lemon Tree*. New York: Sterling Children's Books.

Denise, Anika Aldamay. 2019. *Planting Stories: The Life of Librarian and Storyteller Pura Belpré*. New York: HarperCollins.

Denos, Julia. 2017. *Windows*. Somerville, MA: Candlewick.

Derby, Cindy. 2019. *How to Walk an Ant*. New York: Roaring Brook Press.

de la Peña, Matt. 2018. *Carmela Full of Wishes*. New York: G.P. Putnam's Sons Books for Young Readers.

de Regil, Tania. 2019. *A New Home*. Somerville, MA: Candlewick.

Derting, Kimberly. 2018. *Cece Loves Science*. New York: Greenwillow Books.

Derting, Kimberly, and Shelli R. Johannes. 2019. *Cece Loves Science and Adventure*. New York: Greenwillow Books.

de Sève, Randall. 2018. *Zola's Elephant*. New York: Houghton Mifflin Harcourt.

Desmond, Jenni. 2015. *The Blue Whale*. New York: Enchanted Lion Books.

DiCamillo, Kate. 2016. *Raymie Nightingale*. Somerville, MA: Candlewick.

Doerrfeld, Cori. 2019. *Goodbye, Friend! Hello, Friend!* New York: Dial Books for Young Readers.

Donaldson, Julia. 2016. *Detective Dog*. New York: Henry Holt.

Durango, Julia. 2017. *The One Day House*. New York: Charlesbridge.

Easton, Emily. 2018. *Enough! 20 Protesters Who Changed America*. New York: Crown Books.

Eaton, Maxwell, III. 2018a. *The Truth About Hippos*. New York: Roaring Brook Press.

———. 2018b. *The Truth About Bears*. New York: Roaring Brook Press.

Eggers, Dave. 2018. *What Can a Citizen Do?* San Francisco: Chronicle Books.

———. 2019. *Tomorrow Most Likely*. San Francisco: Chronicle Books.

Elliott, David. 2018. *In the Past*. Somerville, MA: Candlewick.

Farrell, Alison. 2019. *The Hike*. San Francisco, CA: Chronicle Books.

Ferry, Beth. 2019. *Ten Rules of the Birthday Wish*. New York: G. P. Putnam's Sons.

Fleming, Candace. 2016. *Giant Squid*. New York: Roaring Brook Press.

Fleming, Meg. 2018. *Sometimes Rain*. New York: Simon and Schuster.

Fox, Mem. 1994. *Tough Boris*. Orlando, FL: Harcourt Brace Jovanovich.

Frazee, Marla. 2018. *Little Brown*. New York: Beach Lane Books.

Freedman, Deborah. 2019. *Carl and the Meaning of Life*. New York: Penguin Random House.

Fulton, Lynn. 2018. *She Made a Monster: How Mary Shelley Created Frankenstein*. New York: Knopf Books for Young Readers.

Gall, Chris. 2019. *Go for the Moon: A Rocket, a Boy, and the First Moon Landing*. New York: Roaring Brook Press.

Gardner, Kate. 2018. *Lovely Beasts: The Surprising Truth*. New York: HarperCollins.

Gianferrari, Maria. 2018. *Hawk Rising*. New York: Roaring Brook Press.

Grady, Cynthia. 2018. *Write to Me: Letters from Japanese American Children to the Librarian They Left Behind*. New York: Charlesbridge.

Grimes, Nikki. 2016. *Garvey's Choice*. New York: Wordsong.

Guglielmo, Amy, and Jacqueline Tourville. 2018. *How to Build a Hug: Temple Grandin and Her Amazing Hug Machine*. New York: Atheneum Books for Young Readers.

Harrison, Vashti. 2018. *Little Dreamers: Visionary Women Around the World*. New York: Little, Brown.

Hartline, Aaron. 2018. *Box Meets Circle*. New York: Disney-Hyperion.

Haughton, Chris. 2014. *Shh! We Have a Plan*. Somerville, MA: Candlewick.

Heder, Thyra. 2017. *Alfie (The Turtle That Disappeared)*. New York: Harry N. Abrams.

Heiligman, Deborah. 1996. *From Caterpillar to Butterfly*. New York: HarperCollins.

Herrera, Juan Felipe. 2018. *Imagine*. Somerville, MA: Candlewick.

Hillenbrand, Will. 2019. *Mighty Reader and the Big Freeze*. New York: Holiday House.

Hirst, Daisy. 2018. *I Do Not Like Books Anymore!* Somerville, MA: Candlewick.

Hopkinson, Deborah. 2018. *Ordinary, Extraordinary Jane Austen*. New York: Balzer and Bray.

Jacoby, Sarah. 2018. *Forever or a Day*. San Francisco: Chronicle Books.

Jarvis. 2016. *Alan's Big, Scary Teeth*. Somerville, MA: Candlewick.

Jenkins, Steve. 2015. *How to Swallow a Pig: Step-by-Step Advice from the Animal Kingdom*. New York: Houghton Mifflin Harcourt.

———.2016. *Animals by the Numbers: A Book of Animal Infographics*. Boston: Houghton Mifflin Harcourt.

———. 2017a. *Apex Predators: The World's Deadliest Hunters, Past and Present*. New York: Houghton Mifflin Harcourt.

———. 2017b. *Who Am I? An Animal Guessing Game*. New York: Houghton Mifflin Harcourt.

———. 2019. *Look Again: Secrets of Animal Camouflage*. New York: Houghton Mifflin Harcourt.

Johnston, Tony. 2019. *The Magic of Letters*. New York: Neal Porter Books.

Keating, Jess. 2017. *Shark Lady: The True Story of How Eugenie Clark Became the Ocean's Most Fearless Scientist*. Naperville, IL: Sourcebooks Jabberwocky.

———. 2018. *Cute as an Axolotl: Discovering the World's Most Adorable Animals*. New York: Knopf Books for Young Readers.

Kerascoët. 2018. *I Walk with Vanessa: A Story About a Simple Act of Kindness*. New York: Schwartz and Wade Books.

Kilpatrick, Karen, and Luis O. Ramos, Jr. 2019. *When Pencil Met Eraser*. New York: Imprint.

Kostecki-Shaw, Jenny Sue. 2011. *Same, Same but Different*. New York: Henry Holt.

Kraegel, Kenneth. 2017. *Green Pants*. Somerville, MA: Candlewick.

Krull, Kathleen, and Paul Brewer. 2018. *Starstruck: The Cosmic Journey of Neil deGrasse Tyson*. New York: Crown Books.

Kuefler, Joseph. 2017. *Rulers of the Playground*. New York: HarperCollins.

Latham, Irene, and Charles Waters. 2018. *Can I Touch Your Hair? Poems of Race, Mistakes, and Friendship*. New York: Carolrhoda Books.

Lê, Minh. 2018. *Drawn Together*. New York: Disney-Hyperion.

Lebeuf, Darren. 2019. *My Forest Is Green.* Toronto, ON: Kids Can Press.

Lehrhaupt, Adam. 2018. *Idea Jar.* New York: Simon and Schuster.

Lendroth, Susan. 2018a. *Natsumi!* New York: G. P. Putnam's Sons.

———. 2018b. *Hey Ho, to Mars We'll Go! A Space-Age Version of "The Farmer in the Dell."* Watertown, MA: Charlesbridge.

Lies, Brian. 2018. *The Rough Patch.* New York: Greenwillow Books.

Lloyd, Megan Wagner. 2016. *Finding Wild.* New York: Alfred A. Knopf.

London, Jonathan. 2015. *Hippos Are Huge.* Somerville, MA: Candlewick.

———. 2018. *Little Fox in the Snow.* Somerville, MA: Candlewick.

Lowell, Barbara. 2019. *Sparky & Spike: Charles Schulz and the Wildest, Smartest Dog Ever.* Petaluma, CA: Cameron Kids.

Lukoff, Kyle. 2019. *When Aidan Became a Brother.* New York: Lee & Low Books.

Luyken, Corinna. 2019. *my heart.* New York: Dial Books for Young Readers.

MacLachlan, Patricia. 1998. *What You Know First.* New York: HarperTrophy.

———. 2019. *Chicken Talk.* New York: Katherine Tegen Books.

Magoon, Scott. 2019. *Linus the Little Yellow Pencil.* New York: Disney-Hyperion.

Mahin, Michael. 2018. *When Angels Sing: The Story of Rock Legend Carlos Santana.* New York: Atheneum Books for Young Readers.

Maier, Brenda. 2018. *The Little Red Fort.* New York: Scholastic.

Marcero, Deborah. 2018. *My Heart Is a Compass.* New York: Little, Brown.

McAnulty, Stacy. 2019. *Moon! Earth's Best Friend.* New York: Henry Holt.

McCloskey, Kevin. 2018. *Snails Are Just My Speed.* New York: Toon Books.

McCloskey, Shanda. 2018. *Doll-E 1.0.* New York: Little, Brown.

McKissack, Patricia C. 2019. *What Is Given from the Heart.* New York: Schwartz and Wade Books.

Meddour, Wendy. 2019. *Lubna and Pebble.* New York: Dial Books for Young Readers.

Méndez, Yamile Saied. 2019. *Where Are You From?* New York: HarperCollins.

Messner, Kate. 2018. *The Brilliant Deep: Rebuilding the World's Coral Reefs.* San Francisco: Chronicle Books.

Moore, Lindsay. 2009. *Sea Bear: A Journey for Survival.* New York: Greenwillow Books.

Mora, Oge. 2018. *Thank You, Omu!* New York: Little, Brown.

Morales, Yuyi. 2018. *Dreamers.* New York: Neal Porter Books.

Moss, Marissa. 2019. *The Eye That Never Sleeps: How Detective Pinkerton Saved President Lincoln.* New York: Harry N. Abrams.

Na, Il Sung. 2018. *The Dreamer.* San Francisco: Chronicle Books.

Narita, Kate. 2018. *100 Bugs! A Counting Book.* New York: Farrar, Straus and Giroux.

Neal, Kate Jane. 2017. *Words and Your Heart.* New York: Feiwel and Friends.

Numeroff, Laura. (1985) 2010. *If You Give a Mouse a Cookie.* New York: HarperCollins.

Oliveros, Jessie. 2018. *the remember balloons*. New York: Simon and Schuster.

Otoshi, Kathryn. 2015. *Beautiful Hands*. Novato, CA: Blue Dot.

Pak, Kenard. 2016. *Goodbye Summer, Hello Autumn*. New York: Henry Holt.

Pallotta, Jerry. 1986. *The Icky Bug Alphabet Book*. Watertown, MA: Charlesbridge.

———. 2009–2019. *Who Would Win?* New York: Scholastic.

———. 2012. *Whale vs. Giant Squid*. Who Would Win? New York: Scholastic.

Parr, Todd. 2001. *It's Okay to Be Different*. New York: Little, Brown.

———. 2016. *Be Who You Are*. New York: Little, Brown.

Persico, Zoe. 2019. *Georgia's Terrific, Colorific Experiment*. New York: Running Press Kids.

Pfeffer, Wendy. 1994. *From Tadpole to Frog*. New York: HarperCollins.

Piedra, Tony. 2018. *The Greatest Adventure*. New York: Scholastic.

Pilkey, Dav. 2000–2016. *Ricky Ricotta's Mighty Robot*. New York: Scholastic.

Reidy, Jean. 2019. *Truman*. New York: Atheneum Books for Young Readers.

Reynolds, Peter. 2018. *The Word Collector*. New York: Scholastic.

———. 2019. *Say Something*. New York: Scholastic.

Reynolds, Peter, and Paul Reynolds. 2014. *Going Places*. New York: Atheneum Books for Young Readers.

Reynolds, Shauna LaVoy. 2019. *Poetree*. New York: Dial Books for Young Readers.

Rhodes, Jewel Parker. 2018. *Ghost Boys*. New York: Little, Brown.

Richards, Dan. 2019. *Penny and Penelope*. New York: Imprint.

Robinson, Christian. 2019. *Another*. New York: Atheneum Books for Young Readers.

Rosenstock, Barb. 2014. *Ben Franklin's Big Splash: The Mostly True Story of His First Invention*. Honesdale, PA: Calkins Creek.

———. 2018. *Otis and Will Discover the Deep: The Record-Setting Dive of the Bathysphere*. New York: Little, Brown.

Roy, Katherine. 2017. *How to Be an Elephant: Growing Up in the African Wild*. New York: Roaring Brook Press.

Ruiz, Cecilia. 2018. *A Gift from Abuela*. Somerville, MA: Candlewick.

Salas, Laura Purdie. 2019. *Snowman - Cold = Puddle: Spring Equations*. Watertown, MA: Charlesbridge.

Sanders, Joshunda. 2019. *I Can Write the World*. Houston, TX. Six Foot.

Sanders, Rob. 2018. *Peaceful Fights for Equal Rights*. New York: Simon and Schuster.

Santat, Dan. 2017. *After the Fall: How Humpty Dumpty Got Back Up Again*. New York: Roaring Brook Press.

Scanlon, Liz Garton, and Audrey Vernick. 2018. *Dear Substitute*. New York: Disney-Hyperion.

Seeger, Laura Vaccaro. 2012. *Green*. New York: Roaring Brook Press.

———. 2018. *Blue*. New York: Roaring Brook Press.

———. 2019. *Why?* New York: Neal Porter Books.

Shetterly, Margot Lee. 2018. *Hidden Figures: The True Story of Four Black Women and the Space Race*. New York: HarperCollins.

Silva, María Quintana. 2019. *The Last Tree*. Madrid, Spain: Cuento de Luz.

Silvestro, Annie. 2019. *Bunny's Book Club Goes to School*. New York: Doubleday.

Sisson, Stephanie Roth. 2018. *Spring After Spring: How Rachel Carson Inspired the Environmental Movement*. New York: Roaring Brook Press.

Smith, Heather. 2019. *A Plan for Pops*. New York: Orca Books.

Spires, Ashley. 2014. *The Most Magnificent Thing*. Tonawanda, NY: Kids Can Press.

———. 2017. *The Thing Lou Couldn't Do*. Toronto, ON Canada: Kids Can Press.

Spiro, Ruth. 2018. *Made by Maxine*. New York: Dial Books for Young Readers.

Stead, Philip. 2016. *Ideas All Around*. New York: Roaring Brook Press.

Swanson, Matthew. 2017. *Everywhere Wonder*. New York: Imprint.

Tanco, Miguel. 2019. *Count on me*. New York: Tundra Books.

Tapper, Alice Paul. 2019. *Raise Your Hand*. New York: Penguin Workshop.

Tey, Priscilla. 2018. *In-Between Things*. Somerville, MA: Candlewick.

Tsurumi, Andrea. 2019. *Crab Cake: Turning the Tide Together*. New York: Houghton Mifflin Harcourt.

Tullet, Hervé. 2019. *I Have an Idea*. San Francisco: Chronicle Books.

Underwood, Deborah. 2019a. *Ogilvy*. New York: Henry Holt.

———. 2019b. *Reading Beauty*. San Francisco: Chronicle Books.

———. 2019c. *The Panda Problem*. New York: Dial Books for Young Readers.

Verde, Susan. 2018. *Hey, Wall: A Story of Art and Community*. New York: Simon and Schuster.

———. 2019. *Unstoppable Me*. New York: Farrar, Straus and Giroux.

Ward, Jennifer. 2017. *What Will Grow?* New York: Bloomsbury Children's Books.

Wenzel, Brendan. 2018. *Hello Hello*. San Francisco: Chronicle Books.

———. 2019. *A Stone Sat Still*. San Francisco: Chronicle Books.

Wild, Margaret. 2017. *The Sloth Who Slowed Us Down*. New York: Harry N. Abrams.

Willems, Mo. 2015. *I Really Like Slop*. New York: Disney-Hyperion.

———. 2019. *Because*. New York: Disney-Hyperion.

Wilson, Troy. 2019. *Little Red Reading Hood and the Misread Wolf*. New York: Running Press Kids.

Winstanley, Nicola. 2019. *How to Give Your Cat a Bath in Five Easy Steps*. New York: Tundra Books.

Winter, Jeanette. 2011. *The Watcher*. New York: Schwartz and Wade Books.

Winter, Jonah. 2019. *The Sad Little Fact*. New York: Schwartz and Wade Books.

Wittenstein, Barry. 2018. *The Boo-Boos That Changed the World: A True Story About an Accidental Invention (Really!)*. Watertown, MA: Charlesbridge.

Wood, Audrey. 1984. *The Napping House*. New York: Houghton Mifflin Harcourt.

Woodson, Jacqueline. 2018. *The Day You Begin*. New York: Penguin Random House.

Yolen, Jane. 2016. *What to Do with a Box*. Mankato, MN: Creative Editions.

Yoshitake, Shinsuke. 2019. *The Boring Book*. San Francisco: Chronicle Books.

Yousafzai, Malala. 2017. *Malala's Magic Pencil*. New York: Little, Brown.

Yum, Hyewon. 2018. *Saturday Is Swimming Day*. Somerville, MA: Candlewick.

Zagarenski, Pamela. 2018. *The Whisper*. New York: Houghton Mifflin Harcourt.

INDEX

CREDITS

Chapter 5

On a Magical Do-Nothing Day cover image used by permission of HarperCollins Publishers.

The Brilliant Deep cover image used with permission of Chronicle Books LLC, San Francisco. Visit ChronicleBooks.com.

The Dreamer cover image used with permission of Chronicle Books LLC, San Francisco. Visit ChronicleBooks.com.

She Persisted Around the World cover image used with permission from Penguin Random House.

From *Be Who You Are* by Todd Parr, copyright © 2018. Reprinted by permission of Little, Brown Books for Young Readers, an imprint of Hachette Book Group, Inc.

Green Pants. Copyright © 2017 by Kenneth Kraegel. Reproduced by permission of the publisher, Candlewick Press, Somerville, MA.

From *Off & Away* by Cale Atkinson. Jacket illustration © 2018 by Cale Atkinson. Reprinted by permission of Disney Hyperion Books, an imprint of Disney Book Group, LLC. All rights reserved.

From *After the Fall (How Humpty Dumpty Got Back Up Again)* © 2017 by Dan Santat. Reprinted by permission of Roaring Brook Press, a division of Holtzbrinck Publishing Holdings Limited Partnership. All Rights Reserved.

When Sophie Thinks She Can't cover image used with permission from Scholastic, Inc.

Cover image from *The Thing Lou Couldn't Do* by Ashley Spires is used by permission of Kids Can Press Ltd., Toronto. Cover illustration © 2017 Ashley Spires.

From *Box Meets Circle* by Aaron Hartline. Jacket illustrations © 2018 by Aaron Hartline. Reprinted by permission of Disney Press, an imprint of Disney Book Group, LLC. All rights reserved.

Hidden Figures cover image used by permission of HarperCollins Publishers.

Chapter 6

Ada Twist, Scientist by Andrea Beaty, illustrated by David Roberts. Text copyright © 2017 Andrea Beaty. Illustration copyright © 2017 David Roberts. Used by permission of Abrams Books for Young Readers, an imprint of Harry N. Abrams, Inc., New York. All rights reserved.

Starstruck cover image used with permission from Penguin Random House.

Chapter 7

Chapter 8

The Epic Adventures of Huggie & Stick cover image used with permission from Penguin Random House.

What Is Given from the Heart cover image used with permission from Penguin Random House.

From *Blue* © 2018 by Laura Vaccaro Seeger. Reprinted by permission of Roaring Brook Press, a division of Holtzbrinck Publishing Holdings Limited Partnership. All Rights Reserved.

Poetree cover image used with permission from Penguin Random House.

Chapter 9

Apex Predators cover image used with permission by Houghton Mifflin Harcourt.

Don't Let Them Disappear cover image used with permission from Penguin Random House.

In the Past. Text copyright ©2018 by David Elliot. Illustrations copyright ©2018 by Matthew Trueman. Reproduced by permission of the publisher, Candlewick Press, Somerville, MA.

Snowman – Cold = Puddle. Text copyright © 2019 by Laura Purdie Salas. Illustrations copyright © by Micha Archer. Used with permission by Charlesbridge Publishing, Inc.

What Can a Citizen Do? cover image used with permission of Chronicle Books LLC, San Francisco. Visit ChronicleBooks.com.

From *The Truth About Hippos: Seriously Funny Facts About Your Favorite Animals* © 2018 by Maxwell Eaton III. Reprinted by permission of Roaring Brook Press, a division of Holtzbrinck Publishing Holdings Limited Partnership. All Rights Reserved.